How Governors Built the

Modern American Presidency

How Governors Built the Modern American Presidency

Saladin M. Ambar

PENN

UNIVERSITY OF PENNSYLVANIA PRESS

PHILADELPHIA

A volume in the Haney Foundation Series, established in
1961 with the generous support of Dr. John Louis Haney.

Published by
University of Pennsylvania Press
Philadelphia, Pennsylvania 19104-4112
www.upenn.edu/pennpress

Printed in the United States of America
on acid-free paper

10 9 8 7 6 5 4 3 2 1

Library of Congress Cataloging-in-Publication Data

Ambar, Saladin M.
How governors built the modern American presidency /
Saladin M. Ambar. — 1st ed.
     p. cm.
Includes bibliographical references and index.
ISBN 978-0-8122-4396-3 (hardcover : alk. paper)
  1. Presidents—United States—History—19th
century. 2. Presidents—United States—History—20th
century. 3. Executive power—United States—History—
19th century. 4. Executive power—United States—
History—20th century. 5. Governors—United States—
Powers and duties. 6. United States—Politics and
government—1865–1933. I. Title.
JK511.A63 2012
352.230973—dc23
                                        2011040434

*For my mother, Joyce Catherine Thacker, and
my wife, Carmen, and the triplets:
Gabrielle, Luke, and Daniel—the joys of my life*

Contents

Preface

In 2008, Americans elected the first sitting senator to the White House in nearly half a century. It was, in fact, the only presidential contest in the nation's history to field two sitting senators. Amid all the rightful attention to the election of America's first African American president, these other firsts were unfortunately reduced to trivia—intellectual memorabilia to impress friends when reminiscing about this historic event. Such oversights, however understandable, have proven to have a narrowing effect on our understanding of the American presidency and American political development. Americans should think carefully about the effect prior elective office has had on the presidency—and on each of its occupants. By electing Barack Obama the 44th President of the United States, the American people ended nearly thirty years of presidential rule by governors. What this break in electoral practice portends may best be understood when considering a parallel event over 130 years ago.

The oddity of the election of Ohio's Rutherford B. Hayes over New York's Samuel J. Tilden surpasses the brokered political resolution that ended Reconstruction. Beyond Hayes's controversial victory is the story of a resurgent presidential office and the rise of modern presidential power. As Hayes and Tilden were the first two governors to face each other in a presidential election, the 1876 race marked a pivotal moment in the nation's selection of a chief executive. But more important, the moment led to a previously unimagined line of governor-presidents that would shape much of what Americans would come to understand as the basics of presidential authority. This was the era of Grover Cleveland, William S. McKinley, Teddy Roosevelt, Woodrow Wilson, and Franklin D. Roosevelt, governors all, who would go on to become the protomodern leaders most identified with the emerging presidential republic. *How Governors Built the Modern American Presidency* is the first book to examine the role the American governorship has played in reconceiving, and in many respects inventing, the modern presidency.

Today, as Americans grapple with the extent of presidential prerogative power—whether it is called *unitary, imperial,* or simply *modern*—we would be well served to see how today's "Prince," Machiavellian in an ability to garner personal power in the name of republicanism, first began to emerge. As governors, and later as presidents in their own right, the executives discussed in this book were part of a broader practical and theoretical construction of an executive-centered polity. In short, modern presidential power, however elusive to define, was ultimately crafted from the states up. This book is about the often forgotten link between our national and state executives, and how both presidents and governors have laid claim to extraconstitutional authority for themselves and their successors.

Outline of the Book

In the Introduction, I explore the ways prior elective executive office has shaped the presidency. Beginning with the election of 1876, I introduce the governorships of candidates Hayes and Tilden as early harbingers of the type of outsider politics that governors would come to define as presidential candidates. The key distinctions between presidents with executive backgrounds and those without are also drawn here. Chapter 1 takes up the Hayes-Tilden race's implications for the ensuing growth of presidential power. Key governorships of the pre-Progressive period are examined as well, including those of Bob La Follette, Grover Cleveland, and Hiram Johnson.

Chapter 2 explores the governorship of Theodore Roosevelt. TR's Albany tenure is presented as a window into his presidency and the emergence of innovations in executive practice in the United States. The theoretical as well as practical approaches Roosevelt employed are discussed as part of the broader trajectory of executive power emanating from statehouses in America at the time.

Chapter 3 analyzes the governorship and executive philosophy of Woodrow Wilson. Wilson's political writings and theories are explored and linked to his only prepresidential political experience as governor of New Jersey. Wilson's deconstruction and reinterpretation of the founding is presented along with his modern contributions to party relations, his bold moves in the legislative arena, and, finally, his innovative turn in press relations.

Chapter 4 explores the governorship of FDR in New York. Roosevelt's strategic political mind is analyzed and his seemingly antiphilosophical bent uncovered and scrutinized. Here, in the person of FDR as Albany leader, a powerful but by no means unchallenged governor, we can discern the outlines of the fireside chats, later efforts at establishing party unity under the executive, and the contours of the New Deal. Importantly, Roosevelt's modern executive acumen—the one that most comes to define the emergence of the modern presidency—can be seen drawing from the wellsprings of his predecessors in New York State, including Al Smith, Grover Cleveland, and Samuel Tilden.

In Chapter 5, I weigh the implications of executive power's centrality to American politics at the turn of the last century. By largely missing the governorship's role in the process of erecting the modern presidency, we have made an unintended secondary omission. This is the inability to see American executive power's growth as part of the narrative of the Progressive Era—an era in which governors challenged old conventions, opting for new tactics directed toward garnering popular support and progressive policy outcomes.

The most basic contribution of this book is to fold the institution of governor into any analysis of the modern presidency, and to revise the tendency in the discourse of presidential studies to minimize the role of prior elective office. It is time to bring the executive, writ large, into presidential studies.

*   *   *

This book is the product of many people and countless conversations that have shaped my thinking about politics over the years. In some ways, it grew out of a conversation over twenty years ago, when, as a fairly typical New Yorker, I was bemused and unimpressed on a visit to my girlfriend's home in Little Rock, Arkansas. After inquiring about the lack of a visible skyline from the approach to the quaint airport, I began to hear tall tales about the gifts of their young governor. Coming from the Empire State, I thought I knew what a real governor was all about. He was eloquent, ethnic, and nationally known. He was, in short, Mario Cuomo. I've since come to appreciate how easy it is to underestimate small beginnings in politics, and, more importantly, how easy it is to overlook the role governors play in American life. The following year, I spent a summer in Princeton, New Jersey, at the university's summer public policy program for students of color. There I met Michael Hanchard, who first sparked my interest in pursuing a career in political science. I have been in pursuit of the implications of executive power and the prospects of making a contribution in academia ever since.

Those good hosts in Arkansas, Manuel and Gwendolyn Twillie, are now my in-laws and have been indispensable in providing me time, lodging, and overall encouragement over the years. All sons-in-law should be so blessed.

Along the way, I have been introduced to marvelous researchers and thinkers in the field of American politics, not the least of which was the legendary Wilson Carey McWilliams, whose insights need no recounting here. Suffice it to say, I was privileged to be among his last students at Rutgers University. It was Carey who introduced me to my friend and mentor Daniel J. Tichenor, whose guidance and suggestions have been indispensable to the completion of this book and overwhelmingly responsible for whatever good qualities lie herein. Likewise, Dennis Bathory's generosity and keen sense of American political thought has been invaluable. It has been difficult to write about Tocqueville, even as sparingly as I have, knowing Dennis's insights are looming, and yet the joy is in hoping my views meet the muster of his probity. I have also been richly rewarded by the work and depth of analysis provided by Jane Junn, whose perspectives on the democratic implications of *How Governors Built the Modern American Presidency* have been a lodestar for me throughout. Innumerable others at Rutgers have been instrumental in challenging me to grow as a scholar in the very best sense. These include, but are in no way limited to, Beth Leech, Milton Heumann, Richard Lau, Gordon Schochet, Lisa Miller, and Ruth Mandel. I wish to single out Benjamin Peters for his particular encouragement and friendship. I am most appreciative of the time taken by these and other colleagues and friends, in reading this book.

My research was generously supported by a fellowship at the Miller Center of Public Affairs at the University of Virginia. I wish to thank the Miller Center and Sidney M. Milkis, in particular, for serving as my mentor as a Miller Fellow. His thoughtfulness, support, and encouragement have been an invaluable part of this journey. Sid is a one-of-a-kind scholar and his acute insights have been powerful reminders of just how challenging and worthwhile research into the presidency can be.

In the course of conducting this research, I have been well served by the staff at the Franklin D. Roosevelt Presidential Library at Hyde Park, New York, and the Seeley G. Mudd Manuscript Library at Princeton University. Wallace Dailey, the Curator at the Theodore Roosevelt Collection at the Harvard College Library, was particularly helpful to me in obtaining documents related to Roosevelt's governorship. I am also indebted to the Library of Congress and its Manuscript Division housing the Theodore Roosevelt Papers, along with Penn State University and Emory University, for their assistance in helping me obtain reels from the Theodore Roosevelt Collection. To be certain, the librarians and staff of the Fairchild-Martindale Library at my home institution, Lehigh University, were exceedingly helpful to me along the way, as was my research assistant Colleen Casey. This kind of work cannot be done without such supportive individuals and institutions, and I am grateful to them.

*   *   *

I would be remiss if I didn't thank the students whom I have taught history over the years. They have been remarkable reminders to me of the higher purpose underlying education—that in the unfettered exchange of ideas a stronger citizen body is forged. They have been absolutely wonderful, even as they awaited papers that were not always returned the very next day.

It goes without saying, but not without appreciation, that I am most grateful to my wife, Carmen, who, for more than twenty years now, has simply been my very best friend.

Introduction

The Hidden Prince: Unveiling the Presidency's Executive Narrative

Hence it appears that, except as to the concurrent authority of the President in the article of treaties, it would be difficult to determine whether that magistrate would, in the aggregate, possess more or less power than the Governor of New York.
—Alexander Hamilton, *Federalist* 69, 1788[1]

It used to strike me, when I was trying to understand your history, that there had been a certain diminution at one time in the authority and power and influence of the State Governor. . . . I think it no less interesting to observe that of late years the tendency seems to have been for the power and influence and authority of the State Governor to increase and be revivified . . . your people seem to be looking more and more to your Governor as the representative of the consciousness and conscience of the people of the State.
—Ambassador James Bryce, 1910[2]

Prelude

In late summer of his first year as governor, Woodrow Wilson attended the fourth annual conference of governors, held in Spring Lake, New Jersey. The so-called "House of Governors," instituted by President Theodore Roosevelt in 1908,[3] was illustrative of the growing power of state executives during the Progressive Era, and a locus for debating just what direction that newly found power should take. As the conference's host governor, Wilson unexpectedly found himself in the middle of a heated exchange with another, less prominent, newly elected governor. The *New York Times* reported that discussion over executive powers turned "warm" when Alabama's Emmet O'Neal questioned the merits of the increasingly popular use by state legislatures of the initiative, referendum, and recall in the states.[4] These innovations of progressivism were said to restore democracy to the people, giving ordinary citizens direct access to legislation, public policy, and their political leaders.[5] Importantly, all three features had the tendency to weaken the strength of parties while bolstering the authority of executives.[6]

Governor O'Neal impugned these measures as catering to "every popular impulse and yielding to every wave of popular passion."[7] Wilson, for his part, stood firm: "The people of the United States want their Governors to be leaders in matters of legislation because they have serious suspicion as to the source of the legislation, and they have a serious distrust of their legislatures . . . what I would urge as against the views of Gov. O'Neal is that there is nothing inconsistent between the strengthening of the powers of the Executive and the direct power of the people."[8]

O'Neal was unimpressed. "I would rather stand with Madison and Hamilton," he began, and—in a direct shot at Wilson's infatuation with the British parliamentary system—then continued, "than to stand with some modern prophets and some of our Western statesmen."[9] However crafty and acerbic O'Neal may have been, his retort would recede into the mists of history's losing arguments. Indeed, Wilson's support for a more plebiscitary executive was hardly novel, as American governors had been making the case for expanded executive authority for over a generation. Because states were less constricted than the federal government in amending their constitutions, they often took the lead in recasting legislative-executive relations.[10] The British ambassador and scholar James Bryce underscored this development in his visit to the Governor's Conference in 1910. Governors had so increased their visibility and power since Bryce's famous study of America twenty years earlier that he had, by the early twentieth century, become inclined to see them as fonts for the expression of popular sentiment.[11] "You are all," Bryce said in his closing remarks to the assembly of governors meeting in Washington, "the servants of and desirous to be the exponents of public opinion."[12]

At that same 1910 gathering, Wilson, now campaigning for governor, sounded his views on executive power in his keynote address: "Every Governor of a State is by the terms of the Constitution a part of the Legislature. . . . He has the right of initiative in legislation, too, though he has so far, singularly enough, made little use of it. . . . There is no executive usurpation in a Governor's undertaking to do that. He usurps nothing which does not belong to him of right. . . . He who cries usurpation against him is afraid of debate, wishes to keep legislation safe against scrutiny, behind closed doors and within the covert of partisan consultations."[13]

Wilson's arguments, including his all but forgotten encounter with Governor O'Neal, were emblematic of the longstanding fight over the meaning of executive power in the United States. Importantly, these battles had been fought increasingly in the states. Indeed, the nation's governors were in many respects modeling emerging forms of executive leadership that would become common in the modern presidency. Much of the change in the nation's party dynamics and development of direct primaries was attributable to these "hustling candidates" who emerged in the states in the late nineteenth century. As John F. Reynolds writes, "Landing a [presidential] nomination after 1900 required travel to greet delegates and voters, oratorical skills, and even advertising. These new rituals of democracy were already in evidence when it came to local offices during the 1880s. Many of the more proactive gubernatorial aspirants had mastered the necessary political skills by running for lesser offices such as mayor."[14]

In the arc of political history marked by the end of Reconstruction and the rise of the New Deal, it should not be surprising that the nation's governors would emerge as the chief architects of a nascent presidential republic. These were the "modern prophets" most responsible for reinventing executive theory since the founding. While Alexander Hamilton, the most vigorous early supporter of presidential power, argued that the American president was altogether different from the British king, his early effort to compare the new chief magistrate to the nation's most powerful governor was instructive. The president was not a king, Hamilton reasoned in *The Federalist*; he was more like a governor. Hamilton may have been premature in his comparison, but by the early twentieth century the American president and the nation's governors had, in fact, started to resemble each other more and more. While governors were often overlooked as significant political actors throughout much of the nineteenth century—James Madison famously referred to them as "ciphers"—they were to become disproportionately responsible for theorizing and, at times, introducing some of the most basic features of modern presidential leadership.

Unfortunately, one of the glaring omissions in studies of the American presidency has been the limited attention paid to presidential background. The effect of this omission has been to diminish the significance of the contributions of governors, who were at the fore of the shift toward an executive-centered republic. Despite how well this period (1876–1932) has been covered by historians and political scientists alike, there are strikingly few analyses of the shared trajectories of the governorship and presidency during this time. The presidency is the ultimate executive office, yet not all presidents have had prior executive experience. Moreover, those presidents most often associated with the rise of the modern presidency were all once governors. These perspectives on American political history hold important implications when evaluating the origins, evolution, and democratic character of the modern presidency.

Governors and the Modern Presidency

What do we mean when we speak of the modern presidency? The scholarly distinction between modern and premodern has mostly concerned the movement of presidential behavior away from adherence to the more formal and expressed powers of the office to use of those informal and expanded powers claimed by later presidents. These informal powers are often extra-legal and supraconstitutional. While a wide-ranging debate over the precise meaning of a modern presidential office persists,[15] there is broad consensus that changes in presidential leadership beginning around 1900 were characterized by a number of important developments. These included a president more disposed to leading the legislative branch and the newly adopted role of the president as unqualified party leader.[16] Critically, modern presidents have also been distinguished from their predecessors for their institutionalization (and exploitation) of press and media relations—phenomena especially peculiar to the modern age.[17] In addition, modern executive behavior has been characterized by the emergence and expansion of the administrative state, a development occurring in both the American governorship and presidency at this time. Finally, modern presidents have led with a deep and abiding belief in executive-centered government—a theoretical view shared by self-professed conservatives and liberals alike. Taken together, these variables of legislative, party, media, administrative, and executive governing philosophy constitute the central purview of modern presidential leadership, and are the focus of the individual and institutional studies in this book.

While not all-encompassing, these aspects of the modern presidency represent the core features of a "new" presidential office. While there is no single moment by which the modern presidency can be said to have emerged, it is the broad departure by presidents in these areas of leadership that separates their practices from earlier chief executives.[18] It was during this period (1876–1932) that the process of modernization involving these important variables underwent significant change. Yet, tellingly, before scholars began to identify these categories of authority with the modern presidency, they were first employed—experimentally and often peremptorily—by America's governors.

Some of the protagonists in this tale of the development of executive authority are familiar. They include Woodrow Wilson, Teddy Roosevelt, and FDR. But the cadre of state executives that helped redefine modern executive leadership includes significant, but more obscure, figures as well, such as Samuel J. Tilden, Robert M. La Follette, and Hiram Johnson. It is not customary to see the origins of modern executive power in the likes of such late nineteenth- and early twentieth-century governors. Yet these governors purposefully contributed to the rise of America's Prince—a leader full of prerogative power, guile, and extraconstitutional authority. The construction of this singular power was achieved in the name of the people and progressivism, and this presentation gave it a hidden dimension that remains to be fully explored. Continuing to search for the roots of modern presidential power solely at the national level adds to the difficulty of the enterprise.

The Cluster Phenomenon: The Case for Governors

During the Constitutional Convention of 1787, Massachusetts Governor Elbridge Gerry made an intriguing yet unsuccessful appeal for electing the president. Gerry reasoned that executives—namely, governors—should be charged with electing the nation's chief executive. It was counterintuitive, he argued, for legislators, who knew little of the requirements of executive governance, to make such a critical choice. Meanwhile, James Madison recorded in his notes on the Constitutional Convention that part of the opposition to Gerry's plan was the argument that governors would never reduce themselves to "paltry shrubs" by supporting such a great national "Oak."[19] Nevertheless, Alexander Hamilton would pay Gerry's argument an indirect compliment when, as Publius in *Federalist* 69, he drew a connection between the presidency and the governorship. "Hence it appears," Hamilton surmised late in his argument, "that except to the concurrent authority of the President in the article of treaties, it would be difficult to determine whether that Magistrate would in the aggregate, possess more or less power than the Governor of New York."[20] Hamilton's carefully crafted illustration fortified his support for the new executive institution in several ways. To alleviate fears of a revived monarchy, he downplayed the significance of presidential power by comparing it to the then quite mild authority of the office of governor. And yet, by introducing the familiar example of his own New York State, Hamilton employed the strongest governorship of the period to make his case. The exceptional nature of New York gubernatorial authority helped provide the conceptual beginning for what would become an overly robust national executive.[21] Perhaps this is not what he had in mind, but in minimizing the latent strength of New York's governor, Hamilton effectively veiled an American Prince, cloaking Machiavellian executive power in the modesty of federalism.[22]

Hamilton's deftness went unrewarded for most of the nineteenth century. Despite episodic flourishes of prerogative power, the presidency was largely far removed from the vigorous authority Hamilton had tried to cultivate. The early insignificance of the governorship as a pathway to the presidency likewise underscored how relatively inconsequential the office of governor would be during a century dominated by legislatures.[23] Not a single president would be elected directly from a governorship until 1876. Yet, between 1876 and 1932, five presidents were so elected, and eight had prior experience as state executives.

The clustering of governor-presidents—American voters have interrupted the latest cycle dating from President Jimmy Carter to George W. Bush—raises questions beyond a governorship's proximate impact on a given president. In effect, America has had what may be categorized as two compact *regimes of governor-presidents*, a fact that illuminates the nature of voter preferences, and the ebb and flow of executive authority's acceptance and elevation in our politics. As we shall see, the simple dichotomy of executive and nonexecutive presidents (those lacking gubernatorial experience) enriches our understanding of presidential conduct and invites new perspectives on the changing values associated with executive behavior. Put simply, executive background and the clustering of governor-presidents are either epiphenomenal to the founding of the modern presidency or a central part of its narrative. The governorships presented in this book, and the broader analysis of presidential behavior over time, suggest the latter.

Hayes to FDR: A New Narrative for the Modern Presidency

In his lengthy study of the governorship and presidency, the political scientist Joseph E. Kallenbach reasoned that "prior public service, especially in an elective post, is practically an indispensable requirement for the presidency."[24] Yet over 40 percent of all presidents have not held elective *executive* office of any kind. Kallenbach's particular attention to elective office is vital in that elections are the most illuminating democratic phenomena. They help reveal voter aspirations, larger political trends, and perceived candidate qualifications for leadership. The frequently worn path to the White House by vice-presidents and secretaries of state early in the Republic offers insights into the nature of nascent American political values and early popular conceptions of leadership. While there were a handful of governors who would go on to occupy the White House in the nation's early development, no sitting state executive was elected from the time of George Washington through Ulysses S. Grant.

Given the limited number of presidents in American history, some have argued that studies of the presidency of necessity devolve into biography. This criticism, while not without some merit, oversimplifies the breadth of research in the field of political science. Scholars such as Richard E. Neustadt, Sidney M. Milkis, Forrest McDonald, and Stephen Skowronek, for example, have engaged in more than mere biographical analysis.[25] In addition, excellent analyses of the institution have been introduced by Andrew Rudalevige, William Howell, and Kenneth Mayer.[26] Some have nevertheless argued that given the limited number of individuals involved, the so-called "problem of n" presents too high a statistical bar for drawing meaningful conclusions about the presidency. Every president is different, after all—what can we possibly know about what amounts to now forty-four different offices? This problem can be mitigated by considering presidential background. For instance, years of public service can be aggregated among presidents: during the period between Washington's and Grant's presidencies—some eighty-eight years—presidents served a combined 339 years in public office prior to their presidencies. Yet only thirty-four of these years—roughly 10 percent—were spent in prior elective executive office.[27]

The transformation is therefore stunning when we consider that, in the period from Rutherford B. Hayes to Franklin D. Roosevelt, presidents were twice as likely as their nineteenth-century counterparts to have had prior elective executive experience.[28] In addition, these Gilded Age and Progressive Era presidents represented the first cadre of governor-presidents. Perhaps one explanation for this clustering is that the modern presidency was somehow responsible for enlivening the importance and overall dynamism of state executives. However, the evidence suggests the causal arrow worked largely in the other direction. Empowered, yet distant, state executives built a set of practices and theories that ultimately shaped presidential behavior and, indeed, made acceptable a broad executive-centered approach to governance in America. Modern executive power was being created in the states first—from the ground up.

Hence, modern presidents did not so much transform executive behavior as state executives transformed the modern presidency. The paramount executives of this era, Grover Cleveland, Theodore Roosevelt, Woodrow Wilson, and FDR, were pivotal in their drive toward executive leadership and presidential power. Given the specific advantages of their Hudson progressive pedigree, they were the preeminent protomodern executives of the age. But they were not alone. Other governors were critical to the invigoration of executive practices and frequently pushed the bounds of acceptable executive behavior. Wisconsin governor Robert M. La Follette and California's Hiram Johnson are just two of the larger personalities whose behavior extended well beyond their states to affect the most basic attitudes held by early twentieth-century presidents. As Alan Ware has demonstrated, Progressive Era reforms in the states were largely a response to the rapid changes in urbanization and industrialization taking place in the nation, compelling new policies and new party candidates.[29] Governors were most often the prime movers in these endeavors.

While this early progressive period represented the first meaningful break with prior trends with respect to presidential background, the presidential election of 1876 likewise introduced a new scenario in American politics. Republican Rutherford B. Hayes of Ohio and Democrat Samuel J. Tilden of New York affirmed a different kind of presidential campaign and presentation to voters. As sitting governors, they were the first moderns to employ the now rote images of the "Washington Outsider" or "anti-establishment" candidate. Hayes's and Tilden's viability was built on the premise that both scandal and economic crisis were best addressed by those without vested interests in the nation's capital—men whose hands were clean of the antidemocratic excesses for which the legislative branch was increasingly excoriated in the popular press. The rapid and psychologically disconcerting industrialization taking place in America helped pave the way for a more popular form of counter-vailing executive power. As broadly presented by Emile Durkheim and others, the preconditions for this authority could be found in social forces that were being altered by new and disturbing economic realities.[30] In the American political context, the result was to erect state and, later, national executives powerful enough to stand up to the twin machines of industrial capitalism and political bossism.

The governors presented in this book are selected in part because they are the first actors in the regime of governors[31] elected to the presidency directly from state offices. The governorships reflecting the antimachine predilection in this cohort include those of Hayes, Cleveland, Roosevelt, Wilson, and FDR. These cases best highlight the essential features of statehouse-to-White House executive distillation. One reason for the salience of this particular set of executives is that the Hudson corridor (New York and New Jersey) provided executives with a disproportionately powerful megaphone in the form of press coverage. While Ohio produced a significant number of presidents during the period, they were less reflective of the overriding trend toward executive-centered governance. Nevertheless, Hayes's governorship was more in line with the greater emergent executive narrative than some of his Ohio brethren, and is thus included to add further breadth of understanding to national executive trends.[32]

Not all of these governors would go on to attain the presidency. The often overlooked Tilden, for example, authored one of the defining executive legacies of the early and late Progressive Era. His electoral loss in 1876 was significant on a number of levels, not the least of which being that his national campaign exemplified the way Hudson figures would present themselves to the national electorate for decades to come. Beyond Tilden extends a field that includes the most influential Progressive Era figures and champions of executive authority in this period. Robert M. La Follette of Wisconsin and Hiram Johnson of California produced governorships whose respective contributions provided regional and ideological cohesion to the landscape of early twentieth-century attitudes toward executive power and presidential authority. La Follette's and Johnson's governorships provided object lessons for expanding executive latitude at the national level. Indeed, La Follette's executive style and policies were cribbed widely by TR, Wilson, and FDR alike. La Follette is perhaps the most inspirational figure of what can only be described as an evolving movement, led by governors, to present a new vision for executive behavior in the United States.

Each of these executive stories revolves around the aforementioned variables that make up critical components of the modern presidency. These begin with leadership of the legislative branch—namely, the setting of legislative goals and the executive's direction of the legislative agenda. Second, modern presidents have come to be identified as leaders of their party. This represents a break with early republican notions of the president as party representative, or figurehead. As we shall see, it was governors who helped break this subordinate identification with party, as party leadership and, at times, defiance frequently came to be seen among voters as powerful and appealing qualities in their executives. The third element in the subnational origins of the modern presidency is the great emphasis placed on press and media relations by these governors and governor-presidents.[33] The changing dynamic of press coverage of governors, marked by the institutionalization of press relations within the executive office, foreshadowed a key innovation in presidential practices. Finally, as the administrative capacities of the states grew, new ideological arguments were presented by governors to both justify and sustain the changes occurring in their executive offices. The relationship between ideology and public policy became increasingly important in this era as state executives sought new powers for their progressive agendas. With these developments in mind, it is essential to reconsider the traditional understandings of the relevance of presidential background and prior public office. In doing so, this work will cast some light back on the institutional nature of American political development, and make the case for the significance, if not centrality, of the American governorship to the birth of the modern presidency.

Why Presidential Background Matters

The governorship is a political institution. It is not simply a touchstone for discourse within federalism. As a political institution, the governorship has meaning that crosses state and institutional boundaries, while also serving as a gateway for understanding the presidency. In the last quarter of the nineteenth century, governors emerged as a sort of deus ex machina—heroic figures cast into a narrative gone awry—as increasingly powerful private interests consolidated undue authority in the political arena. Executive power shed its early image as an embarrassment of republicanism as it became an instrument of progressivism. Executives, not legislatures, were now seen as best able to confront the antidemocratic forces growing apparently beyond all scale. "I would trust a governor quicker than I would a legislature every week,"[34] remarked one member of the Ohio Constitutional Convention of 1912. Such exhortations were no longer derided for their presumed monarchist character. It is no coincidence that governor-presidents account for 91 percent of all presidential vetoes in this period, an era in which a clear majority of presidential vetoes in American history occurred.[35] While presidents were just beginning to reconsider the relationship between formal and personal power, governors were instrumental figures in fusing the two. Central to this effort were their appeals to the public, which helped overturn traditional notions of what an executive could or could not do.[36]

In almost every way, governors began to cross the line in the early progressive period. They did so literally, as when Governor La Follette delivered his annual address in person to the Wisconsin legislature. They did so figuratively, as when Woodrow Wilson threatened to govern "unconstitutionally" in New Jersey. And they would frequently do so when at odds with their own party, as was the case when TR served as governor of New York. These early efforts in executive power-building have unfortunately been separated from the broader story of the growth of executive power in America. And where excellent institutional analysis of the American governorship can be found, it is seldom connected meaningfully to the larger question of executive behavior or the institutional development of the presidency. In short, presidential background, a subset of a subset of political science, has been addressed as part of a very limited approach to understanding the evolution of the presidency. And, when it has been invoked, it has been all too often through an ahistorical lens. Such approaches have tended toward character studies, biography, psychology, and personality studies. Institutionally based literature on presidential background is very limited, save for efforts at assessing prior office as a pathway to the White House. All too often, exceptions notwithstanding, the presumption has been that prior executive office among presidents is largely a personal or biographical affair, rather than an historic or institutional one. The executive as category, in short, is missing.

Beyond the adoption of informal power, the modern presidency has also come to mean the institutionalization of the office of president. The growth of its bureaucracy, aura of personal and prerogative power, and overall importance as an agency for perpetual emergency management, mark today's presidency as decidedly different from what went before it. Richard E. Neustadt's mid-twentieth-century analysis of the political environment inhabited by presidents of that time has come to best represent this understanding of the distinction between moderns and others: "The weakening of party ties, the emphasis on personality, the close approach of world events, the changeability of public moods, and above all the ticket splitting, none of this was usual before the Second World War.... Nothing really comparable has been seen in this country since the 1880s. And the eighties were not troubled by emergencies in policy."[37]

It is hard to refute the increasingly institutionalized nature of the presidency. But what has been absent from most discussions of what is modern about today's presidency is the idea that not only has the office been institutionalized, but so have all of its occupants, as presidents are unquestionably shaped by their prior political offices. By hearkening back to the 1880s, Neustadt indirectly (and unintentionally) linked today's presidency to an era whose political climate served as the incubator for new forms of executive power, and for the modern presidency. This was the period that launched the political careers of Grover Cleveland, William McKinley, Teddy Roosevelt, Woodrow Wilson, and a host of dominant state executives, a period defined by new and radical interpretations of the nature of the executive role in republican government. Like most who subscribe to the idea of the modern presidency as a distinct political phenomenon in American political development, Neustadt drew from critical experiences before FDR. As such, both Woodrow Wilson and Theodore Roosevelt have been seen as crucial precursors to the invigoration of the presidency. And while Neustadt did not make the case explicitly in his discussion of the 1880s, it is worth considering just how comparable and informative the politics of that period were to those encountered by modern executives.

However critical the TR and Wilson presidential narratives are for understanding the modern presidency, though, they do not go far enough. This approach suggests somehow that Roosevelt and Wilson either invented, or sublimely fell into, a new language of American executive power, one with no discernible or meaningful antecedents. To extend the linguistics meta-phor, American governors best represent the most proximate Linear B of the modern presidency. It was they who developed the institutional roots of dis-course, practices, and theories that ultimately grew into modern executive parlance in the United States. All classical periods have their founders; the modern presidency's was most closely tied to late nineteenth-century execu-tives and to governors in particular. There may have been a share of clerks (to use Neustadt's term) in the White House before the iconic FDR, but not all executives were worthy (or unworthy, as it were) of this appellation.

So where are the key indicators of the birth of the modern presidency to be found? For the political scientist Jeffrey Tulis, little has been more critically suggestive of the rise of the modern presidency than the dramatic increase in rhetoric among twentieth-century presidents. Tulis sees the will-ful use of popular rhetoric as a reflection of new forms of democratic politics and changing values within the polity. As he explains, "Rhetorical practice [among presidents] is not merely a variable, it is also amplification or vulgar-ization of the ideas that produce it."[38] In Tulis's model, there is ample evidence to suggest that prior executive office played a role in altering the rhetorical dispositions of American presidents, while also serving as a fundamental variable in the creation of the modern presidency. As others have rightly noted, however, Tulis's conclusions are contingent upon a more restricted sense of what constitutes "rhetoric."[39] Whether or not one accepts a more limited definition of rhetoric, such as confining it to speechmaking only, we are left to ponder where the earliest and most significant rhetorical strate-gies were employed among American executives.

In considering the value of the rhetorical presidency as a portent of the modern executive office, it is worth remembering that the genetic coding of American presidents has changed considerably over time. To start, the politi-cal DNA of chief executives has trended toward prior executive experience to a much greater extent in the second half of American political develop-ment than in the first. In Tulis's model, for example, Andrew Johnson is the great statistical outlier of his time, having "violated virtually all of the nineteenth-century norms encompassed by the doctrine."[40]

But what if Johnson's break with prior presidential norms reflects a greater willingness among former governors to defy the traditional encumbrances upon public utterances? What if the subsequent transformation of presiden-tial rhetoric can be traced to the parallel rise in prior executive experience? Interestingly, Johnson was the first former governor to occupy the White

House since the administration of James K. Polk over twenty years earlier. Governors, after all, were the earliest executives to perfect the art of public appeals; they were, more than any other institutional constituency in America, predisposed to prerogative power and the denigration of legislative authority. Can it be mere coincidence that those presidents with prior elective executive experience in Tulis's study average close to twice as many speeches per year as their nonexecutive counterparts?[41] It would seem the rhetorical presidency may well have been presaged, if not begun, by the popular rhetorical governorship. To be certain, hostility toward "up-start" executives in the early 1900s was not restricted to presidents alone. As John F. Reynolds points out, "Complaints of 'executive usurpation' found expression in legislatures in New Jersey, Colorado and elsewhere, manifesting a more activist executive branch at the state as well as the national levels."[42]

Looking at the tables provided below, we can see that those presidents most often linked to the turn in rhetorical practices associated with the modern presidency were those with disproportionate backgrounds in executive office and as governors. The examples of Andrew Johnson, Rutherford B. Hayes, and William McKinley, along with their more prolific successors Theodore Roosevelt and Woodrow Wilson, serve to remind us that the modern presidency is very much linked to this corresponding rise in executive experience. Tables 1 and 2 show the political experience of American presidents as it relates to the number of years spent in prior executive administration and elective executive office. The capital "X" denotes a sitting governor or one elected directly to the White House; the lowercase "x" reflects a conventional governorship. "Y" represents a governorship under the Articles of Confederation, and "T" represents a territorial governorship.

As Mel Laracey and others argue, Tulis does not capture the totality of rhetorical practices among nineteenth-century presidents in his *The Rhetorical Presidency*. Granted, even if Tulis mostly discusses presidential speechmaking (albeit with clear policy preferences), he nevertheless demonstrates an important dynamic of new presidential behavior. That there was such willingness to openly convey personal political views in this new manner by presidents—especially by those who were former governors—is but another reason to explore the relationship between the modern presidency and governorship.

As scholars continue to debate the origins, meaning, and very existence of the modern presidency, there will hopefully be more space to consider the

Table 1. Years of Public Service for U.S. Presidents

President	Public Office	Executive Administration	Elective Executive	Governor
George W. Bush	6	6	6	X
Bill Clinton	12	12	12	X
G. H. W. Bush	16	12	8	
Ronald Reagan	8	8	8	X
Jimmy Carter	8	4	4	X
Gerald Ford	25	1	0	
Richard Nixon	14	8	8	
Lyndon Johnson	27	5	3	
John F. Kennedy	14	0	0	
Dwight D. Eisenhower	0	0	0	
Harry S. Truman	20	10	10	
Franklin D. Roosevelt	13	11	4	X
Herbert Hoover	13	9	0	
Calvin Coolidge	20	7	7	x
Warren G. Harding	12	2	2	
Woodrow Wilson	2	2	2	X
William H. Taft	25	14	0	
Theodore Roosevelt	14	12	3	X

relevance of prior political experience in assessments of the American presidency's development. The growth of elective executive office in presidential background is unmistakable. Consider the two halves of American political history. During the tenures of the last twenty-one presidents from Grover Cleveland to George W. Bush, presidents have been over three times as likely to have had prior experience as elected executives as their twenty-one counterparts from George Washington to Chester Arthur. Further, the period from FDR to George W. Bush represents a near quadrupling of years served in some executive capacity compared to those in the first half of the nation's history. By whatever means one considers the presidency, it is clear that, over time, executive experience no longer proved embarrassing or prohibitive of political advancement. And governors were "ciphers" no more.

Table 2. Years of Public Service for U.S. Presidents

President	Public Office	Executive Administration	Elective Executive	Governor
William McKinley	18	6	6	X
Benjamin Harrison	11	0	0	
Grover Cleveland	6	6	6	X
Chester Arthur	8	7	0	
James Garfield	20	0	0	
Rutherford Hayes	9	5	5	X
Ulysses S. Grant	0	0	0	
Andrew Johnson	26	9	7	x
Abraham Lincoln	10	0	0	
James Buchanan	35	5	0	
Franklin Pierce	13	0	0	
Millard Fillmore	18	2	2	
Zachary Taylor	0	0	0	
James K. Polk	18	2	2	x
John Tyler	23	2	2	x
William Harrison	24	13	0	T
Martin Van Buren	22	6	4	x
Andrew Jackson	12	1	0	T
John Q. Adams	24	18	0	
James Monroe	26	14	3	x
James Madison	23	8	0	
Thomas Jefferson	23	9	6	Y
John Adams	26	8	8	
George Washington	16	0	0	

Note: X = elected president as a sitting governor; x = former governor; T = territorial governor; Y = governor under Articles.

Why Hudson Progressives?

The modern presidency was built upon a demonstrable intensification of and emphasis on executive background, coupled with a sudden and related proliferation of governor-presidents. These were clustered as a group during late state development in the United States. New York's governors were particularly crucial figures in this era, and, as such, they began to be featured prominently in the national press. Their status as iconoclasts went as far back as Tilden, and the ensuing increase in press coverage from the last quarter of the nineteenth century through FDR demonstrates just how important

New York's (and, to a lesser degree, New Jersey's) governors were in redefining the stature of state executives. As can be seen in the following chart, the significant contributions of Tilden, Cleveland, TR, and ultimately FDR are revealed in the increased press attention they garnered. The *New York Times*'s increased coverage of New York's governors since the paper's inception through the governorship of FDR reveals the elevated status of this crucial cadre of state executives in the last quarter of the nineteenth century and beyond (see Figure 1).

A similar pattern of coverage for governors can be seen in other national papers as well, including the *Chicago Tribune* and the *Washington Post*. This broader look at the Hudson executive influence will be taken up in Chapters 3 and 4.

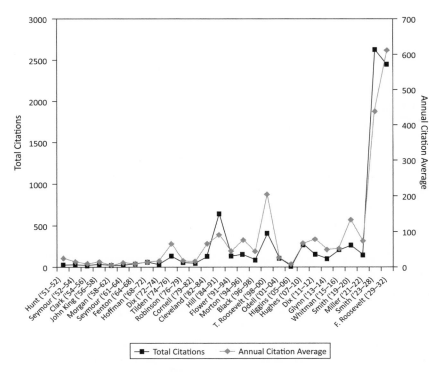

Figure 1. Governors of New York and *New York Times* citations, 1851–1932

In looking to New York and New Jersey, this book explores a particular variety of progressive political development—namely, a Hudson strain linked to executive-led reform, disproportionate press and media influence, and a peculiar mix of large-scale, private, antidemocratic institutions and patronage opportunities. Coupled with enduring and expansive executive constitutional authority, these elements made the case of the Hudson Progressives unique. It was this combination of factors that gave the region's executives a superior platform to innovate at the state level, while playing the lead in invigorating the warrants of executive authority. They did this primarily and initially at the state level, while, in the process, accruing the greater share of presidential possibilities for themselves. It is therefore essential to examine these protagonists as some of the earliest exemplars of what would become modern presidential authority.

Conclusion

Given the rising importance of the governorship as part of the overall elevation in executive power in the United States, it is insufficient to consider modern executive authority to be solely a function of presidential practices. For instance, Wilson's threat to govern unconstitutionally and his appeals to the public were both innovations developed during his governorship (and patterned after other governors such as La Follette). The same can be said for TR's strengths as party leader, and, on occasion, party challenger. Nearly all the chief builders associated with the birth of modern presidential power were once governors whose policies and theories of governance were largely replicated later on the presidential stage. In turn, these governor-presidents influenced the practices of their gubernatorial counterparts, producing an intriguing dialectic in American executive politics. Moreover, as I will later describe, the bases of modern presidential leadership and practices were informed by other state executives as well. The shifting tectonic plates of executive authority converged around the nation's governors and its early modern presidents at the turn of the last century. To miss this is to overlook one of the important stories of American political development and the rise of American executive power.

Thus far, I have avoided making any normative arguments about the nature of this transformation in executive background as it applies to the modern presidency. I will take up this argument more directly in the conclusion of the book. In short, the relationship between prior executive office and the birth of the modern presidency begs new approaches to understanding the broad set of political, sociological, and economic factors driving the popular appeal of both state and national executives. The *anomie* of modern industrial society had its consequences for both individuals and the nature of the state. One of these consequences was the elevation of executive power as a counterweight to the large, faceless institutions that were increasingly prevalent in society. In the American context, this elevation of the executive grew primarily among Progressive Era governors who gained a host of new institutional powers and tools to stoke popular sentiment in their favor. This was a mutually induced process, as voters sought antimachine and often antiparty leaders often with extralegal (and at times anticonstitutional) perspectives on executive governance. While the rise of modern industrial capitalism in America brought its own staggering implications for the reshaping of republican values, so too did the emergence of the outsized executive. This is one of the great ironies of progressivism in America: it extolled the virtue of popular ends, but, in its untethering of executive power, simultaneously extolled the virtue of personalist leadership. We are still trying to untangle the benefits and costs of this transformation in American politics.

Chapter 1

Emerging Executives of the Second Republic, 1876–1912

I would go back as far as Hiram Johnson when he
destroyed boss rule.
—Gubernatorial candidate Ronald Reagan, describing
his party philosophy, 1966[1]

In the end of course, there will be a revolution, but it will
not come in my time.
—Hiram Johnson, 1920[2]

Introduction

Just months into his first campaign for the presidency, Governor Franklin D. Roosevelt was forced to attend to some unfinished business in Albany. Despite his reluctance to assault his party or New York's political machine, FDR nonetheless confronted New York City's errant, albeit famously colorful mayor. For years, Jimmy Walker had provided ample ammunition to his political foes through his personal and political excesses. Over time, he had grown to personify graft and big city corruption. If Roosevelt were to win the Democratic nomination, he would have to satisfy the progressive elements of his party, who, since the time of Samuel J. Tilden, had come to expect the use of executive power as the chief means of protecting the people's trust. Moreover, as the historian Richard L. McCormick has noted, New York's increasingly powerful "governorship inevitably encouraged anyone who attained it to distance himself from the [Party] boss."[3] It was in this context that Roosevelt launched his late assault upon Walker, ultimately compelling the mayor's resignation.

The importance to late nineteenth-century politics of Roosevelt's row with Walker, which will be discussed more fully later, is its indebtedness to past executive practices. Here, the political legacy of New York's governors—and of Tilden specifically—figured into FDR's and the state's claims against Walker. It was Tilden who brought down Boss William Tweed some sixty years before Roosevelt's fight with Walker. That victory regained the power of removal for New York's governor—still a point of some contention in 1932.[4] As Roosevelt's Seabury Commission argued to the state's attorney general at the time, "the justification for the position taken by [FDR] was actuated by the same considerations which served as guides for his illustrious predecessors, Governors Tilden, Cleveland and Hughes."[5]

Yet, like so many of the early progressive governors at the fore of the transformation of executive power in America, Samuel J. Tilden remains an obscure figure. His place in history holds a spare vestige of importance—the losing subject of the tainted bargain that ended Reconstruction. Yet Tilden was hardly an irrelevant figure in his time. One *New York Times* feature on Woodrow Wilson in 1910, weeks before his election as governor of New Jersey, captured just how significant a figure the former New York governor remained: "*Wilson—A Tilden, But a Tilden Up to Date*," ran the late September headline. The *Times* would go on to tout Wilson as "a man with all the Tilden characteristics and an appreciation of the fact that conditions have changed since Tilden's day."[6] In New Jersey, Wilson would face tremendous opposition, but also great opportunity for support among progressives—provided he demonstrated credentials worthy of the Tilden legacy.[7]

Undoubtedly, the election of 1876 marked the end of Reconstruction and the restoration of white home rule in the South, but it also heralded a new era of notoriety for state executives. The reform impetus sweeping the country at the time found its most vocal expression in the states, where governors led the way.[8] Tilden's governorship reflected an early but growing movement by voters to grant greater power and voice to their executives. The shift from legislative to executive authority was purposeful, as governors were called upon to respond to the demand for specific policies that would fundamentally alter the relationship between the people, their government, and private enterprise in the states.

Besides serving as the immediate impetus ending Reconstruction, the election of 1876 has been seen as the beginning of an era of deep partisan divisions and hotly contested presidential elections. Few have seen it as the beginning of the end of America's "First Republic."[9] Formerly, American electoral politics had been typified by a *Virginian* philosophical approach to the presidency, buoyed by more limited conceptions of executive authority.[10] As the political scientist Rowland Egger noted, "The executive apparatus which emerged [from Virginia's 1776 Virginia Constitutional Convention] was weak in constitutional stature, confused in lines of authority, and wholly and irresponsibly subservient to the legislative will."[11] While late nineteenth-century American politics was certainly defined by a reform impulse, it was also joined to new and provocative executive practices. One example of this was the virtual disappearance of legislative overrides of executive vetoes in the states, which fostered greater control over policy making by governors.[12]

In truth, James Madison's view of governors as "little more than ciphers" reflected an executive model steeped in stringent modesty. It was legislative-, not executive-centered, government that concerned Madison initially. "Experience had proved a tendency in our governments to throw all power into the Legislative vortex,"[13] Madison wrote in his notes on the Constitutional Convention. Yet, with the convention debates behind him, and fresh examples of the misuse of presidential authority arising, Madison questioned, as Jack Rakove has suggested, "whether Hamilton was using the energy of the executive to attract support to the government, or the government to attract support to the executive."[14] Andrew Jackson's and Abraham Lincoln's muscular uses of executive authority serve as notable exceptions to the *Virginian* conceptualization of the presidency, and are reminders of the sharp turn in late nineteenth-century executive behavior.[15] Governors were at the fore of this turn; they were the "kings of state progressivism," as described by Robert H. Wiebe, who "expanded the discretionary power of the executive."[16]

Governors in the Age of Reform

Reform governors were of two minds regarding the types of changes they wanted to introduce into the political system. On the one hand, they generally favored process-oriented goals. These were tools to make democracy less of an abstract concept. Hoping to turn voters into demilegislators, both progressive theorists and politicians supported direct primaries over the old convention system. They also tended to support local initiatives and referenda over what they deemed to be the corrupt brokering over legislation all too common in American statehouses. While this orientation had its critics, even among progressives, the movement toward what Richard Hofstadter referred to as a kind of "mechanical" democracy came to represent a good deal of the reformist impulse around 1900.[17]

Next, reform governors sought more fundamental changes in public policy. In their efforts to upend a system weighted heavily in favor of private business and its interests, state executives implemented policies designed to limit the power of utilities, railroads, canal agencies, custom houses, and the "trusts," which had come to embody the immoderation of the period. Whether it was a fight over "Canal Rings" as with Tilden, or a battle over the taxation of franchises as with TR, reform-minded governors sought personal power on behalf of the people. As Hofstadter outlined in *The Age of Reform*:

> Somewhat more congenial to [reform] traditions was the idea that the evils against which the Progressives were fighting could be remedied by a reorganization of government in which responsibility and authority could be clearly located in an executive, whose acts would be open to public view. The power of the boss, they argued, like the overweening power of great corporations, was a consequence of the weakness of the political executive and the more general division of authority and impotence in government. Spokesmen of this view scoffed at the inherited popular suspicion of executive power as an outmoded holdover from the days of the early Republic when executive power was still identified with royal government and the royal governors.[18]

Ronald Reagan's curious conjuring of the great Progressive Era governor Hiram Johnson can only be fully understood in the context of such executive-led reform. What Johnson did in California fifty years before Reagan took office in Sacramento was part of this wider movement toward executive leadership and experimentation. In short, progressive governors reenvisioned the role of executives in the name of protecting "the interests of the people" (or "the *individual*" as Reagan put it to his "Meet the Press" host, Sander Vanocour).[19] This idea—that the executive is uniquely responsible for guarding the public and its interests—lies at the heart of the modern presidency. The root of this form of governance, however, was planted during a period of comparatively weak presidential authority. It was state executives who first began to take the legislative initiative, often in contradistinction to their national counterparts. When Woodrow Wilson described the presidency as a "big governorship," in *Congressional Government*, it was in many respects an admission of relative presidential weakness.[20] Today, as political scientists continue to question the true effectiveness or democratic quality of Progressive Era tools such as the initiative or recall, there is little debate about the centrality of executive power in American politics today.

In the early 1900s, there were few prominent examples of strong executives at the national level. Woodrow Wilson's admiration for Teddy Roosevelt, however grudging, is well known; however, his equally important regard for Grover Cleveland is little remembered today. Some of this is no doubt owed to the personal animosity noted by historians between the two men, focused upon a letter Cleveland penned in which he described Wilson as lacking "intellectual honesty."[21] Wilson's imbroglio with Cleveland—a Princeton trustee opposed to then Princeton President Wilson's graduate school plan—was part of a broader battle dating to before Wilson's time in public office. "[P]ractically all the darts are supplied by the Princetonians who hate me," Wilson would write in early 1912.[22] What has also no doubt been a contributing factor in underestimating Cleveland's influence on Wilson is the effect of the natural supplanting of one great party figure of the period for another—such was the case when Cleveland eclipsed Tilden.[23] And yet it was Cleveland who first helped shape Wilson's questioning of the nineteenth-century model of executive subservience to the legislature. And it was Wilson's perception of Cleveland's status as someone whom we would today describe as "outside the Beltway" that foreshadowed the role all governor-presidents would come to play—that of Washington outsider.

Wilson wrote of this phenomenon, which was fast becoming an integral part of the executive story of his age: the emergence of state executives as national leaders and reformers. "It has not often happened," Wilson remarked, "that candidates for the presidency have been chosen from outside the ranks of those who have seen service in national politics." Wilson empathized with Cleveland's status as an "'outsider,' a man without congressional sympathies and points of view."[24] It was the outsiders who were best positioned to claim credit for breaking up the trusts, disrupting the "rings," and, in the somewhat anachronistic language employed by Reagan, "destroying boss rule." Likewise, these outsiders were prone to outright leadership of, if not an assault upon, political parties. The early paucity of governors on the national scene, as noted by Wilson, would become reversed in short order by a progressive line of governors who helped build a new executive model in America's Second Republic. As the historian Herbert Margulies has pointed out, "Much of progressivism's achievement occurred on the national level, where the movement is associated with men like Theodore Roosevelt, Woodrow Wilson, and Robert M. La Follette. Yet it is a suggestive coincidence that each of these three served first as reform governor before moving to the White house or the Senate chambers. The fountainhead for the progressive movement was the state."[25]

Wilson would put it best himself: "The whole country . . . is clamoring for leadership," he would say, "and a new role, which to many persons seems little less than unconstitutional is thrust upon our executives."[26]

Beyond the Election of 1876: Forging New Pathways

In some respects, the election of 1876 was the first national election. Democrats nominated Samuel J. Tilden of New York that June in St. Louis at the first convention ever held west of the Mississippi.[27] The use of telegraph technology, which in 1844 produced the first news transferred via wire (Henry Clay's Whig Party nomination!), had become commonplace by 1876. Tilden had in fact installed a telegraph line into the executive chamber in his governor's office in New York to monitor the news out of St. Louis.[28] One of the reasons governors became national figures was that rail and wire technology finally brought the hinterlands of America out of the periphery and into the core of the nation's political consciousness. Tilden's reputation as the man responsible for bringing down Boss Tweed spurred national calls for his nomination, including some from distant California.[29] Subsequently, Hayes would become the first president to visit the Pacific states, and it was his administration that saw the installation of the first telephone in the executive mansion.[30] In the period following its centennial year, the United States had truly become a *national* republic.

Nonetheless, it was Samuel Tilden's losing campaign that contributed genuinely significant innovations to modern electoral politics. Countering Hayes's efforts to wave "the bloody shirt" of the Civil War ("are you for the rebellion, or are you for the *Union*?"[31]), Tilden sought to extend his message in unconventional ways. The Tilden machine that fought Boss Tweed's was now churning out its own propaganda—establishing a literary bureau, a 750-page campaign text book, and a speakers' bureau that coordinated Tilden's far-flung appearances. It was dubbed the "perfect system."[32] As Tilden biographer Alexander Flick noted, Tilden was one of the first party leaders to employ publicity based on the psychology of advertising, in the form of newspapers, pamphlets, and circular letters.[33] Much of this political innovation dated from Tilden's earlier campaigns for governor, where his organizational skills were ahead of their time. As the reporter William C. Hudson noted years later in his reflections on Tilden, it was Tilden "who invented the exhaustive canvass of each town as a basis for campaign work." Such practices had their rewards. "He once showed [me] a book containing the names of 50,000 Democrats," said Hudson, "with whom he could directly communicate."[34] In many respects, Tilden's were the first exhortations from the modern "war room." His New York-based campaign ultimately devised a crude but innovative form of national polling as well. Using newspaper clippings and individually crafted reports delivered across the country by his aides, Tilden was able to assess regional strengths and weaknesses.

Critically, Tilden's electoral appeal was based on his reputation as a reformer. Referring to Washington, the *New York World* editorialized about Tilden, "Would to God that some Hercules might arise and cleanse *that* Augean stable as the city and state of [N]ew York are cleansing."[35] The efforts to portray both Hayes and Tilden as "clean government" men were essential to the campaign of 1876, and all subsequent gubernatorial bids to the White House. From *Credit Mobilier* to Watergate, the regimes of governor-presidents have followed periods of grave popular doubt about federal corruption centered on the presidency.

The myriad scandals attached to the Grant administration, the economic panic of 1873, and widespread disaffection with Reconstruction, helped state executives immensely, if for no other reason than that they were spared by a press and citizenry obsessed with cabinet and senate-based scandals. Gilded Age politics bore little resemblance to the perceived halcyon days of Webster, Clay, and Calhoun. The caricatures of U.S. senators popularized in *Puck* were summed up in words by Henry Adams, when he described the United States in his 1880 novel *Democracy* as "a government of the people, by the people, for the benefit of Senators."[36] Such popular disaffection with Washington "insiders" would not be seen again until the post-Watergate era, which launched the second historic wave of governor-presidents that began with Jimmy Carter.

Hayes, Tilden, and the Political Geography of 1876

In highly contested late nineteenth-century presidential elections, the critical but frequently unpredictable states of Ohio and New York proved instrumental to breeding national candidates for the office. In the first twenty-five elections held after the Civil War, New Yorkers or Ohioans won the White House seventeen times.[37] Nine of these victories belonged to governor-presidents who articulated an antimachine and executive-leaning politics. As the most populous state in the union, with thirty-five electoral votes, New York was a frequent king-maker in presidential politics. After Pennsylvania, Ohio followed with twenty-two electoral votes, and its growing immigrant population and sizable Irish community made it a battleground state for years to come. New York's Horatio Seymour advised Tilden to portray Hayes as anti-Irish, eschewing more genteel self-promotion, such as "Tilden and Reform." "The word 'reform' is not popular with the workingmen," Seymour insisted.[38] Tilden nearly pulled out Ohio, losing by just 6,636 votes.[39]

Hayes would have his own difficulties. Even as governor, representing the incumbent party, with its association with Washington's scandals, proved daunting. To make matters worse, Hayes had only marginal support from New York's highly influential Republican party boss Roscoe Conkling, who was denied the nomination at the Republican convention in Cincinnati.[40] Conkling's power came from Republican control over New York's most coveted patronage bonanza, the Custom House. As early as 1828, the Custom House's duties were paying all federal expenses apart from interest on the debt.[41] By 1876, it was the largest federal office in the United States and was responsible for 70 percent of all customs revenue.[42] As President, Hayes would ultimately direct some token reform efforts regarding the Custom House, such as naming Theodore Roosevelt senior collector of customs to the Port of New York (over Conkling's objections). Agitated, Conkling used his senate committee power to delay the appointment, catching Roosevelt in the crosshairs of a titanic political battle, one that may have debilitated, if not killed, him outright. The seeds of TR's reformist bent were in part attributed to his father's physical demise and the Custom House battle with Conkling.[43] The possibility that Hayes would lay down the law to Conkling once president proved too great a risk; Conkling effectively sat on his hands during the national campaign, greatly hurting Hayes's chances.

Indeed, after Hayes's electoral victory, his administration did in fact go after Conkling, in many respects exercising an extraordinary amount of executive and federal authority. Hayes's attack on the New York Custom House also proved highly symbolic. It served notice to other cities similarly victimized by petty, machine-based corruption.[44] Hayes's efforts against Conkling should be seen in light of his overall executive-centered leanings, which, in the words of the historian H. Wayne Morgan, ultimately "sustained Executive rights" while helping to "restore presidential authority."[45]

Tilden, for his part, turned down the position of collector offered to him by President Polk over thirty years before his presidential bid.[46] Nearly every politician of ambition coveted this plum of the New York political machine. Tilden was among the few to spurn the office. In time, Tilden's Jeffersonian aversion to centralization made him an opponent of what would become a more robust executive approach forwarded by TR, Wilson, and, ultimately, FDR. Nonetheless, this "conservative" aspect of Tilden's philosophy made him equally opposed to centralization of municipal authority that violated the public interest. As the issue of municipal corruption increased in prominence nationally, Americans became fearful the nation was moving away from its founding principles. David McCulloch captured the sentiment well: "For most Americans the evils of the Tweed Ring were the natural outgrowth of the essential evil of big cities. . . . The golden age of representative government had lasted less than a hundred years, learned men were saying gloomily. Jefferson had been right about what cities would do to American life. The future now belonged to the alien rabble and the likes of Tweed."[47] Tilden interpreted his executive role as requiring him to serve as a buffer between the public and New York's political machine. Like so many antimachine governors who would follow during the Progressive Era, he launched an attack on municipal corruption, including that of Tweed. It was a struggle that forced reconsideration of the governor's power of removal, discussed at the beginning of this chapter. Along these reformist lines, Tilden's inaugural address targeted the Canal Ring of private interests that had abused governmental outlays to the state's canals, and he likewise targeted the corruptibility of the famed Custom House itself.

Such shots across the bow were intended not only for New Yorkers, but also "our sister States" who stood to benefit from "an improved polity, wise legislation, and good administration."[48] Despite losing his presidential bid, Tilden's gubernatorial administration stood as an early symbol of reform, one not forgotten by later progressives. The immodest but always revealing Theodore Roosevelt knew the parameters that defined his executive legacy. "I think I have been the best Governor of my time," he claimed, "better either than Cleveland or Tilden."[49] Roosevelt would eschew the Jeffersonian plot line of early reformers, favoring a national politics and more overt forms of executive power. But it was Tilden who destroyed Tweed, first with a bold, if not unglamorous, affidavit, followed by targeted legislation during his governorship. Tweed's end was indeed ignominious, spiraling downward amid his flight to California, then Spain, and, ultimately, a return to New York in handcuffs. He would die in prison in 1878. "I guess Tilden and [Democratic party regular Charles S.] Fairchild have killed me at last. I hope they will be satisfied now," he said.[50]

Rise of the Hudson Progressives

Why were Hudson progressives so successful? First, Tilden and later New York governors had far more authority in New York than did Hayes and his counterparts in Ohio. While both men came to their governorships at a time when New York and Ohio lacked as much as an executive mansion, Tilden at least held the nation's most powerful executive state office.[51] Here, early American executive institutional development, like much of what can be explained about American political life, is attributable to geography. By and large, New York and New Jersey escaped the more conservative executive constitutional realities confronting states south of Pennsylvania.[52]

Not all Hudson governors were uniformly "progressive," of course. Nevertheless, the recurrence of progressive executive leadership and its popular support gave the New York and New Jersey variety of progressivism a geopolitical legacy with enduring national importance. As well detailed by the political historian Charles Thach, New York's constitutional oddity was in granting the state's executive exceptional authority. One of the rationales could not have been more unpredictable, as New York invigorated its governor in the aftermath of the so-called "Doctors' Riots." These were a series of citizen attacks against the city's physicians, caught, of all things, digging up graves for cadavers to be dissected for medical research. Once it was discovered that "respectable" citizens' bodies were part of this project (where "strangers" and "negroes" had been used formerly), New Yorkers took matters into their own hands.[53] As the former editor of the *New York Tribune* Joel Tyler Headley recounted in his short history of the riots, "The Mayor and the Governor seemed to have an unaccountable repugnance to the use of force."[54] In his classic study of the American presidency, Thach credits the riots against the doctors with compelling New York to strengthen its executive, forwarding a "body of constitutional interpretation, in which, indeed, may be found some of the most important of American constitutional principles."[55] More than that of any other state, New York's constitution played a profound role in shaping the framers' arguments for a strong "energetic" presidency.[56] Coupled with a disproportionately influential press and a growing popular antagonism to the region's large political machines and bosses, Hudson politics would evolve to favor executive-centered solutions.

Despite somewhat weaker constitutional grants of power, other governors found ways to test the limits of their executive authority. Hayes, for example, was hardly docile in his efforts to exert executive influence in Ohio. Unlike New York's governor, Ohio's chief executive was far closer to one of Madison's "ciphers." First, Ohio's governor lacked veto power. The governor also lacked authority over the state budget and held very limited appointive powers. Yet Hayes used the appointments he had at his discretion in unprecedented ways. As was increasingly common, Hayes sought to use his stature as governor to project an image of himself as being above party. He did this most effectively through his appointment of a fair number of Democrats to state offices, a rarity for most governors at the time. "I was assailed as untrue to my party," Hayes recalled, "but the advantages of minority representation were soon apparent, and the experiment became successful."[57]

Hayes took honor to extremes, however, when he pledged in his acceptance letter to seek only one term if elected president in 1876. Hayes thus peremptorily made himself a lame-duck.[58] Nevertheless, the reform issue was effectively muted by Hayes's nomination—a preview of sorts for when New Jersey's progressive Democratic governor, Woodrow Wilson, effectively divided the progressive vote to his advantage in the 1912 presidential election. As Roy Morris, Jr. writes, "Hayes's many years of honest service as governor of Ohio, far from the quicksands of Washington," made him a formidable counter, if not equal, to Tilden's reputation as the outsider standard-bearer of reform.[59]

While Tilden's leadership of New York's Democratic legislature made his veto power largely unnecessary, Hayes employed his limited executive authority in Ohio and later as president in more confrontational ways.[60] As governor, he wielded power on behalf of conservative interests during the 1876 Ohio coal strike, ordering the Ohio militia "to protect the coal operators' property and the strikebreakers' 'right to work.'"[61] Hayes would take similar action as president, putting down the Great Strike of 1877. In this instance, he responded to governors' calls for aid, as some 100,000 railroad workers engaged in a mass work stoppage—the largest in the nation's history. Hayes's action was unprecedented, as he employed federal troops for the first time in a dispute between labor and private industry.[62] "The strikes have been put down by *force*," Hayes would say, "but now for the real remedy. Can't something be done by education of the strikers, by judicious control of the capitalists, by wise general policy to end or diminish the evil?"[63] The tendency to overemphasize Hayes's use of executive power toward conservative ends, as is often the case with Cleveland, obscures the larger story of how the expansion of presidential authority owes its beginnings, humble as they were, to a period well before the presidency of FDR. The use of power in the name of conservative policies still tends to increase power. This has been especially true of presidential power.

In addition to intervening in the Great Strike, Hayes took bold executive action elsewhere. He vetoed a widely popular bill excluding Chinese immigrants. He struck a blow against senatorial courtesy by calling for Chester A. Arthur's resignation from the Port of New York Custom House, initiating his battle with Conkling and appointing John Jay's grandson to investigate New York's corruption (along with commissioners for Philadelphia's, New Orleans's, and San Francisco's custom houses).[64] His so-called "popular baths" were public addresses delivered outside of Washington to support his legislative agenda, earning him the moniker "Rutherford the Rover."[65] In fact, Hayes has been credited with delivering more speeches on tour while president than his six immediate predecessors combined.[66] Ari Hoogenboom has summarized Hayes's contributions to the executive turn away from First Republic principles of executive leadership well: "Despite his small staff, Hayes strengthened the office of the presidency. His concept of his office differed from that of his immediate predecessors, who had either embraced or enhanced the Whig approach to the presidency. . . . Although he had been a Whig and was hoping to revive and realign southern Whigs, he moved away from the Whig ideal of a weak president who was subservient to Congress and deferential to his cabinet."[67]

Despite Hayes's limited constitutional authority, his Ohio tenure included innovations that would become common among the state's progressive class to come. He established Ohio's modern university (which would become Ohio State University); he pushed the legislature to ratify the fifteenth amendment and reforms aimed at protecting the mentally ill and the incarcerated—areas where he did have a degree of executive authority as governor. Likewise, he was an early advocate of civil service reform and railroad regulation in Ohio.[68] He was, as one historian described him, "an early progressive."[69] In many respects, this aspect of Hayes's legacy is lost in the fallout of what the election of 1876 has come to represent in the popular imagination. This is understandable, but it should not obscure the layered object lesson from the election of 1876. Tilden and Hayes helped spawn a new thinking in executive leadership, positioning the American governorship as a popular and characteristically "honest" executive institution for democratic reform. While the transition to a modern presidential republic was still at least a quarter century away, its contours could be seen in the shadows of Reconstruction's demise.

The Cleveland Connection: Beyond Bourbon Leadership

Grover Cleveland is said to have come out of the conservative business wing of late nineteenth-century Democratic politics. His tariff and hard money policies spoke to a so-called Bourbon interest in preventing "control of the government by farmers, wage earners and inefficient, irresponsible officehold-ers."[70] Henry F. Graff has explained the Bourbon movement well: "Bourbon Democracy was a name inspired not by the Kentucky whiskey but by the backward-looking restored monarchy in France, of which Talleyrand, the irrepressible French diplomat, had quipped that its people had learned nothing and forgotten nothing. It was a form of Jeffersonianism dedicated to small, mostly inert government, aimed more at protecting business than promoting the substantial needs of a larger population."[71]

Taken at face value, there is much to commend in this view of Cleve-land's presidency. Indeed, Horace Samuel Merrill's summation of Cleveland as a "narrow legalist" is not so much wrong as it is incomplete.[72] Cleveland's governorship and presidency—particularly his first term—demonstrate a stronger affinity for executive leadership and power than he is often given credit (or damnation) for. It was Cleveland, as governor-president, who contributed mightily to the governing philosophy of Theodore Roosevelt and Woodrow Wilson. And it was Cleveland's Democratic interregnum that presaged the preemptive politics of late twentieth-century presidencies such as Bill Clinton's.[73] Most importantly, Cleveland's use of executive authority helped strengthen the presidency and reinforce the idea of the president as both national and legislative leader. FDR would look to Cleveland's presidency on occasion for insights, without provocation, and certainly without a Bourbon agenda in mind.[74]

It was during Cleveland's first term that he invoked "executive privilege," employing this still somewhat exotic constitutional concept more forcefully than any president to that point during peacetime. Alyn Brodsky has called it

"Cleveland's greatest achievement: retrieving for the executive branch many of the prerogatives that had fallen to the legislative branch through a succession of presidential mediocrities."[75] The impetus for Cleveland's claim was the Tenure of Office Act. Congress had passed this piece of legislation in its effort to derail the Democratic presidency of Andrew Johnson; the act effectively turned over all removal authority to the United States Senate, detaching it from the president's appointive powers. As David A. Crockett has recounted:

> In February, 1886, the Senate began asking the administration for information regarding executive branch suspensions. Citing the advice-and-consent clause, Cleveland sent only information on appointments, while retaining confidential letters and documents. The president himself would be the judge of whether such things could be released to the Senate. The Senate replied saying it would block all future appointments, and the stage was set for a showdown. Cleveland then sent a public message to the Senate, arguing that the Senate had no constitutional authority over dismissals and suspensions, and that sending confidential documents about appointments would embarrass and injure the president and his advisors, who would be unable to offer frank advice.[76]

Cleveland delivered a response to the Senate essentially declaring the Tenure of Office Act unconstitutional, arguing he was "not responsible to the Senate" concerning dismissals.[77] Cleveland ultimately prevailed, signing the repeal of the Tenure of Office Act in March of 1887 and restoring balance to executive-legislative relations.[78] In true progressive fashion, Cleveland would later claim he helped free "the presidency from the Senate's claim of tutelage," making the office "again *the independent agent of the people*."[79] While Cleveland's act was restorative, it was also, in a sense, precedent-setting. As one Hayes biographer concluded, "The modern presidency does not begin with Grover Cleveland, but Cleveland made a necessary contribution to its development when he contested the claims of the Republican Senate and thereby helped to right the balance between the legislative and the executive branches of the federal government."[80]

Similarly, Cleveland's Bourbonism must be qualified when examining another aspect of his executive performance. Cleveland was anything but conservative in his use of the presidential veto, exercising it more than any other president but FDR, who governed nearly twice as long.[81] Prior to the presidency, Cleveland was known first as the "Veto Mayor" of Buffalo and then as New York's "Veto Governor." His willingness to favor strong executive government countered his self-proclaimed Whiggish sentiments.[82] His 301 first-term vetoes were a record, and his combined total of 584 dwarfed the combined bills vetoed prior to his terms in office (132). Cleveland's most controversial veto while governor was employed to defend legalistic and high-minded purposes. His veto of the five-cent fare bill drew in a young assemblyman, Theodore Roosevelt, forging an early bipartisan alliance with the "twenty-five year old rising star of the Republican Party and a leader of its reform wing."[83]

Cleveland's deep and studious analysis of the bill convinced him that, while a boon to a public desperate for affordable public services, it was nevertheless unconstitutional; if passed, it would negate a contract between the state and the wealthy Jay Gould, who owned the elevated line in question. Gould stood to benefit greatly by keeping the fare at ten cents. "The State must not only be strictly just, but scrupulously fair," Cleveland said in his speech to the assembly.[84] Cleveland's principled stand earned him great respect and admiration for his political courage, not the least of which from Roosevelt. Both Cleveland and TR benefited from their early reform alliance, with the two future presidents depicted by one cartoonist as presiding over the demise of the Tammany Hall "tiger."[85] While Cleveland's Bourbon democracy may be critiqued for its establishment biases, Cleveland's liberal use of the veto became a hallmark of modern executive leadership, the modern presidency, and a singular contribution of later governor-presidents.[86] Such a prolific use of the veto necessarily tempers the one-dimensional view of Cleveland as legislatively neutral or weak. FDR, for one, took evident pride in being linked with Cleveland—both as president and as New York governor—through their shared proclivity to veto. "It is to me tremendously interesting," noted Roosevelt in a letter to Cleveland's widow in 1941, "that President Cleveland and I seem to have a veto record not even approached by anyone else in the White House." Mindful of their similarly high veto tallies in Albany, Roosevelt concluded, "I am very happy in the association which this record brings out."[87]

Of the top quartile of vetoes given between 1829 and 2000, governor-presidents account for 70 percent.[88] And though governor-presidents make up less than 40 percent of all presidents, they account for a surprising 64 percent of all presidential vetoes. The following chart puts the Cleveland veto record in perspective. While a preeminent vetoer, Cleveland was part of a cadre of governor-presidents whose use of the veto was unparalleled in American history.

Even when controlling for Cleveland's and FDR's vetoes, governor-presidents still veto disproportionately, accounting for over half of all presidential vetoes. More to the point, however, is the fact that Cleveland's executive background was hardly incidental to his behavior as president. Cleveland's deep executive experience is emblematic of the influential role executive background has played in presidential behavior. As Cleveland biographer H. Paul Jeffers recounts:

> [Buffalo's City Council] crowned Grover Cleveland with a halo of political courage and enshrined his street-cleaning veto as the beginning of the most astonishing and rapid ascent from political obscurity to the pinnacle of governmental power in the annals of the United States. American historians and Cleveland biographers agree that if the Buffalo Common council had overridden the veto of the street-cleaning contract, Grover Cleveland could not that very year [1882], have become governor of New York, and only two years after that, have been elected the twenty-second President of the United States.[89]

Purely quantitative analyses of presidential vetoes tell only part of the story of the modern presidency. At a minimum, the veto record of former governors in the White House begs a reconsideration of the role of executive background in presidential politics. Certainly, behind Cleveland's use of the veto was the belief that it was the executive's responsibility to provide honest and efficient government to the people. Theda Skocpol is also correct in pointing out that Cleveland's presidential veto record was strongly tied to his antagonism toward the costs of veterans' pensions.[90] But Cleveland's veto record before the presidency clearly aligns with his later use of the veto as part of a broader executive philosophy, one increasingly shared by state executives at the time. This emergent theory of executive power was matched by shifting constitutional dynamics in the states as the executive veto grew in strength and popularity.[91] Cleveland himself saw an inherently popular role in the executive function, and this sentiment guided his attacks on Tammany Hall and the New York Democratic political boss of the time, John Kelley. As

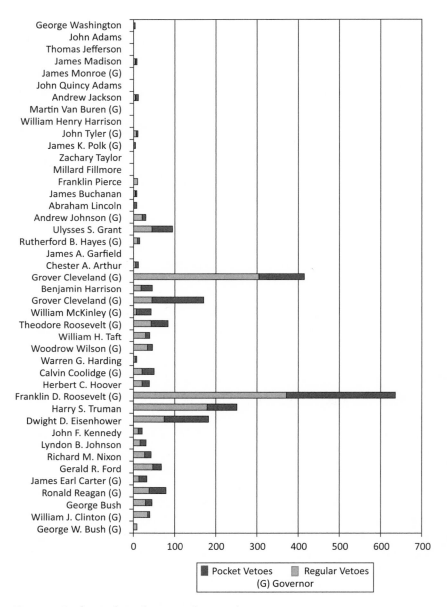

Figure 2. Pocket and regular vetoes by president

H. Wayne Morgan has pointed out about Cleveland's governorship, "Every ringing veto enlarged his public aura of honesty and independence from bread-and-butter Democrats."[92] To be sure, the use of the veto among presidents since Eisenhower has less to do with executive philosophy than with divided government. But this was not true during the rise of the modern presidency, when the warrants to veto were far more restricted, and, when challenged, were disproportionately so by former governors well versed in the practice.

Following in the footsteps of Tilden, Cleveland sought a leadership role independent of party bosses, thereby enhancing his national stature. Cleveland's early progressive support for smaller government in the interests of efficiency did not necessarily translate into a smaller executive; indeed, only the executive was powerful enough to stand up to the "interests." And there was no executive in the nation—short of the president—greater equipped than New York's governor to draw attention to the need for reform. Tilden's 1876 campaign demonstrated that Democrats could win, and that reform executives, especially Hudson progressives, could parlay their independence into national prominence. As Henry Graff has argued, "The governorship of New York was regarded as second in importance only to the presidency itself, because of the state's central location, its growing population, and its economic primacy."[93] Stephen Skowronek likewise has observed that in Cleveland's meteoric rise, "Success in a new kind of [reform] politics seemed to herald a new kind of government." To go one step further, a new kind of executive was essential to this new politics.[94]

If the use of the veto marked Cleveland's first presidential term, his second was shaped by the use of force in domestic disputes. The economic depression of 1893 enhanced the hand of executives nationally and Cleveland's use of presidential prerogative was part of a "Search for Order." "Inevitably this new value system, consciously in conflict with that of nineteenth-century America, led the new middle class to see 'the need for a government of continuous involvement' and to emphasize executive administration," wrote Robert H. Wiebe in his classic work on the period.[95] There is perhaps no better example of such active executive behavior from this time than when, in 1894, Cleveland put down the march on Washington of unemployed laborers known as "Coxey's Army" and the Pullman Strike in Chicago. Where Hayes had acted with the support of local officials, Cleveland did so over their opposition.[96]

Such intervention was atypical; it involved executive interference in state disputes deemed of a national character, and was unsolicited by state authorities.[97] Cleveland later used his emergency powers in an effort to grab hold of the economic situation responsible for the uprisings, lobbying to repeal the Silver Act of 1890. This was seen as "an unprecedented invasion of Congressional prerogative," with powerful implications for the presidency.[98] Cleveland was clearly breaking new ground in federal-state relations. Illinois's Democratic governor John P. Altgeld, for one, protested Cleveland's willingness to use force against the states, arguing that Cleveland was in violation of the law.[99] Nevertheless, Cleveland remained unshaken in his belief that he was acting in the public's best interest. The highly mixed record of Cleveland's presidential terms, particularly his second, should not detract from Cleveland's clear role in establishing a more powerful presidency.

If the modern presidency is measured by administrative expansion, centralization, White House staffing, and the dissemination of daily mail, there may well be little to see in Cleveland's presidency that speaks to a fundamentally altered national executive.[100] Yet if we look to executive prerogative, the assertion of executive authority in legislative matters, and the distinction of executive privilege, Cleveland offers as open a window as any into the beginnings of modern presidential leadership. Unfortunately, Cleveland's contributions to the presidency are buried in an obscurity defined by the oddity of his nonsuccessive terms, his physical size, and his purported support for "rum, Romanism, and rebellion."[101] Also, public fascination with Cleveland's personal scandal persists.[102] Finally, FDR's mammoth historic presidency has cast a shadow over the once highly regarded Cleveland (and nearly every other president since). Cleveland and FDR are perhaps now more popularly linked anecdotally, as it was Cleveland who once wished away any presidential ambitions for the then five-year-old Roosevelt upon first meeting him.[103]

In truth, none of the early progressive state executives demonstrated *in toto* the features of modern executive leadership best exemplified by FDR. But taken together, they do reflect the composite elements that TR, Wilson, and FDR would employ in turn and that ultimately demarcated new ground in the presidency. Equally significant is this group's executive connection to later presidential practice. To paraphrase Justice Louis Brandeis, legislatures may well have been the "laboratories of democracy," but it was late nineteenth- and early twentieth- century statehouses that became the laboratories of modern executive leadership.[104] As we shall see, no governorships were more prolific in this regard than the executive administrations of Hiram Johnson of California and Robert M. La Follette of Wisconsin.

Progressive Fury: La Follette's and Johnson's Executive Leadership

When Woodrow Wilson delivered his first presidential message to Congress in person, he is said to have introduced one of the signature procedures identified with the modern presidency.[105] Yet before Wilson challenged the sanctity of the separation of powers associated with the once hand-delivered annual message, Governor Robert M. La Follette had already done something very similar. While Wilson revived this executive ritual on the national stage, La Follette resurrected it from the earliest Empire State governors. The practice had been employed on a routine basis by New York's governors until 1821, when the state changed its constitution.[106] Reveling in the novelty of the move—in all likelihood borrowed from La Follette—Wilson bragged that he "had put one over on Teddy [Roosevelt]."[107] La Follette's action set a precedent in Wisconsin politics, to be sure, but it was also symbolic of more overt forms of executive leadership of legislatures across the country. Progressive Era notions demanded an active executive and both La Follette and Johnson were pacesetters in this regard. Like Wilson, La Follette would earn a reputation for a distinctive and "increasingly messianic conception of political leadership."[108]

Bob La Follette and the Wisconsin Executive Idea

La Follette and Johnson reflected different ends of progressivism's democratic theory; although La Follette was less sanguine about direct democracy, both governors supported a strong, Hamiltonian executive.[109] It was La Follette's veto of the Hagemeister bill while governor that earned him the reputation for introducing a confrontational brand of executive politics in Wisconsin. The bill was a direct-primary proposal full of loopholes favored by local politicians, but it did not go far enough in principle for La Follette. La Follette's opposition was manifold, but largely a product of his desire to retain control over local jurisdictions within the state.[110] As Allen Lovejoy has recounted,

"[T]he Hagemeister veto message is remarkable for its revelation of La Follette's conception of the executive in a democratic government," for it showed La Follette believed "it was the duty of the executive to call attention to the legislature to any negligence on their part to fulfilling their obligations."[111]

In the eyes of the national press, the veto was "manly" and La Follette "nervy."[112] Nonetheless, Wisconsin's legislature censured him for it, "[charging] that the Governor had transcended all bounds of legislative propriety and constitutional rights in attacking the motives of the legislature."[113] La Follette was an "unconstitutional governor" at least a decade before Wilson; the difference was that Wilson proudly gave that appellation to himself. For his part, La Follette argued in characteristically caustic fashion that "no bread is often better than half a loaf."[114]

La Follette's branch of progressive philosophy grew out of Wisconsin's peculiar ethnic and agricultural backdrop. It was a distinctly Midwestern brand of reform that would ultimately make its way out to California. But for La Follette, it began with the Grangers. "As a boy on the farm," he recalled, "I heard and felt this movement of the Grangers swirling about me; and I felt the indignation which it expressed in such a way that I suppose I never fully lost the effect of that early impression."[115] Some of La Follette's indignation was fueled by the combined national travails surrounding the Panic of 1873 and the Grant administration's unseemly railroad scandal, known as Credit Mobilier.[116] As was the case with Hiram Johnson, La Follette's early progressivism aspired to stem the flood of industrialization's grosser excesses, which favored railroad monopoly over the interests of ordinary citizens.[117]

Many years later, echoes of the Granger farm movement could be heard in La Follette's disappointment with the Hepburn Act and President Roosevelt's perceived compromise with big business.[118] The act lacked the power to fix rates unilaterally, a sine qua non for La Follette.[119] Roosevelt was far more pragmatic on the issue. "I do not represent public opinion: I represent the *public*," TR would declare. "I must not represent the excited opinion of the West, but the real interests of the whole people."[120]

The early Granger antirailroad struggle was for cheaper rates to eastern markets and federal regulation of the industry.[121] Two-thirds of Wisconsin's population lived in rural areas and was dominated by farmers. Yet manufacturing was becoming a dominant source of wealth in the state and represented the rising importance of industrial wealth and urbanization.[122] In addition, two-thirds of Wisconsin's residents were foreign-born by the late nineteenth century, and the state's ethnic composition (predominantly German and

Scandinavian) had to be considered carefully. Above all, farm interests—especially dairy—took political precedence. As these interests ran counter to those of the corporate rail lines, La Follette's passion on the issue was well placed. Railroad regulation was "the most important work in the government of this republic for this generation of men," he argued.[123] In Wisconsin, as in California during its struggles with Southern Pacific, executive leadership in fighting the railroad industry was in popular demand. The railroad and lumber interests had dominated the state for decades, with the legislature reduced to introducing periodic and largely unsuccessful feints at reform.[124] In Wisconsin, the corruption of the railroad powers resembled a western version of New York's Custom House.

Like so many progressives of his day, La Follette maintained a governing philosophy that was built upon popular electoral support with the promise of executive leadership over the legislature. The instrument of choice for accomplishing this end was the direct primary.[125] La Follette championed the idea as a candidate for governor in 1896, after failing to earn the Republican Party nomination.[126] His first major speech on the subject, "The Menace of the Political Machine," delivered at the University of Chicago in 1897, called for an end to all caucus and convention systems in favor of the direct primary and the administration of the Australian ballot.[127] It was a call whose messianism typified the emergence of Second Republic executives:

> You will place the nominations directly in the hands of the people. You will restore to every state in the union the government given to this people by the God of nations. To every generation some important work is committed. If this generation will destroy the political machine, will emancipate the majority from its enslavement, will again place the destinies of this nation in the hands of its citizens, then "Under God, this government of the people, by the people and for the people shall not perish from the earth."[128]

It would take until the election of 1904 and La Follette's second term as governor for the direct primary to become a reality in Wisconsin politics. Countering the charge that the direct primary was unconstitutional, La Follette argued that "many of the accepted institutions of the United States are not part of that document."[129] La Follette's indirect claim of divine mandate reflects what Nancy Unger has called the purported "omniscience" at the heart of La Follette's veto of the Hagemeister bill; it was certainly this and more—a hallmark of a transformed national executive whose connection to the people carried overtly spiritual portents. For all of his attempts to associate himself with Lincoln, La Follette's rhetoric, and indeed, that of the age, abandoned the Lincolnesque quality of righteous humility. Woodrow Wilson's later view of his executive authority would push even further. "I owe you nothing," Wilson told the Democratic national party chairman the day after being elected. *"Remember that God ordained that I should be the next President of the United States."*[130] Nevertheless, as David Thelen has noted, "insurgent voters accepted this messianic and plebiscitarian concept of leadership because they believed, based on local experiences, that their leader would have to be a superman to defeat the corporations."[131] In many respects, La Follette's and other progressives' advocacy for the direct primary produced unreasonable expectations from voters about what adoption of the measure could ultimately do.[132]

Of course, La Follette's leadership of the legislature reflected his belief in executive primacy. La Follette biographer Fred Greenbaum has called his tactics "strange and frightening" to his opponents, who were unaccustomed to such pushiness from the governor.[133] "It was very well known that I was the only man in the capital who could crowd that legislature to do its duty," La Follette boasted.[134] Employing a legislative strategy that foreshadowed FDR's efforts against his own party years later, La Follette spared little in the way of party loyalty in his reelection campaign of 1904. La Follette biographer Carl Burgchardt captured this preemptive party purge well:

> In 1900 La Follette had disregarded the election of the legislature. In 1902 he had endorsed certain candidates. But in 1904 he campaigned in the districts of his political opponents. In addition for the first time La Follette openly endorsed Democrats who were running against [Republican] Stalwart candidates. La Follette urged voters to support men who stood for reform, and he pleaded for citizens to disregard party affiliation. La Follette needed a powerful rhetorical weapon in 1904 to influence the election of the legislature. In April and May of 1904 he had experimented with a new tactic, which he called "reading the roll" to the people of Wisconsin. After considering a specific issue, such as the railroad commission bill, he then would read the official vote of the legislature, usually including only the "wrong" votes of Stalwarts. By the fall of 1904 "reading the roll" had become a central feature of La Follette's campaign speeches.[135]

From delivering his annual message to legislators in person to "reading the roll" against members of his own party, La Follette established unprecedented executive practices in Wisconsin. "The Wisconsin Idea," as La Follette's progressive reform programs came to be known, would gain national attention and influence. When Wisconsin did adopt the direct primary, it became the first state to do so, altering electoral politics for decades to come. Yet there was more to the Wisconsin Idea than the direct primary law. La Follette also pioneered state-university relations, fostering far greater interaction between higher education and government than was thought either permissible or desirable at the time.[136] While La Follette's vision begat a failed presidential bid in 1924, the ranks of former La Follette supporters that would soon litter the administration of FDR speak to his influence.[137]

When Louis Hartz wrote, "La Follette was about all that remained of the high enthusiasm of the Progressive movement," in 1924, he was stating a partial truth.[138] Much of La Follette's and progressivism's brand of executive politics endured well into the twentieth century. La Follette's reforms did indeed "serve as models that were copied, in whole or in part, by many other states and by the national government."[139] Like Cleveland, La Follette's strong executive served as a prototype for later models.[140] And, as we shall see, La Follette's emphasis on executive intervention in the public interest was not lost on the next generation of progressives, who would not only do much more than La Follette, but also, in many ways great and small, largely *because* of him.[141]

Hiram Johnson and the California Exception

The University of Wisconsin's Frederick Jackson Turner famously stamped the frontier as the dominant force in American political development in 1893. "The meeting point between civilization and savagery," as he described it, had been officially declared "closed" by the 1890 U.S. Census Bureau. Yet, for the renowned writer and historian Carey McWilliams, California was the exception to the exception of America. California had never, in fact, belonged to the frontier, and this reality had a profound influence on future political and economic developments in the state.[142] As Spencer C. Olin, Jr. noted, "California differs from other states because it skipped the frontier phase of land development. Because of early Spanish and Mexican grants, California began with land monopoly."[143] The result was one of heightened social and economic stratification, with a severe labor problem piled on top of real social instability.[144] Practically speaking, the railroads became the dominant political force in the state. As George Mowry put it, "California, like so many of her sister commonwealths at the turn of the century, had only the shadow of representative government."[145] The railroads were the de facto political power in California.

Southern Pacific's dominance was part of the prize won by southern Democrats when they exchanged restoration of white home rule for the Hayes presidency back in 1877. The company's new route was purported to foster industrial development in the South. While the compromise was largely an economic bust for the South, one of the unintended consequences was that it helped create a political megalith in California.[146] Southern Pacific became a veritable Standard Oil and Tammany Hall rolled into one.[147] As the historian R. Hal Williams has described it, "Except for a few years in the late 1880's, when hostility toward the railroad temporarily subsided, Californians viewed the decades between 1870 and 1900 as a continuous struggle to free their state from railroad thralldom."[148] As can be imagined, the railroad loomed large in Hiram Johnson's early life and political career: "The dominant power in the city of Hiram Johnson's childhood [Sacramento], the Southern Pacific was the dominant power at the state Capitol as well. As the largest single employer and landholder in the state, it had the most to win, the most to lose, and by all odds the most to preserve through its manipulation of the political process."[149] Before Hiram Johnson's governorship, there had been mostly token, unsuccessful efforts at thwarting Southern Pacific's political lock on the state. Johnson's father had been, much to his son's shame, part of a conservative line of leaders and businessmen who owed their allegiance to Southern Pacific. Despite initially opposing bossism in Sacramento, Johnson's father ultimately succumbed to it.[150] But the rise of progressivism in the state, along with Johnson's own doggedness and political guile, was crucial to turning the tide against the railroad. More to the point, Johnson's political success marked the beginning of a wildly democratic popular insurgency in California, one with executive implications for later state and national leaders. Newcomers accounted for much of this transformation. By 1890, nearly half of all Californians were from the Midwest, and that percentage would only increase. These Midwesterners would play an even greater role in southern California politics than in the state as a whole. The spirit of populism, Protestantism, and progressivism had traveled westward.[151]

Johnson's rise in state politics was assisted, in part, by the creation of a neo-Republican organization, the Lincoln-Roosevelt League. The organization's name captured both its progressivism and detachment from the more staid national image of the Republican Party (a similar development would occur in New Jersey). Moreover, the political dynamics originating in Wisconsin wound their way into California politics. In time, Southern Pacific's hold on Republican candidates began to wither, beginning with the establishment of the League in 1907. A new primary law that all but eliminated nominating conventions delivered another blow. Hiram Johnson took advantage of this opportunity, getting the necessary signatures to launch a campaign against the railroad interests.[152] Johnson's gubernatorial victory in 1910 was a profound and precedent-setting break in California politics. Its tone was reminiscent of Tilden's triumph over Tweed, Cleveland's rebuke of Tammany Hall, and La Follette's direct primary challenge to the rail and lumber interests of Wisconsin. Johnson tapped into a wave of Roosevelt-inspired progressivism, one equally focused on the executive in its political philosophy. Large pictures of Roosevelt were never far from Johnson throughout the gubernatorial campaign, and Johnson's victory earned him instant comparisons with the "Rough Rider."[153] Robert Cleland described the connection well: "The people saw in him only the fearless champion of the Lincoln-Roosevelt League, the two-fisted champion of the common man." Johnson had become "the California Roosevelt, the nemesis of the political machine."[154]

As Herbert Croly noted, a host of progressive statesmen assumed the imprimatur of the people's will. Hiram Johnson was no different, supporting not only the direct primary in California, but also the referendum, initiative, and recall. Like La Follette in Wisconsin and Woodrow Wilson in New Jersey, Johnson rejected "the whole theory of checks and balances as a denial of popular government."[155] While Croly belonged to a class of progressives more disposed to elite representation, his political writings should not be read as necessarily antithetical to those of progressives like Johnson. Whether or not an "Athenian" school of popular government was favored over more elitist interpretations, Progressive Era governors exercised an almost universally adhered-to belief in the supra-authority of the executive. And at the presidential level, later governor-presidents, especially TR, Wilson, and FDR, thought so almost as an article of faith.[156]

In legislative matters, Governor Johnson took the early lead. He backed the initiative, referendum, and recall with each bill passing, including a surprisingly wide margin allowing for judicial recall. He also pushed for and won the establishment of a railroad commission that greatly reduced Southern Pacific's political influence in the state. And Johnson led the call for civil service reform, bringing the merit system to California, professionalizing its workforce for decades to come. While the bureaucracy grew considerably, it was efficient, modern, and sufficiently expert by the time Ronald Reagan took office some fifty years later.[157] As Reagan biographer Lou Cannon points out, the executive connection to popular democracy in California was built upon the premise that the legislature was part of the defect of checks and balances, one that had to be overcome in the interests of the people: "Coming from another direction, the Progressives in the early twentieth century also distrusted the Legislature. Instead of fearing that the Legislature would be too responsive to the passions of the majority, the Progressives were concerned that it would not be responsive at all. The Progressive remedy was 'direct democracy,' including the initiative and the referendum. When the Legislature failed to act, the people could."[158]While Governor Ronald Reagan would lose in his initiative effort years later, his willingness to wield it as a political weapon reveals an important thread of Second Republic executive philosophy: democracy is best forwarded when executive representation is its vessel.

Johnson's success as governor was built upon this premise. A relative neophyte as doctrinaire progressive, he cut his teeth in long meetings in the East with Bob La Follette and Teddy Roosevelt.[159] More important, Johnson guided the legislature through a loyal and well-oiled political machine of his own, one that drew inevitable comparisons with Southern Pacific.[160] At the end of his first year as governor, Johnson's administration passed a remarkable twenty-three amendments to the state constitution.[161] Johnson's was a bootstrap progressivism if nothing else, and he understood his executive role with a visceral sense of authority and duty. As Richard Lower notes, "In 1911 Johnson and the California legislature captured the attention of progressives throughout the nation—in no other state had so bold a set of reforms been put into place in so short a span of time."[162] The following year, Johnson traveled to Ohio to speak at its Constitutional Convention, offering the state his insights about what progressive reform entailed.[163] A circle of sorts was completed, as Midwestern progressivism wheeled its way west and back home again.

When Johnson joined Theodore Roosevelt on the 1912 Progressive Party ticket, the two ex-Republicans and Woodrow Wilson represented a triumvirate of progressive executive leadership that, while not monolithic, was demonstrably modern in both ideas and governance.[164] It was not the high-water mark of modern American executive political development, but it was a crucial doorway to what was to come. As Sidney M. Milkis writes, "FDR consciously patterned his leadership after that of Woodrow Wilson and Theodore Roosevelt, seeking to reconcile the strengths of these leaders."[165] It was reconciliation more of kindred spirits than of adversaries, at least with respect to the role of executive authority. Taken together, Hiram Johnson and Robert M. La Follette, as well as any, helped demonstrate the possibilities of executive power in this emergent presidential republic.

Conclusion: The Progressive Turn

At the beginning of the twentieth century, American executives orchestrated a radical departure from Virginian notions of a limited presidency. This movement was led by a progressive line of governors—protomoderns, if you like—who exercised executive authority and held governing philosophies so largely detached from what came before that one can't help but look upon them as edifiers of some new regime. What did come before them—namely, a First Republic defined by notions of limited executive power—had become, for a variety of reasons (mostly to do with nascent progressivism), a nonportable executive philosophy. What the election of 1876 effectively initiated was a march toward executive power that would shape the office and expectations of the modern presidency for well over a hundred years. From Grover Cleveland's invocation of executive privilege to Bob La Follette's first personally delivered address to the legislature, modern executives were establishing precedents and brokering new relationships between themselves and the public that previously had been sporadic or nonexistent. The forty-year reign of progressive governors discussed here constituted a detour in American political development, one with lasting implications for the presidency.

The legacy of late nineteenth- and early twentieth-century executives requires understanding their connections to the modern presidency as a whole. Many of these state executives either became or greatly influenced modern presidents in ways that we may now only be beginning to appreciate. When Hiram Johnson, in the twilight of his life and senate career, spoke of a "revolution" to come, he was speaking of liberal government's redefinition, complete with new purposes for executive leadership. That revolution did in fact take place. And Johnson and his cadre of progressive executives provided its cri de guerre. In laying claim to guardianship status, Second Republic executives advocated a form of democracy emanating from the popular will, yet manifestly singular in voice and execution. Such was Woodrow Wilson's retort to the fading notion that ours is a "government of laws and not of men." "You know that [line] doesn't taste right," he insisted, just days before his election as governor of New Jersey. "Every government is a government of men and not of laws," he said, concluding the thought with the assertion that "Government is personal, gentlemen, the responsibilities of government are personal."[166] Such sentiments, challenging as they were to worn constitutional theories, foretold the blossoming of prerogative power and party decline in the United States. Whether or not this reality would ultimately best conform to republican virtues will be taken up later. It is to those executives who embodied this newly crafted executive creed that we now turn.

Chapter 2

Theodore Roosevelt and the New American Executive, 1881–1911

Wherever public opinion has been vigorously demanding
the adoption of a progressive state policy, the agent to
which it has turned for the carrying out of that policy
has been a candidate for governor. . . . These executives
have usually been accused of usurpation of power, but
the accusation has not had any practical effect.
—Herbert Croly, *Progressive Democracy*, 1914[1]

I think, my dear Governor, that you put the party in a
most unfortunate position. . . . to the average man it
looks as though the Republican Governor of this great
commonwealth has become intoxicated by the sounding
brass and tinkling cymbals of these sensational
Democratic newspapers, and he shoved the conservative
Republican party in a Populistic whirlpool.
—Republican Party Boss Thomas Platt, *Letter to Theodore
Roosevelt*, May 6, 1899[2]

Introduction

In early 1900, some twenty months before assuming the presidency, Governor
Theodore Roosevelt was embroiled in but the latest of the many political fights
of his life. Already in a battle with New York's conservative Republican party

boss Thomas Platt over Roosevelt's growing opposition to trusts, TR added further fuel to the fire. Like so many Hudson progressives before him, Roosevelt found himself at odds with New York's political machine—in this instance, it was with the "Easy Boss" Platt, who demanded that Roosevelt reappoint one of his trusted men, one Louis Payn. TR refused to rubber-stamp the appointment, only to find his political career threatened by the state's party leader. Roosevelt was undaunted and called Platt's bluff, girding himself with the knowledge that he was in the right, and that other governors had survived similar battles.[3] In the end, TR forced Platt and the party to back down and accept one of Roosevelt's alternates for the appointment. A *New York World* cartoon captured Roosevelt's posture in the matter well, depicting the governor "serving" Payn—drawn appropriately enough as a crow—to Platt for breakfast.[4] Ever prideful, Roosevelt wrote a memorable line to a friend a few days later: "I have always been fond of the West African proverb: 'Speak softly and carry a big stick; you will go far.' "[5]

Like so much of what has been written about Roosevelt, this aphorism is presumed to have originated in the White House. Indeed, it has become part of popular lore that TR's "big-stick" philosophy grew out of presidential foreign policy making. Not only is this untrue, but it also masks some of the more important aspects of how the modern presidency took form, and, crucially, it underestimates the role played by governors in establishing new and often brazen features of executive politics. Moreover, such personalist forms of leadership were not initiated by Roosevelt—as president or otherwise. They had long since been part of a trajectory of executive behavior coming out of the states that helped redefine the terms of acceptable presidential conduct. "Big stick" executive politics began in progressive statehouses, not international vistas.

It is therefore no accident that Herbert Croly, perhaps progressivism's grandest theoretician, drew inspiration for his model of executive politics from America's early twentieth-century governors. Writing shortly after TR's presidency, Croly was uncertain as to whether or not the Rooseveltian model of executive power could be sustained. One of Croly's biggest fears was that the Republican party's conversion to progressivism under Roosevelt was "hollow" and would lead to the loss of true progressive reforms.[6] As Roosevelt would in turn be inspired by Croly's *The Promise of American Life*, so had Croly been moved by TR's presidency, one replete with even greater progressive possibilities.[7] The challenge for Croly and other reform advocates at the time was to find a way to normalize executive authority and bypass those legislative checks and party loyalties threatening popular reform. For answers, Croly looked to the states. He was particularly drawn to the executive successes found in Governor Robert La Follette's Wisconsin, and in an Oregon plan rife with executive authority. Here, Croly argued, "the electorate would be intrusting power not to a party, not to a system, but to a man."[8] Interestingly, Croly (and later Woodrow Wilson) was drawn to the ideas of a little-remembered Oregon legislator, William S. U'Ren, who stood at the fore of theorizing progressive reform's relationship with executive power. Beyond Roosevelt, presidential models proved less instructive.

As has been noted, one of the Progressive Era's great ironies was that in seeking democratic ends, progressives often eschewed democratic means and structures. "Governors who reject [extralegal measures] and who remain scrupulously loyal to the old theory of the separation of powers are considered weak and poor-spirited," Croly argued.[9] Croly had the presidency in mind in his analyses of state practices and gubernatorial projects around the country. His perfunctory effort to tamp down concerns for executive excess was notable if not convincing:

> [The governor's] legal powers, when reinforced by public confidence, would give him an enormous advantage over any other specific branch of government. Might not that advantage be so overwhelming as to degrade the legislature into an insignificant and unnecessary part of the governmental mechanism? Could not such a powerful administration easily arrange the convenience of a subservient legislative majority? Would not the result be to bestow upon the once omnipotent American legislature about as much power and dignity as had the legislative assembly during the early years of the second Napoleonic empire?[10]

Croly offered a pithy remedy to his query: voters would have the recall option available to them as a check against a presumptive American Prince. As for legislative leadership, Croly was even more dismissive. "The legislature represents those minor phases of public opinion which have sufficient energy and conscience to demand some vehicle of expression."[11] Finally, and unapologetically, Croly argued for an American charismatic:

> A vague popular aspiration or a crude and groping popular interest often requires incarnation in a single man. . . . His exhortation and

explanations and his proposals to convert such aspirations and interests into action bring them to a head and start them on a career of
adjustment to the general interest. Even the most sophisticated soci-
eties are rarely able to feel much enthusiasm about a principle or a
program until it becomes incarnated in a vivid personality and is
enhanced as a result of the incarnation. In the case of less sophisticated people, such as compose the majority of modern democracy,
no program is likely to be politically effective unless it is temporarily
associated with an effective personality.[12]

Roosevelt embodied this ideal for Croly; however, Croly also saw the
portent of new-styled executive leadership in Grover Cleveland and in governors more generally.[13] "The best reform legislation now enacted usually orig-
inates in executive mansions," Croly wrote in 1909 in *The Promise of American
Life*.[14] Croly's writings undoubtedly spoke to a broad set of progressive theories, not the least of which was progressivism's ties to the unrestrained executive, and the related breakthrough moment for governors in presidential
politics. "The subordination of the executive to the legislature would conform to the early American political tradition," Croly warned at the time.[15]
The dated and constitutionally conscious Virginian model of executive governance was under assault—and no more so than in New York. As the historian
Richard L. McCormick described, "For a century, a slow trend had taken its toll
on the power of state lawmakers by shortening their sessions, forbidding them
to pass certain kinds of laws, and burdening them with procedural limitations.
[By] the 1890s these pressures continued from those who distrusted the legislature to deal with increasingly specialized matters of governance. Every state
executive of the period sought in a different way to lessen legislative powers."[16]
    By the time TR became president, executives at the national and state levels
had already crossed significant constitutional thresholds. From TR's initial
tutelage in executive politics as assemblyman during Cleveland's governorship in Albany, to Woodrow Wilson's last year in Trenton, governors were at
the fore of a period of unprecedented executive vitality and experimentation. State executives and governor-presidents led the turn away from Croly's
passé legislative state to a more robust presidential republic.[17] As James P. Young
noted, "The result was a number of measures that set in motion the long-
term decline of the party system—the rise of the direct primary and the resort
to devices such as the initiative, referendum, and recall that had their roots
in populism."[18] There was no more pivotal figure in this narrative than Teddy

Roosevelt, who formed a bridge between Cleveland and Wilson as the new executive archetype. It was Roosevelt's governorship that may have best anticipated modern presidential practices, in part, because New York's constitution along with the state's newspapers came to extol the virtues of the grand executive. As such, one of the more important starting points for grasping modern executive practice in the United States is to be found in the governorship of Theodore Roosevelt.

Order from Disorder and the Hudson Executive

The historian Robert Wiebe once described the period after Reconstruction as the birth of "a society without a core." Wiebe was part of a growing number of historians and intellectuals who associated the intersection of material wealth and industry with the loss of individuality and local autonomy. The Panic of 1873, coming amid the corruptions of the Grant administration and soon followed by the divisive resolution of the election of 1876, was the beginning of an era of great social unrest in America. Undoubtedly, at the heart of the new urban industrial order was a yearning for greater meaning, as the once presumed sense of community and belonging felt by many Americans began to slip away.[19] This "distended society," as Wiebe described it, failed to extend economic growth to the citizenry as a whole. Walt Whitman's lament captures the sense of disorder:

> I saw to-day a sight I had never seen before and it amazed, and made me serious; three quite good-looking American men, of respectable personal presence, two of them young, carrying chiffonier-bags on their shoulders, and the usual long iron hooks in their hands, plodding along, their eyes cast down, spying for scraps, rags, bones, etc. If the United States, like the countries of the Old World, are also to grow vast crops of poor, desperate, dissatisfied, nomadic, miserably-waged populations, such as we see looming upon us of late years—steadily, even if slowly, eating into them like a cancer of lungs and stomach— then our republican experiment, notwithstanding all its surface-successes, is at heart an unhealthy failure.[20]

The era's economic imperative, outlined by Whitman, became foundational to later American conceptions of justice and fairness, and served as the backdrop to a new theory of American rights. The sense of alienation—both economic and psychological—was instrumental in creating the conditions that foreshadowed Franklin D. Roosevelt's "reappraisal of values."[21] As Woodrow Wilson would famously remark, "government does not stop with the protection of life, liberty, and property; it goes on to serve every convenience in society."[22] As president, Wilson, and later FDR, would design an agenda rooted in this basic premise, while orchestrating presidencies built on plebiscitary leadership and executive primacy. But they would each do so first, and with great effect, as governors.

Roosevelt's and Wilson's executive philosophies were seemingly validated by such disillusionment and social disconnection, as progressives clamored for immediate action. The vigor found in their governorships was also partly the product of political history. The shared Hudson River border between New York and New Jersey mirrors a similar executive political heritage. Indeed, the two states actually shared one governor until 1738.[23] New York's port and the Hudson River gave the two states an outsized geopolitical significance. By the mid-eighteenth century, the port had become an international commercial boon, carrying with it untold patronage possibilities. Tom Lewis's history of the Hudson captures this reality well: "As shipping increased in the nineteenth century, the port expanded its wharves to both sides of Manhattan Island, as well as to Staten Island, Brooklyn, and the New Jersey Shore—771 miles of wharfage in all. The day Lincoln arrived [for his Cooper Union address], steamships from Le Havre, Liverpool, Hamburg, Baltimore, Savannah, and Havana docked in New York; other ships embarked for Glasgow, Marseilles, Liverpool, Hong Kong, and Barbados."[24]

Both states were early progenitors of strong governorships with lasting, if intermittently, executive-centered constitutions. While New York's governors have held a consistently powerful place in the state's government, New Jersey has seen more wild swings in its executive's authority. In the end, Roosevelt's and Wilson's governorships were notable beyond the strength of their personalities. Their success as national examples was made possible by the plausibility of their executive actions—a product of the constitutional authority presented by both their states and media-dominant locales.[25]

The Hudson model of progressive-executive reform was unique, as the region was the font of capital, news-generation, and "heroic" national personalities going back as far as Martin Van Buren's governorship. Moreover, the tradition of independent executive leadership had been established in

New York at least as early as Samuel J. Tilden, and had only been bolstered in the interim by Grover Cleveland's tenures as both governor and president. It is hard to imagine today Theodore Roosevelt ever standing in the shadow of Samuel J. Tilden. Yet Tilden had helped expand the realm of executive possibilities by the time Roosevelt took the oath of office in Albany on New Year's Eve of 1898. In essence, Roosevelt, like Cleveland before him, had to demonstrate that he was a worthy successor to the progressive line of Hudson leadership. Barely a month into Roosevelt's term, the *New York Times* revisited this theme:

> Mr. Tilden's exposure of the canal frauds when he was Governor was a master stroke of policy as well as morals. The Republican Party was sunk in corruption. All over the land the cry went up for reform. Governor Tilden's work in New York made him the most conspicuous reformer in the Nation. . . . There is the same opportunity in New York now for a great reformer, the same field, the same work. . . . But this time it is no Democratic Tilden, it is the Republican Roosevelt who is called to do the work. He is going to be the great reformer of the day. Upon him the eyes of the country will be fixed. Who knows where the fame of his work will carry him?[26]

Despite the fact that progressive hopes were riding on TR's success, the demands on New York's governor were particularly burdensome. The popular pressure to address the dual evils of bossism and patronage loomed large in the state's history. As Stephen Skowronek has noted, the state's centripetal force was geopolitical in nature and had been for some time:

> [Between 1877 and 1882] reform progressed through two distinct phases. The first centered on the New York Customshouse. Here reform rode a confluence of interests among a faction of the Republican party, a reform-minded President, the merchants of New York, and reform leaders. . . . The electoral compromise of 1877 set the political conditions for civil service reform's first success in American government. . . . The Port of New York was the lifeline of American government, accounting for well over 50 percent of all federal revenues. . . . More than any other single office, the New York Customshouse symbolized the fusion of party and state, and more than any other single

office, it focused the interests of merchants and gentlemen reformers against spoils administration.[27]

To meet the challenge of corruption, New York's governor had to navigate the perilous waters of party and boss confrontation, and an increasingly powerful press—all while leading a reform agenda ambitious enough to draw popular support, yet modest enough to garner legislative victories. In short, reformers wanted an executive big enough to stand up to the cold and patently undemocratic interests of canals, custom houses, and machines, yet not so big as to dwarf the will of the people. Paradoxically, in winning for a time some of the more cherished concessions demanded by progressives, Roosevelt's governorship initiated other steps away from lasting democratic protections, widening the gap between the executive and the people. Roosevelt's time in Albany foreshadowed similar developments in his presidency. As Sidney Milkis and Michael Nelson point out, "By itself, Roosevelt's ability to get a considerable part of his program enacted in the absence of a national crisis and in spite of the tepid support, and sometimes the outright resistance, of his party indicated that a new era of presidential leadership had arrived. From now on, government action would be much more likely to bear the president's personal stamp than in the past."[28] This state of affairs was largely due to the decline of parties and voter turnout, and the advent of more direct executive appeals for popular support. "The civic republican model," noted the political scientist John Gerring, "in which the people courted statesmen, now stood on its head."[29] Roosevelt expressed this burgeoning freedom from bossism well: "I myself am a cog in the New York machine," he recognized, "but the machine must do right or this cog will begin to turn independently."[30]

Not all were pleased with the rise of such independence. By 1905, Louis Brandeis joined the chorus of disaffected progressives, albeit privately, deploring then President Roosevelt's "kingly attitude."[31] By this time, the prerogatives of the new American executive were evident in a variety of venues. Indeed, when the first mayor of a newly consolidated New York City Robert Van Wyck gave a two-sentence inaugural address in 1898, it was an invocation of an executive zeitgeist. "Mr. Mayor, the people have chosen me to be mayor," Van Wyck began. "I shall say whatever I have to say to them." And, stunningly, that was that.[32] Van Wyck's record ultimately demonstrated, and in some respects foreshadowed, the extremes of the plebiscitary leader: rhetoric was for the people, reform for the campaign, and power, ultimately and increasingly, was to the executive. Undoubtedly, Roosevelt's tenure as New York governor is a window into his later contributions to the modern presidency as a whole. Mastery of legislative and party leadership, the routinization of executive-press relations, and an executive-centered governing philosophy are all on display. And yet it is also a window into how that philosophy so precious to Croly and other reformers had in some respects become detached from the very ends from which it emanated. "The bestowal upon an executive of increased official responsibility and power will be stigmatized by 'old-fashioned Democrats' as dangerously despotic," dismissed Croly.[33] Such assertions presumed a great deal of the American electorate and, even more, of conscientious and enlightened executive statecraft.

ROOSEVELT'S ALBANY EXECUTIVE

By the time Theodore Roosevelt took the oath of office as the youngest president in American history, he was arguably the most famous person in the United States. Roosevelt's notoriety was hardly accidental, as few politicians knew how to stage their own photographic and print legacy as the great game-hunter and Rough Rider-turned-corruption-fighter.[34] Today, Roosevelt has come to hold a near mythic place in presidential history. Much of what is written about him touches upon his role in ushering in the modern presidency. In positing Roosevelt as the "father of the rhetorical presidency," Jeffrey Tulis places him at the epicenter of the institution's coming of age:

> Roosevelt's [railroad regulation] argument was that a change in autho-
> rized practices was necessary to fulfill the purposes of the underlying
> founding theory of governance. So Roosevelt criticized the founding
> theory from within, displaying some of the dilemmas of governance
> built into the original arrangements. . . . [This] serves as a paradigm
> of rhetorical leadership properly conceived and exercised. Franklin
> Roosevelt's campaign to pass the Social Security Act and Reagan's
> achievement of tax reform are two very similar successes in American
> political history . . . [It] also helps to explain how Woodrow Wilson's
> subsequent rejection of the constitutional perspective of the founders
> took hold when it did.[35]

Notably, the exceptional executives cited here were all former governors. It is well to remember how the rhetorical and other political skills they brought to bear on the modern presidency were honed first during their tenures as governor.

Roosevelt's Media Command and Legislative Leadership

It is nearly impossible to separate Roosevelt's handling of the press from his legislative accomplishments and position within his party. Newspapers had long since been largely affiliates of either parties or corporate interests, with few forwarding a progressive agenda. The latter were most enthusiastic about Governor Roosevelt's willingness to take on New York's corporations, which had been largely exempt from paying taxes on the public franchises they owned. To fight corporate power, early progressives sought executive leadership. As Roosevelt biographer Wallace Chessman reminded, "The New York Sun recalled that when Cleveland came to Albany he regarded his task as 'essentially executive,' whereas Governor Roosevelt has shown, more strikingly than in any other instance in recent years, that the office is likewise essentially legislative."[36] Cleveland's example comported well with Roosevelt's own executive philosophy. "In theory the Executive has nothing to do with legislation," wrote Roosevelt. "In practice, as things now are, the Executive is or ought to be peculiarly representative of the people as a whole."[37] Progressives saw this new "legislative executive" as an essential part of the war against both the spoils system and more general machine-based corruption. A Hamiltonian executive with a sense of Jeffersonian popular appeal was thus indispensable to the leadership model Roosevelt sought to employ while governor.[38]

New York's governorship produced a recurring progressive "bully pulpit" in the years leading up to TR's tenure. From advocacy for clean government to a young Franklin Roosevelt's publicity campaign for the direct election of senators, the position had gained authoritative resonance as keeper of the progressive flame.[39] As Chessman noted, "New York afforded a scope for executive leadership unsurpassed outside the national capital. Here was a premier place to explore the problems disturbing the urban-industrial society, and to advance solutions that might mark the way for others. Here was that rare rostrum assured of national prominence and attention."[40] Certainly, New York endured its share of antireformist and reactionary governors. But it was adherence to the state's reform tradition that created national political opportunities. It could not have been lost on Roosevelt that between the Civil and Spanish and American Wars, New York governors had been major party candidates in five of the seven presidential elections.[41] For Roosevelt to be the eighth, he would have to do so in the tradition of a progressive Hudson line of executives with true reform accomplishments. To this end, Roosevelt cultivated the image of a reformer, instituting the unprecedented practice of holding two daily question-and-answer sessions with members of the press.[42] Accordingly, the *New York Times* credited Roosevelt with "[tearing] down the curtain that shut in the Governor."[43]

The unseemly relationship between secrecy and monopolistic power had been one of the great evils attacked by progressives in the era. Yet, Roosevelt's 11 A.M. and 5 P.M. press sessions were more theatrical than illuminating. "It is not publicity in this manner that news of importance is gained," the *Times* noted about these early press conferences. "At [one] conference the writer attended while in Albany . . . the most famous of all the Albany correspondents was conspicuous by his absence."[44] While Roosevelt's meetings institutionalized press relations under the auspices of assisting the public, they were held with the governor's benefit in mind. The daily sessions were opportunities to leak information of Roosevelt's choosing and to assess potential hazards. He may not have been the first to employ the "trial balloon" for proposed policies, but Roosevelt regularized the practice, and would go on to establish the first White House press room.[45] One biographer deemed Roosevelt's Albany press relations "the most revolutionary change from past practice."[46]

Since the press was Roosevelt's most effective means of speaking directly to the people, he fostered the relationship early on; press conferences became his counter to boss control in New York. "I therefore made no effort to create a machine of my own, and consistently adopted the plan of going over the heads of the men holding public office and of the men in control of the organization, and appealing directly to the people behind them," Roosevelt explained.[47] As Stephen Ponder noted, Roosevelt used the press "to shape public opinion that drew both from his notion of expanding executive power as a 'steward of the people' and from the Progressive view that properly informing the public was necessary to create support for reform."[48]

Indeed, Roosevelt's governorship produced unprecedented press coverage. Since the inception of the *New York Times*, no other New York governor garnered the number of annual citations as Roosevelt did during his two-year tenure in Albany. The *Times* would cover no other governor as closely or as widely until Franklin Roosevelt's tenure. While Tilden's and Cleveland's terms changed the scope of *Times* coverage, Roosevelt's set a new standard, dwarfing

Table 3. Governors of New York and *New York Times* Citations, 1851–1900

Governor	Years	Total Citations	Yearly Average	Rank
Theodore Roosevelt (R)	1898–1900	408	204.0	1
Frank S. Black (R)	1896–1898	87	43.5	7
Levi P. Morton (R)	1894–1896	152	76.0	3
Roswell P. Flower (D)	1891–1894	133	44.3	6
David B. Hill (D)	1884–1891	642	91.7	2
Grover Cleveland (D)	1882–1884	131	65.5	5
Alonzo B. Cornell (R)	1879–1882	45	15.0	10
Lucius B. Robinson (R)	1876–1879	52	17.3	8
Samuel J. Tilden (D)	1874–1876	133	66.5	4
John Adams Dix (R)	1872–1874	33	16.5	9
John T. Hoffman (D)	1868–1872	55	13.7	13
Reuben E. Fenton (D)	1864–1868	36	9.0	15t
Horatio Seymour (D)	1861–1864	25	12.5	14
Edwin D. Morgan (R)	1858–1862	19	4.7	17
John A. King (R)	1856–1858	29	14.5	12
Myron H. Clark (Fusion-R)	1854–1856	18	9.0	15t
Horatio Seymour (D)	1852–1854	30	15.0	11
Washington Hunt (Whig Anti-Rent)	1851–1852	25	25.0	N/A

Note: Dates are from December 31 to December 30 for years cited.

his predecessors in terms of annual citations. The effect of Roosevelt's institutionalization of press relations can be seen in Table 3:

The political benefits that would redound to Roosevelt from such sizeable and largely favorable press coverage would be evident in his most impressive legislative accomplishment.

The Ford Franchise Bill

Roosevelt's celebrity and effective direction of the New York press helped push forward one of the Progressive Era's most visible, if not most successful, pieces of legislation. In an early move against Boss Platt, Roosevelt cherry-picked from four bills in the legislature, focusing on "one proposing a general state tax on all such power and traction [franchise] privileges, in order to replenish the state treasury."[49] Such defiance marked Roosevelt out as a committed and innovative progressive, willing to stand up to the strongest of machines. It was Platt's mentor Roscoe Conkling, after all, whom TR believed had destroyed his father's political career.

Roosevelt had to work to cultivate a reformer's cachet, however; the New York press had been most unforgiving of him for holding Saturday morning breakfasts with Platt, and for his seeming penchant for last-minute compromise. The fact was that Roosevelt carved out a centrist position within the progressive movement. As John Milton Cooper, Jr. reminds, "One close observer later commented that [Roosevelt's] insistence on balance and qualification had usually prevented him from being a real orator."[50] Roosevelt would not go down the overly strident rhetorical path of Bryan, a veritable Robespierre, "grotesque" and "pitiable."[51] As Roosevelt explained in his consideration of taxing franchises, "The line of cleavage between good and bad citizenship does not follow the line dividing the men who represent corporate interests from the men who do not; it runs at right angles to it. We are bound to recognize this fact, to remember that we should stand for good citizenship in every form, and should neither yield to demagogic influence on the one hand, nor to improper corporate influence on the other."[52]

While the Ford franchise tax bill on corporations (as it came to be known) was ultimately adopted and properly viewed as a welding by Roosevelt of "conservatism to reform,"[53] it was largely hailed as a heroic moment in progressive policy making. "The Governor knew how to tax franchises," opined the *New York Herald*, "and his good strong jaw and his bright shining teeth were set in an unalterable resolve not to yield."[54] Such praise nevertheless masked some of the more practical difficulties of implementation and enforcement of the bill, which did not pass legal muster until Roosevelt was no longer governor.[55] But it was such challenges—balancing the need to institute change with the need to hold the center—that became characteristic of later progressive reforms hewn out by governor-presidents. As well stated by Nathan Miller, "fearing radicalism on the one hand and the excesses of the great corporations on the other, Roosevelt saw himself as a mediator, or honest broker, between these contending forces who had the interests of all Americans in mind."[56] In this vein, Roosevelt "would go after bad individuals and evil corporations, but would chastise as demagogues those who opposed wealth as such or the impoverished as such."[57] Thus, the Ford bill captured both Roosevelt's progressive daring and the politics of his legislative pragmatism. "One of the reasons why I am so anxious to see corporations pay their full share of taxes," Roosevelt explained, "is because I want to prevent any just discontent becoming a factor in the socialistic movement."[58] That said, his belief in executive primacy pushed him further than earlier models of executive leadership would have countenanced.

In his first annual message, Roosevelt in fact proposed an intriguing remedy to what he described as "overlegislation." He called for an "[amendment to] the Constitution so as to provide for biennial sessions of the legislature."[59] Roosevelt effectively wanted to turn the New York state legislature into an every-other-year institution. This fell in line with other proposals common to the era, such as the push for more democratic and unicameral legislatures.[60] Progressive democracy was seen as primarily executive in nature; "degenerate" or regressive democracy was legislative. "Legislatures have degenerated into the condition of being merely agents," wrote Croly, "rather than principals in the work of government."[61] Such conclusions paved the way for support for the initiative and referendum. Increasingly, powerful state executives were taking on the responsibilities of legislation. "More than half of my work as Governor was in the direction of getting needed and important legislation," Roosevelt claimed.[62] The Ford bill was a prime example of executive intervention in legislative affairs, down to Roosevelt's personal vetting of the constitutionality of particular provisions with state senators.[63]

For starters, Roosevelt used his relationship with the press to push the Ford bill, "[authorizing] the newspaper correspondents to make the public statement that he hoped the Assembly would pass the Ford bill."[64] In addition, he used the governor's special emergency powers to get it passed. Roosevelt recalled the episode in some detail in his autobiography: "I had made up my mind that if I could get a show in the Legislature the bill would pass, because the people had become interested and the representatives would scarcely dare to vote the wrong way. Accordingly, on April 27, 1899, I sent a special message to the Assembly, certifying that the emergency demanded the immediate passage of the bill. The machine leaders were bitterly angry, and the Speaker actually tore up the message without reading it to the Assembly."[65] Roosevelt's recollections of his heroism, including his threat to visit the legislature "in person" if the bill was not passed, reflect the personal brand of executive politics that characterized the era. While TR's memory was typically self-serving, there is little question that the passage of the Ford bill was one of the early educative executive experiences that prepared him for the White House.[66] Unsurprisingly, he considered it "the most important law passed in recent times by any American State legislature."[67] The episode was TR's first foray into antitrust legislation and thus is properly seen as "[laying] the roots and objectives of the Square Deal."[68] Beyond this, the politics of the passage of the Ford bill involved some of the hallmarks of modern presidential leadership: legislative intervention, party defiance, and executive direction of the press. Despite theoretical opposition to "overlegislation," what Roosevelt and other progressives inveighed against was legislative leadership. At the close of the 1899 session, Roosevelt had in fact signed twice as many bills into law as had his predecessor, Governor Black.[69] And by learning to tactically "separate bills from party politics," Roosevelt helped construct a "common element of twentieth-century policymaking."[70]

In shepherding a new civil service law in Albany as governor, Roosevelt truly reflected an antispoils position held at the time. Yet, if such acts presaged the "Square Deal," others portended an Anglo-centered nationalism and imperialism that called into question the most basic of constitutional checks. "I would not put him in a position," worried the great progressive Carl Schurz, "in which he would exercise any influence upon the foreign policy of the republic."[71] Roosevelt's democratic leanings were complicated at best. As Sven Beckert has noted, Roosevelt fought New York's political machine in part because it represented an anti-elitist suffragist movement that threatened to turn New York City into what Roosevelt described as a "Celtocracy."[72] In all, Roosevelt's governorship cannot be separated from his ultimate executive record. Much of this legacy included Roosevelt's progressive engineering of legislation while governor. If, in fact, Roosevelt's Albany press relations "prefigured his management of presidential correspondents in Washington, using both a combination of the carrot and the stick," they likewise were a microcosm of his ability to "go over the heads" of the legislature and party opposition to win legislation to his liking.[73]

Beyond the "Too-Compliant Party Man"

As early as his Inaugural Address as governor, Roosevelt indicated that he would not govern on the basis of party. "It is only through the party system that free governments are now successfully carried on, and yet we must keep ever vividly before us that the usefulness of a party is strictly limited by its usefulness to the State," he argued.[74] The combative tone was set at the inaugural ceremony itself. "Equally conspicuous for their absence were the representatives of the Republican Party organization, without whom no inauguration of the past would have been considered complete," recorded the *New York Times*.[75] Sensing the early confrontations to come with Platt and Republican leaders, Roosevelt later warned, "the too-compliant party man needs to be told that we can give our money and our labor to our party, but cannot sell our country for it, nor our honor, nor our convictions of right and wrong."[76] Platt's reaction to such sentiments was predictable. Writing to Roosevelt over a month later, he attempted to make his expectations clear: "I assumed that you would easily appreciate the fact that anything done by you as Governor of New York tended to commit your whole party, and especially those of us who were associated in the public mind with your candidacy, and I had small doubt that you would give fair consideration to this fact before you began to move in any novel direction,—novel, I mean, as to party policy."[77] Unfortunately for Platt, Roosevelt learned as early as his time in the Albany Assembly that reform carried with it political currency when tied to party defiance. When then Governor Cleveland called upon Roosevelt in 1883 to assist him in breaking ranks with New York Democrats in pushing civil service reform, the lesson was not lost on Roosevelt. By helping Cleveland successfully break with Tammany Democrats from the Republican aisle, Roosevelt was lauded for his "rugged independence" and called a "controlling force on the floor superior to that of any member of his party."[78]

The political dynamics of the Ford bill were therefore not foreign to Roosevelt. The bill was sponsored by an opposition Democratic senator, and thus placed Roosevelt at cross-purposes with Platt and New York's Republican machine. "[T]o my very great surprise," Platt would lament, "you did a thing which has caused the business community of New York to wonder how far the notions of Populism as laid down in Kansas and Nebraska have taken hold upon the Republican party of the State of New York."[79] Notwithstanding the backlash from party stalwarts, many of the new, independent executive progressives emerging during this period owed similar success to a willingness to move beyond pure party affiliations and leadership. Roosevelt was truly a leader in this regard. The passage of the Ford bill was thus seen instantly as a victory not only over corporate power in New York, but also "over the organized leadership of [Roosevelt's] own party."[80]

Likewise, Roosevelt's willingness to make gubernatorial appointments on his own terms only heightened his sense of executive autonomy. Despite walking the line between New York's Independents, progressive Democrats, and his own Republican party, Roosevelt was creating a personal governorship not altogether different from the type of plebiscitary presidency described by contemporary political scientists. The *New York Sun* appropriately credited Roosevelt's "individuality" with providing "for one of the most successful extraordinary sessions of the State Legislature in the memory of men now interested in New York State politics."[81] And despite strong condemnation of Roosevelt's seeming fascination for war, the *Times* likewise applauded TR for his independence: "There is not a selfish line in his [Inaugural Address], not a hint of any personal or party motive. He suggests no legislation for partisan advantage. . . . We have been accustomed to see our Governors shape their message to the requirements of the organization or the views of the boss. Mr. Roosevelt's message is all his own."[82] Roosevelt thus understood that, fundamentally, his power within the party was in many respects tied to his ability to win favor directly with the people. As such, he carefully selected opportune times to rally the public against the legislature.[83]

While it is well established today that national party decline was concomitant with the rise of progressivism, what has not yet been broadly accepted is the role governors played in this unfolding political dynamic. As Theodore Lowi has argued, "In political terms, the twenty-year period beginning around 1870 constituted an era of social movements. And from these movements there issued a cascade of demands for government action, ranging from outlawing monopolistic practices to the cheapening of the currency, to the improvement of working conditions as well as the conditions of the poor. . . . Since as we have seen, the states were doing most of the governing, it was naturally and rationally to the states that the social movements looked for redress."[84] State legislatures could not, and did not, do what aggressive, independent-minded governors did in attempting to address the broad social discontent common to the era. The early movement toward a more executive-centered state was thus most discernible in the actions of the nation's governors, and Roosevelt's political lineage in Albany was the critical dimension of this narrative. His movement from the statehouse to Washington was part of the broader national shift toward popular support for overtly executive leadership.

Roosevelt's Executive Philosophy and Management

As governor and as president, Roosevelt believed that the executive was permitted the ability to act unless otherwise expressly prohibited by the

Constitution. He likewise believed that the legislature ought not to enact any law unless it was demonstrably enforceable. Roosevelt thus came to regard all legislative acts as cumbersome until having passed executive scrutiny. "I have always sympathized with the view set forth by Pelatiah Webster in 1783 [that] Laws or ordinances of any kind . . . which fail of execution, are much worse than none," he wrote.[85] Following a Hamiltonian bias toward energetic executive administration, Roosevelt's exemplars at the national level are not surprising.

> The course I followed, of regarding the executive as subject to the people, and, under the Constitution, bound to serve the people affirmatively in cases where the Constitution does not explicitly forbid him to render the service, was substantially the course followed by both Andrew Jackson and Abraham Lincoln. Other honorable and well-meaning Presidents, such as James Buchanan, took the opposite and, it seems to me, narrowly legalistic view that the President is the servant of Congress rather than of the people, and can do nothing, no matter how necessary it be to act, unless that Constitution explicitly commands the action.[86]

Part of Roosevelt's view of an independent executive stemmed from his intellectual interests and values. The basis of good government for Roosevelt was expertise mixed with action; he therefore saw academia as filling a practical role in public life. He frequently vetted his own ideas through the lens of academics whom he respected, "seeking advice from college professors and experts on such subjects as taxation, canal improvements, education, labor, and conservation. Among his visitors was Woodrow Wilson, who spent a weekend at Sagamore."[87] Along these lines, Roosevelt worked methodically to find an appropriate tax on franchises in weighing the merits of the Ford bill, ultimately deciding to tax the corporations as realty. "I do not know," he confided to one state senator, "—and if you do know, you are the first man I have met who does—exactly the best form in which to tax these corporations. Men like Comptroller Roberts, Prof. Gunton and Prof. Ely and the like differ radically."[88] These insights provided Roosevelt intellectual fuel for his newly instituted cabinet meetings of New York's top state officials. Roosevelt's evaluation of the Ford bill's feasibility and strength is illustrative of his inclusive, directed, sometimes informal, and, more often than not, masterful executive management style. Before long, the leading academic and policy experts of the day had weighed in on nearly every conceivable aspect of the bill.[89] Such efforts at building the meritocratic state were tied to progressive views of executive leadership. As Croly would argue, "Progressive democracy demands not merely an increasing employment of the legislative power under representative executive leadership, but it also particularly needs an increase of administrative authority and efficiency."[90] These were the early steps toward "enlightened administration," thirty years before Franklin D. Roosevelt would mark its arrival in his Commonwealth Club Address.[91]

In seeking expert knowledge in his administration, TR was a fairly typical progressive governor. Robert Wiebe probably overstated the case when he contended that "in the realm of broad policy, each [Wilson and Roosevelt] political leader was his own expert."[92] Each was expert perhaps, but not divorced from outside influence and advice. Modern executive leadership ultimately came to be identified with scientific, energetic, and enlightened government. Yet the implications for republicanism have not necessarily been benign, as popular government has frequently been subsumed within the less representative ranks of administration by elites.[93] As president, Roosevelt's preference for seeking such extraconstitutional counsel proved costly, as he established a retinue of advisory commissions without Congressional approval. The practice has been far from abandoned today, further strengthening presidential authority.[94]

The basic premise of the antispoils civil service movement was that expertise ought to trump personal loyalties or favor. A related faith in moral efficiency as a bulwark against the tyranny of the growing corporate state became essential to the spirit of progressivism. Here, Grover Cleveland was very much the model statesman. Having witnessed in 1883 the ability to make legislative change in Albany over dreaded "patronage," Cleveland would make a familiar, if not unchallenged, advancement as president. Stephen Skowronek notes that "in Cleveland's first sixteen months in office there was a 90 percent turnover in presidential officers."[95] This was in some ways in keeping with Alexis de Tocqueville's notion of a revolution in American politics every four years, but what was different during the Progressive Era, was the linkage of turnover in office with some traceable form of administrative competence.[96] Cleveland's election to the presidency in 1884 was indeed "the crowning achievement of the new independent reform politics."[97] But it was a coronation that would lead to more lasting and profound reigns, led by even bolder and more effective Hudson progressives. A number of factors made Roosevelt's breakthrough of greater consequence:

The strategic environment for state building was more favorable during the Roosevelt administration than at any other time. . . . From a position of party strength and electoral stability, Roosevelt pushed executive prerogatives to their limits. Nurturing the development of substantive administrative powers, he drove a wedge into the institutional relationships established among parties, courts, Congress, and the states. . . . He preferred to rely on an expansive interpretation of executive authority, to move ahead with the professionals' reform agenda on his own initiative, and to bypass Congress as much as possible.[98]

As Roosevelt biographer G. Wallace Chessman has stated, "those who boomed Roosevelt for the Presidency could do no better for their argument than to turn to the record of the governorship. There they found formulated his doctrine on the relation of party to the government and the people; his general theory on the role of the state in the modern society; and his stand on such issues as trusts, transportation, labor, and conservation."[99] Most importantly, these were prescriptions that were culled from a distinct theory of executive-centered leadership—one that sought a marriage between Hamilton's powerful executive and Jefferson's democratic populace.[100]

Such an emphasis on executive-centered government had its detractors. As Sidney Milkis notes, " 'consolidation' of responsibilities in the national government that would follow from Hamilton's commercial and international objectives presupposed executive leadership in formulating policy and a strong administrative role in carrying it out. The power of the more democratic and decentralizing institutions—Congress and state governments—were necessarily subordinated in this enterprise."[101] Ironically, early progressive innovators spawned a popular attachment to executive leadership, one that did serious damage to its *raison d'être*, protection of the people's rights. As Roosevelt biographer Lewis Gould notes, "[Roosevelt] did not view as wise provisions that the framers of the Constitution had included as a possible check against either a well-intentioned president gone wrong or a more sinister executive bent on excessive power."[102]

In writing of former New York governor Mario Cuomo—perhaps the last of New York's Hudson progressives—Alan Rosenthal argued that "governors today, and especially those in the larger states, recognize that the ability to mobilize broad public support through the media is supplanting the traditional small-group persuasive skills needed by their predecessors."[103] This has been true for some time in the modern era, but the building blocks of persuasion, outlined through rhetoric and bolstered by institutional practices and custom, go back at least as far as Roosevelt's Albany days. Those features common to the modern presidency emerged, in part, from executive practices that flowed from an earlier era of executive leaders—none more so than those Hudson progressives who governed near the turn of the twentieth century. For better or for worse, these tracks were laid with no apparent route of return. Perhaps this is why the likes of Theodore Roosevelt and Woodrow Wilson remain of contemporary interest, even when their successors struggle with fulfilling the Hudson progressive tradition.[104]

Conclusion: Rethinking the Modern American Presidency

The modern presidency came of age when ideas of American executive authority moved through radical reinterpretation. Its transformation was defined, in part, when state executives built models of aggressive, party-defying, press-commanding success. And ultimately, the presidency came of age when American industrial capitalism and political machinery were undergoing fundamental changes, and it did so most tellingly from the locus of the Hudson corridor of power. New York's patronage system, newspaper culture, and economic dominance gave its governors outsized significance and opportunities. There, progressives rethought government and how it could work, if not purely, then at least *positively*. Some of Roosevelt's contributions are not without serious normative concern, however. Joseph E. Kallenbach captured the long-term historic implications of Roosevelt's executive philosophy well:

> Theodore Roosevelt's assertion of his stewardship theory of the presidency—an amalgam of the Jacksonian concept of the tribunative function of the office and of a broad Lincolnian view of presidential prerogative power—marked unmistakably the beginning of a new era in the history of the presidency. Although Roosevelt's application of his theory in practice was discreetly tempered by recognition of the limitations imposed by practical political considerations, he set in motion evolutionary changes which were built upon and extended by his successors.[105]

In "going over the heads" of his party and its bosses in New York, and in employing the seldom-used emergency powers of the governor, Roosevelt pushed the limits of modern executive power in the single most important executive forum short of the presidency itself. Roosevelt's skill with the press and legislative leadership were precursors of the modern presidency and his White House tenure. Before Roosevelt's governorship, no American executive in recent memory had acted so forcefully, so colorfully, and with such overt theoretical consideration for executive power. The stage had been set in many respects by other Hudson and western progressives, to be certain, but it was Roosevelt who commanded the stage first.

When asked, before becoming New Jersey's governor, how he would cope with a recalcitrant legislature, Woodrow Wilson famously remarked, "I can *talk*, can't I?"[106] There may be no better summation of modern executive authority's most basic tool. Whether one calls it persuasion, as Richard Neustadt did, or "rhetoric," it is a core sense that what the executive says matters, and may matter *decisively*. As presidential prerogative has been sooner granted than contested in more recent times, it is worth considering some of the less explored paths to this terminus. Those turn-of-the-century "laboratories of democracy" were headed by political scientists (if we may extend the metaphor) with overtly executive predispositions. The Progressive Era witnessed this potent valorization of the executive as "leader." What resulted, in part, in the Second Republic's transvaluation of values, was the sense that republicanism could somehow no longer afford the virtues of an artfully restrained executive. Yet, by FDR's presidency, Hegel's Owl of Minerva had already flown. Perhaps something less than a monster was created in the Brandeisian labs by progressive governors and governor presidents, but something perhaps less than democratic emerged as well. Here, James P. Young's assessment is to the point:

> [Roosevelt's and Wilson's] actions amounted to what has been called a basic change in constitutional structure. At the least, the modern presidency began to emerge in the thought and practice of the two Progressive presidents. . . . We are all probably better off in the regulated world the Progressives created than in what went before; still, one need only scan a newspaper frequently to know that the regulatory state has not tamed the giant corporation or brought full security to all. Nor can anyone claim that democracy is more secure than it was seventy years ago. By many standards it is weaker.[107]

The governorship of Theodore Roosevelt is a critical gateway to understanding the democratic gains and losses inherent in America's modern presidency. If democracy is to be measured by civic engagement, by the voting practices of its members, and by the constraints foisted upon their leaders, Progressive Era executive leadership, particularly as demonstrated by its most powerful exemplars, leaves much to be desired. As Theodore Lowi has lamented, "no entrepreneur would sign a contract that leaves the conditions of fulfillment to the subjective judgment of the other party. This is precisely what has happened in the new social contract underlying the modern government of the United States."[108] Such a contract conjures up Thomas Hobbes's historic frontispiece to his *Leviathan*—the unitary executive embodying, literally, the people and their will. How then, if at all, shall the people get it back? While Lowi and others consider the establishment of the "personal president" a product of the New Deal, much of the record of executive personalist leadership suggests a resurrection of Jacksonian prerogative during the Progressive Era. By simply looking below the surface, at the state level, and to a time before the process began to beg for reconsideration, we can grasp much that prerogative power and the imperial presidency would bring to bear on American political development. Albany was only the beginning.

Chapter 3

An "Unconstitutional Governor": Woodrow Wilson and the People's Executive

Some gentlemen . . . seem to have supposed that I studied politics out of books. Now, there isn't any politics worth talking about in books. In books everything looks obvious, very symmetrical, very systematic, and very complete, but it is not the picture of life and it is only in the picture of life that all of us are interested.
—Governor Woodrow Wilson, Jersey City, New Jersey, 1911[1]

It will not do to look at men congregated in bodies politic through the medium of the constitutions and traditions of the states they live in, as if that were the glass of interpretation. Constitutions are vehicles of life, but not the sources of it.
—Woodrow Wilson, Presidential Address, American Political Science Association, 1911[2]

Introduction

In the days following Woodrow Wilson's election as governor of New Jersey, press coverage offered a conspicuous glimpse into just how significant a rupture Wilson's victory was of the prevailing notions of executive leadership in

America. More than anything, these were reflections upon what the governor-elect suggested for party leadership and the executive's relationship with the legislature. New York's *Evening Post* provided but one example: "Governors are coming more and more to be regarded as party leaders. In Woodrow Wilson's case, the thing was perfectly clear, for he again and again notified voters that, if they elected him Governor, he should regard himself as Democratic leader—he is to be responsible and no boss or machine, for executing the popular will."[3] In similar fashion, the *Jersey Journal* chimed in with a rebuke to Wilson's opponent, Vivian M. Lewis. The paper disparaged Lewis's legal formalism, noting that Lewis "said he would be, if elected, a 'constitutional Governor.' Apparently the people did not take to Mr. Lewis' idea, for Wilson was elected by about [a] 50,000 plurality."[4] The *Journal*, perhaps not unlike a great many voters, thought "this matter of the Executive forcing his views upon the Legislature [is] getting to be altogether too irksome."[5] The "partitions" theory of government that had guided Madison in his view of republicanism was no longer in vogue. As best put by the governor-elect himself: "There is something pathetic in the reliance of Americans upon statutes. The average American always wants a statute to save him from something or somebody. One of the most conspicuous things about the spirit of America is its faith in the law. Our appetite for legislation is notorious. The real way to have good government is to have good men."[6] Where Madison had sought a system sufficient for the moment when "enlightened statesmen" might not be at the helm, Wilson argued for one in which statesmen were strong enough to overcome the strictures of the law. Wisdom was to be found in individual strength and personal leadership. On its own, the law was enfeebling.

Wilson did not arrive at these conclusions overnight. He had begun a reevaluation of his executive philosophy as early as 1908, when his *Constitutional Government in the United States* was published. In truth, his reassessment began much earlier. Over a decade before this final scholarly word on government, Wilson had expressed the essentials of his perspective on executive leadership in an article in the *Atlantic Monthly*.[7] The subject of the article was Grover Cleveland. In examining Cleveland's presidency, Wilson offered an early glimpse at his future executive philosophy as he paid homage to the nation's most successful president since Lincoln. "He has been the sort of President the makers of the Constitution had vaguely in mind: more man than partisan; with an independent executive will of his own," he wrote.[8] Just how representative of the framers' vision of the presidency Cleveland was is an interesting question—at best, Wilson was taking liberties with Madison's understanding of presidential power: "It was singular how politics began at once to centre in the President, waiting for [Cleveland's] initiative, and how the air at Washington filled with murmurs against the domineering and usurping temper and practice of the Executive. Power had somehow gone the length of the avenue, and seemed lodged in one man."[9]

As one of the first presidents to invoke the use of executive privilege in the modern era, and the first to use the veto with astonishing regularity, Cleveland was in many respects the type of executive Madison would have blanched at. In this regard, Wilson was closer to reinterpreting the founding—if not rewriting it—than he was to upholding its legalistic merits. For Wilson, Cleveland represented the popular, if not fully plebiscitary, president. He was, Wilson would say, "a President, as it were, by immediate choice from out of the body of the people, as the Constitution has all long appeared to expect."[10] Wilson also saw fit to laud Cleveland's party leadership and his intrusions into legislation, reminding readers that "the President stands at the centre of legislation as well as of administration in executing his great office."[11]

Moreover, Wilson's trained political eye saw the connection between Cleveland's executive experiences as mayor of Buffalo and governor of New York State. At each turn, Cleveland was party-defiant, a leader of his legislature, and no simple-minded legalist. "Not all of government can be crowded into the rules of law," Wilson said in his tribute to Cleveland.[12] Indeed, Wilson made the extralegal executive a signature part of his leadership philosophy. When running for the governorship, Wilson vowed to make good on his promise of executive independence. "As Governor of New Jersey I shall have no part in the choice of a Senator," he said on the campaign stump. "Legally speaking, it is not my duty even to give advice with regard to the choice. But there are other duties besides legal duties."[13] Indeed, Wilson's first political battle was in exercising these extralegal duties in personally campaigning for the Senate candidate of his choice. But that was in 1911. In 1897, Grover Cleveland was Woodrow Wilson's most proximate model of a modern executive—before there was a Roosevelt administration—and well before Wilson had ventured into politics himself. If anything made the dormant executive as found in Wilson's *Congressional Government* obsolete in 1885, it was the executive legacy handed down by Grover Cleveland.[14] For Wilson, "[Cleveland] made policies and altered parties after the fashion of an earlier age in our history."[15] Time, it seemed, had passed the Founders by.

Wilson's support for an executive-centered government ran parallel to the rising profile of America's governors. At the 1910 Governors' Conference, New York's Governor Charles Evan Hughes proclaimed, "We are here in our own right as State Executive[s]."[16] While Hughes's declaration was in part an admonition against federal encroachment into "states' rights," it was also a proclamation of new-found state executive authority and popular appeal. The *Times* hailed Hughes as "head of the most powerful of the States, whose legislature he has dominated in the full confidence of its people."[17] Such adulation was not lost on Wilson, who echoed these sentiments on executive power during the conference's keynote address.[18] The "real power" of governors over legislatures, reminded Wilson before his new colleagues, "is their ability to convince the people. If they can carry an opinion through the constituencies, they can carry it through the legislature."[19]

Despite the conviction of these remarks, in many respects Wilson was a latecomer. By the time he began to put into practice his executive philosophy as governor, state executives had gained a degree of national prominence for the first time in American history.[20] In the early 1900s, the number of state constitutions that included strong provisions for executive leadership had grown considerably, and would continue to do so for the next half-century.[21] Wilson was particularly impressed with western political innovations, citing, like Herbert Croly, the State of Oregon's experiments in executive power. "I earnestly commend to your careful consideration the laws in recent years adopted in the State of Oregon," Wilson implored in his Inaugural Address as governor. "[Their] effect has been to bring government back to the people and to protect it from the control of the representatives of selfish and special interests," he said.[22]

Oregon's suddenly influential legislator, William S. U'Ren (a Midwesterner originally from Wisconsin), made quite an impression on Wilson, who over time came to support Oregon's "new tools of democracy." These included the initiative, recall, and referendum.[23] Wilson's support for U'Ren's proposed constitutional innovations, radical as they were in their executive orientation, should be put in broader context. As Richard J. Ellis notes, "The lawgiver," as U'Ren's admirers styled him, also proposed abolishing the state senate and creating a unicameral legislature in which members' terms would be four years, making the governor and defeated gubernatorial candidates ex-officio members of the legislature, and permitting the governor to introduce appropriation bills, except those the legislature referred to the voters."[24] While U'Ren would be defeated as a gubernatorial candidate in Oregon in 1914, his influence on executive political theory was nonetheless significant.

Wilson benefited from the lessons of executive-centered progressivism found in the West, as he did from his own state's political legacy. As Wilson biographer Arthur Link noted, "Few governors in the country possessed the sweeping range of patronage that the governor of New Jersey had at his disposal in 1911; he appointed practically all high-ranking judicial and administrative officials."[25] The state's constitution had been revised in 1844, granting the governor "a three year term, a weak veto, and some appointment powers."[26] While seemingly not profound by today's standards of executive authority, the new constitution also held one critical feature endemic to modern executive office: "The constitution did, however, contain the provision that Coleman Ransone suggests opened the way to gubernatorial participation in policymaking: '[the Governor] shall communicate by message to the legislature at the opening of each session, and at such times as he may deem necessary, the condition of the State, and recommend such measures as he may deem expedient.' Eventually, the governor's message became the vehicle for laying out a legislative program."[27] At the time of this addition, New Jersey was already among a handful of states with comparably strong executive authority.[28] Yet because of its vast patronage opportunities and resultant venues for corruption, New Jersey had also long been a choice state for bossism and executive malfeasance.[29] Wilson once referred to New Jersey as "the Bloody Angle," a term from his beloved battle of Gettysburg, emphasizing the state's importance to progressive reform. Wilson, no doubt, saw himself as General Meade.[30]

It was the much lamented loss of Samuel Tilden in 1876 that helped shape Wilson's antagonism toward legislatures, as a congressional committee ultimately decided the New York governor's fate. "When I see so plainly that there is an endeavor to make the will of the people subservient to the wishes of a few unblushing scoundrels," wrote Wilson, "such as some of those in power in Washington, I am the more persuaded that while the government of the Republic is beautiful in theory, its practical application fails entirely."[31]

Tilden's reform record became the standard for future executive reform among Hudson progressives. While Cleveland attained the White House and was highly esteemed among reformers for his honesty, Tilden's defeat was a perpetual scar, and a reminder of the price of taking the machine head on. A *New York Times* feature on Wilson just months before the gubernatorial election captured progressive aspirations for the former Princeton president quite well, referring to Wilson as "a man with all the Tilden characteristics and an appreciation of the facts that conditions have changed since Tilden's day."[32] In New Jersey, Wilson would face tremendous opposition, but also great opportunity for progressive support, provided he demonstrate credentials worthy of the Tilden legacy.[33] Fittingly, Tilden's personal secretary and executor of the late governor's estate ("a descendant from a long line of Jerseymen and a Democrat of the School represented by Samuel J. Tilden") offered a congratulatory note to Wilson on his election as governor of New Jersey, closing a circle of sorts in the political genealogy of Woodrow Wilson.[34]

In this light, Wilson's governorship was hardly new; it trailed emerging national progressive principles and practices, including those honed by Wisconsin's former governor Robert La Follette and other Westerners and shaped to a great extent within the state by New Jersey's progressive (self-styled "New Idea") Republicans.[35] As Arthur Link noted, "[P]rogressive spokesmen knew that Wilson was no pioneer of reform, either in the state or in the nation. Many of them had personally helped [Governors] Hoke Smith in Georgia, Bob La Follette in Wisconsin, Hiram Johnson in California, or Charles Evans Hughes in New York to push through similar reform programs years before. These all paved the way for Wilson's success."[36]

Wilson's governorship was, more than any other, a platform for neo-executive theory to be put into practice. Wilson was the intellectual progenitor of the executive turn in American governance. His understanding of the relationship between public opinion and executive leadership, coupled with his direction of the Democratic Party, was a microcosm of an executive style that most Americans would come to take for granted by midcentury. With his institutionalization of press relations, use of rhetoric, popular appeals, and rupturing of the wall between the executive and the legislature, Wilson held a governorship that is an indispensable component for understanding what modern presidential leadership would come to look like. And, perhaps most importantly, Wilson's tenure served as the bridge between the Progressive Era and New Deal executive leadership—the link between Cleveland, the last of the stronger nineteenth-century executives, and FDR, the quintessential modern executive leader. Ultimately, Wilson's executive philosophy did extend beyond that merely "written in books," as he cagily remarked on the campaign trail for governor in 1910. It would likewise be written into his practices as state executive. "There is no training school for Presidents," Wilson had once remarked, "unless as some governors have wished, it be looked for in the governorships of states." That would prove to be one of Wilson's more ironic musings from *Constitutional Government*. By 1911, his training and, indeed, that of a new American executive leadership were well underway.[37]

Woodrow Wilson's American Executive Zeitgeist

American progressivism was nothing if not keenly aware of time. As its exponents frequently lacked a coherent political philosophy, progressives were more defined by their aspirations than by strict ideology. Nevertheless, progressives were definitionally linked to the idea of democratic triumphalism—the emergence of science, education, and, indeed, civilization over darkness and barbarism. Such darkness represented political immaturity and anachronistic features of society. For Wilson, the Constitution fell within the former category. Wilsonian political science did not seek dissolution of American constitutionalism so much as it wanted to drag constitutional formalism into modernity. In an 1890 lecture on democracy, Wilson addressed the founders from the assumed perch of historical clarity: "We have in a measure undone their work. A century has led us very far along the road of change. Year by year we have sought to bring government nearer to the people, despite the original plan."[38] Much of this sentiment was a product of Wilson's reading of history and of the German philosopher G. W. F. Hegel. As one political scientist has argued, "while Wilson's thought is perhaps most obviously influenced by [Edmund] Burke and Walter Bagehot, both members of the English Historical School, Wilson goes beyond their evolutionary conservatism to adopt a historicism most directly attributable to Hegel."[39]

Hegelian history is best understood as a series of progressions, with each age governed by a spirit relevant to its own conditions. There are no "good" or "bad" epochs per se; each is good for its time, with "the slaughter bench" of history compelling progress, sometimes characterized by overwhelming brutality.[40] Wilson's understanding of the American founding is thus tied to his broader sense of history:

Hegel agrees with the basic precept of the Historical School that one cannot transcend one's own historical environment. Historical contingency makes it impossible to ground politics on an abstract principle. Wilson cited Hegel directly in making this same point in his essay, "The Study of Administration." The political principles of any age, Wilson contends, are nothing more than the reflections of its corresponding historical spirit. Wilson claimed that "the philosophy of any time is, as Hegel says, 'nothing but the spirit of that time expressed in abstract thought.' "[41]

This is a crucial distinction from the founding conceptualization of time. Jeffersonian history was universal, abstract, and timeless. That is, in rooting itself in the Lockean social contract, society is "created" out of truths that defy any particular age or set of circumstances. Human freedom is not subject to context; it is "evident" and intractable. For Wilson, such theoretical musings defied the logic of history. The theme of the universe is change; Darwin must supplant Newton as modernity must render the founders' strict adherence to social contract theory irrelevant. Since power is tied to the necessarily transient sentiments of the people, structure and symmetry held no allure for Wilson. It is why some have suggested that Wilson's executive philosophy reflected the closest thing to a "reversal of the Whig revolution of 1689." [42]

In his 1891 essay on Edmund Burke, Wilson argued, "no state can ever be conducted on its principles."[43] Principles are loose and subject to change. "Good government, like all virtue, [Burke] deemed to be a practical habit of conduct," Wilson wrote. It is "not a matter of constitutional structure."[44] If the personal presidency owes its origins to any theoretical exposition by an American statesman, it is to this one invoked by Wilson. In marrying Burkean traditionalism to Hegelian progress, Wilson espoused an at once conservative and radical doctrine of governance. Since custom is read as temporal, traditional notions of the state are turned on their heads. Instead of tradition reflecting an aversion to revolutionary change, Wilson argues for tradition as epochal. Each people is responsible for creating its own political customs. Constitutional structure is merely a legal appendage to generational understandings. As Jeffrey Tulis rightly notes, "Wilson attacked the founders for relying on mere 'parchment barriers' to effectuate a separation of powers. This claim is an obvious distortion of founding views. In *The Federalist*, nos. 47 and 48, the argument is precisely that the federal constitution, unlike earlier state constitutions would *not* rely primarily upon parchment distinctions of power but upon differentiation of institutional structures."[45] For these reasons, Wilson is seen by some as inaugurating a "postconstitutional presidency."[46] The theoretical change wrought by Wilson is perhaps better understood as a form of *presidential* constitutionalism. As has been suggested, "Wilson agreed with [Theodore] Roosevelt that the president must direct more attention to national problems. But he also believed that executive leadership would be ineffective or dangerous unless it was accompanied by a fundamental change in the government's working arrangements. Such a change would unite the constitutionally separated branches of government."[47] In effect, modern American conceptions of presidential power owe much of their origins to Woodrow Wilson's theory of executive governance. His governorship was among the first forums to put these ideas to the test.

THE CASE FOR THE UNCONSTITUTIONAL GOVERNOR

In early October of his campaign for governor, Woodrow Wilson expressed his executive philosophy in the starkest terms. At the Trenton Taylor Opera House, Wilson upbraided his Republican opponent, Vivian M. Lewis, for suggesting that, if elected, Lewis "would only talk to the Legislature and be bound by the acts of that body."

> If you elect me [said Wilson] I will be an unconstitutional Governor in that respect. I will talk to the people as well as to the Legislature, and I will use all moral force with that body to bring about what the people demand. I am going to take every important debate in the Legislature out on the stump and discuss it with them. If the people do not agree, then no harm will be done to the legislators, but the people will have their way in things. This is serving the spirit of the Constitution. . . . The Governor is elected in this State, and if he does not talk the people have no spokesman.[48]

Wilson was advocating a clean break with the notion of a separation of powers, one that New Jersey's constitution had embraced for decades.[49] Wilson would read between the lines of the document, seeing, as he suggested to his Trenton audience, far greater latitude than imagined. It was a popular message—Wilson's "unconstitutional Governor" line earned him a two-minute ovation.[50]

Three months later and newly elected, Wilson offered, "The thing I am violating is not the Constitution of the State but the constitution of politics."[51] However read, Wilson was at the least inveighing against constitutional for-

malism; at worst, he was close to embracing patently antirepublican principles. In *Constitutional Government*, Wilson rebuked the legalist approach
altogether. "Liberty fixed in unalterable law would be no liberty at all," he
claimed.[52] For all his sense of Jeffersonian populism, Wilson was similarly
dismissive of Jeffersonian natural law, making the startling argument that
the true heart of the Declaration of Independence was to be found not in its
preamble advocating human equality, but in Jefferson's insistence on the
right of the people to alter their government according to generational ne-
cessities.[53] "When you speak of a progressive Democrat," he told a Montclair
audience just before his election, "I understand that you mean not a man
who will always be standing upon a literal interpretation of quotations out of
Thomas Jefferson, but who will try to carry forward in the service of a new
age."[54] For Wilson, the executive was best positioned to determine such imperatives, as he most clearly embodies the will of the people. Since parlia-
ments were literally "talking shops," they could not expect to move beyond
theoretical considerations. In this regard, Wilson does indeed represent a
form of overthrow of the Whig Revolution in 1689, as his words indicate:

> The government of the United States was constructed upon the Whig
> theory of political dynamics, which was a sort of unconscious copy
> of the Newtonian theory of the universe. In our own day, whenever
> we discuss the structure or development of anything, whether in nature
> or society, we consciously or unconsciously follow Mr. Darwin; but
> before Darwin, they followed Newton. . . . The trouble with the
> [Founders'] theory is that government is not a machine but a living
> thing. It falls, not under the theory of the universe, but under the theory
> of organic life. It is accountable to Darwin, not to Newton.[55]

Wilson's theory cannot be divorced from his broader appreciation of
executive background and the requisites for presidential success in the modern era. "Certainly the country has never thought of members of Congress
as in any particular degree fitted for the presidency," he wrote in *Constitutional Government*. And while cabinet officers were well suited for the office
in "our earlier practice" customary in the Whig Era in American politics, "the
men best prepared, no doubt, are those who have been governors of states."[56]
Not everyone would find solace in such executive exuberance. Henry Cabot
Lodge, for one, rebuked Wilson's political theory, arguing that "Mr. Wilson
stands for a theory of administration and government which is not Ameri-

can."[57] Wilson was nevertheless not alone in looking to American state executives for leadership. It was "the new and strong leadership of the Governors," wrote the *New York Times*, that were foisting reform upon the nation; they, and not the nation's presidents, were the parties responsible for "cleansing their legislative halls."[58] Indeed, the closest thing to an exemplary modern president for Wilson was a governor—or a president who had been one. As early as 1885, Wilson recognized that "the presidency is very like a big governorship." In truth, by his election to the governorship of New Jersey in 1910, and with the modern presidency still evolving, the nation's chief executive remained a figure still somewhat less demonstrably powerful and creative than his erstwhile junior executive contemporaries.

Of course, Lodge's lament reflected conventional conservative sentiment against extraconstitutional presidential authority. This is no longer a widely held view among neoconservatives today, who, as Stephen Skowronek notes, have taken progressive arguments for presidential preeminence and placed them within the confines of "original understandings of the Constitution": "In place of a straightforward refutation of the progressives' case for the "modern" presidency, today's conservatives have, in effect, outbid them. They have reinvigorated traditional conservative arguments for resting power on original understandings of the Constitution, but they have jettisoned traditional reservations about the modern presidency, and they have extended the progressive paradigm of presidency-centered government while jettisoning the distinctly progressive premises on which it was built."[59] Such logic relies on Wilsonian and progressive aspirations for presidential government, but it likewise rejects the democratic underpinnings of progressivism, suggesting the warrants for "unitary" presidential leadership were present at the founding all along. However unfaithful to the progressive model, contemporary conservative theories of executive power could not have developed without the ironic contribution of progressive practitioners over a century ago.

The New Boss and the Hudson Press: Wilson's Party Leadership

By the end of Wilson's tenure as governor, he had launched the inexorable transformation of both the Democratic Party and its relationship to its political leadership. After two years of reducing, if not destroying, New Jersey's bosses, Wilson had indeed made his mark as a "Tilden up to date." At an Independence Day conference of Democratic National Committee members held at Sea Girt, New Jersey, one attendee, freshly arrived from Baltimore, put it best to one reporter: "We have come merely for a visit to the new boss."[60] After years of doing battle as well as business with New Jersey's political bosses, Wilson proved more of a supplanter than vanquisher. He, and future presidents, would mark modern presidential leadership by the personal direction of their parties, not the other way around, as it had been at least since the days of Martin Van Buren.[61] At Sea Girt in 1912, the party arrived to receive instructions. As the *Times* reported, "as the committee members left the Governor's home at nightfall, each one in shaking his hand told [Wilson] that the future policy of the Democratic National Committee was to give him 'whatever he wanted and felt called upon to request at its hands.'"[62]

Before Wilson could lead his party, he would have to challenge the political bosses endemic to Trenton politics. While Theodore Roosevelt's governorship was in some ways instructive for Wilson, in most respects his task in New Jersey was more formidable. As James D. Startt expressed it, "The political terrain of New Jersey was a landscape unknown to Wilson. In no state in the union did lenient corporate laws attract more "trusts" than in New Jersey, and in no state did boss-controlled political machines, often in alliance with large corporate interests, wield greater power . . . New Jersey Republican newspapers outnumbered Democratic ones 92 to 52. When the state's 86 independent newspapers are added to the equation, the problematic nature of support for Wilson can be appreciated."[63] If Wilson were to be successful, he would have to employ uncommon skill in molding public opinion. He would do so, as governor, in terms characteristic of modern presidents.

Wilson's press challenges were like pincers; southern New Jersey commuters were beholden to Philadelphia opinion while "the *New York Tribune* for instance, made a habit of targeting [Northern] New Jersey commuters with news and opinion about their state."[64] This difficulty in generating attention and resources across the state, a problem not unfamiliar to modern New Jersey statewide office holders, challenged Wilson to secure and hold the attention of a dispersed press, one highly influential in generating national news.[65] Wilson garnered an unusual amount of coverage from the New York press, which proved advantageous to his future ambitions. Indeed, he was covered more by the *New York Times* than Governor Roosevelt had been during TR's Albany tenure.[66] As will be shown, Wilson's formidable presence in the press was far from accidental, as he would take what was essentially instinctive to Roosevelt and formalize it. In short order, Wilson dwarfed all previous New Jersey governors in press coverage, exploding the trend begun in New York with Samuel J. Tilden. Reflecting the advent of the personal executive, Wilson's governorship was covered more by the *Times* than all previous New Jersey governorships combined (see tables below). The same overwhelming degree of press coverage for Wilson is found in other influential newspapers of the time, including the *Chicago Tribune* and *Washington Post*:

Table 4. Governors of New Jersey and *New York Times* Citations, 1851–1913

Governor	Years	Total Citations	Yearly Average	Rank
Woodrow Wilson (D)	1911–1913	645	322.5	1
John Franklin Fort (R)	1908–1911	50	16.6	6
Edward C. Stokes (R)	1905–1908	33	11.0	8
Franklin Murphy (R)	1902–1905	101	33.6	2
Foster M. Voorhees (R)	1898–1902	40	10.0	9
John W. Griggs (R)	1896–1898	34	17.0	5
George T. Werts (D)	1893–1896	39	13.0	7
Leon Abbett (D)	1890–1893	77	25.6	3
Robert S. Green (D)	1887–1890	16	5.3	11
Leon Abbett (D)	1884–1887	63	21.0	4
George C. Ludlow (D)	1881–1884	8	2.6	14t
George B. McClellan (D)	1878–1881	7	2.3	17t
Joseph D. Bedle (D)	1875–1878	1	0.3	21
Joel Parker (D)	1872–1875	19	6.3	10
Theodore F. Randolph (D)	1869–1872	4	1.3	19
Marcus L. Ward (R)	1866–1869	8	2.6	14t
Joel Parker (D)	1863–1866	13	4.3	12
Charles S. Olden (R)	1860–1863	2	0.7	20
William A. Newell (R)	1857–1860	10	3.3	13
Rodman Price (D)	1854–1857	7	2.3	17t
George F. Fort (D)	1851–1854	8	2.6	14t

Notes: Dates are from January 1 to January 1 of years cited; "t" indicates a territorial governor.

Table 5. Governors of New Jersey and *Chicago Tribune* Citations, 1852–1913

Governor	Years	Total Citations	Yearly Average	Rank
Woodrow Wilson (D)	1911–1913	469	234.5	1
John Franklin Fort (R)	1908–1911	8	4.0	6
Edward C. Stokes (R)	1905–1908	1	0.5	13t
Franklin Murphy (R)	1902–1905	14	7.0	2
Foster M. Voorhees (R)	1898–1902	3	0.8	11
John W. Griggs (R)	1896–1898	9	4.5	5
George T. Werts (D)	1893–1896	4	13.0	9t
Leon Abbett (D)	1890–1893	12	6.5	3
Robert S. Green (D)	1887–1890	1	0.5	13t
Leon Abbett (D)	1884–1887	5	2.5	8
George C. Ludlow (D)	1881–1884	0	0.0	17t
George B. McClellan (D)	1878–1881	7	3.5	7
Joseph D. Bedle (D)	1875–1878	0	0.0	17t
Joel Parker (D)	1872–1875	11	5.5	4
Theodore F. Randolph (D)	1869–1872	0	0.0	19
Marcus L. Ward (R)	1866–1869	2	1.0	12
Joel Parker (D)	1863–1866	4	2.0	9t
Charles S. Olden (R)	1860–1863	1	0.5	13t
William A. Newell (R)	1857–1860	0	0.0	17t
Rodman Price (D)	1854–1857	0	0.0	17t
George F. Fort (D)	1851–1854	0	0.0	17t

Notes: Dates are from January 1 to January 1 of years cited; "t" indicates a territorial governor.

As was the case with its coverage of New York's governors, the *Times* increasingly covered state executives in the last quarter of the nineteenth century. While TR and Wilson were both anomalies in terms of the amount of press coverage they received, they were both part of an upward trend, no doubt tied to the rise of governors' significance in state and national politics.

Table 6. Governors of New Jersey and *Washington Post* Citations, 1877–1913

Governor	Years	Total Citations	Yearly Average	Rank
Woodrow Wilson (D)	1911–1913	1062	531.0	1
John Franklin Fort (R)	1908–1911	12	4.0	5
Edward C. Stokes (R)	1905–1908	11	3.6	6
Franklin Murphy (R)	1902–1905	49	16.3	2
Foster M. Voorhees (R)	1898–1902	12	3.0	8t
John W. Griggs (R)	1896–1898	15	7.5	3
George T. Werts (D)	1893–1896	2	0.7	10
Leon Abbett (D)	1890–1893	18	6.0	4
Robert S. Green (D)	1887–1890	1	0.3	11t
Leon Abbett (D)	1884–1887	9	3.0	8t
George C. Ludlow (D)	1881–1884	1	0.3	11t
George B. McClellan (D)	1878–1881	10	3.3	7
Joseph D. Bedle (D)	1875–1878	0	0.0	13

Notes: Dates are from January 1 to January 1 of years cited; "t" indicates a territorial governor.

Deftly, Wilson worked the Democratic Party–controlled press corps before later seeking some distance from them. Early on, he mastered what today might be called an "embedded" relationship with the press corps:

> Reporters accompanying Wilson during the campaign were drawn not only to his ability as a speaker but also to the man. He made himself accessible to them. . . . [C]arrying a group of reporters and stenographers hurried across the state on rough, dusty, and sometimes impassable roads, Candidate Wilson remained patient and congenial. He was gracious about campaign inconveniences and impromptu demands made upon him. . . . Moreover, Wilson let his regard for the reporters traveling with him be known. He often brought them together to ask their opinion on a point. . . . "We have learned to love this man," [said one].[67]

While not on a two-a-day pace as Roosevelt, Wilson did in fact institute daily press meetings, called "séances," while the legislature was in session.[68]

The person responsible for later regularizing press conferences in the Wilson White House was none other than Wilson's Trenton secretary Joseph P. Tumulty, who had been with Wilson since his first campaign in New Jersey.[69] Tumulty served Wilson in New Jersey as advance man, information-gatherer, confidant, and advisor. Tumulty had proven so valuable that Wilson stood firm in his appointment of Tumulty as his private secretary while president, despite vehement anti-Catholic opposition from within Wilson's circle.[70] As he had advised in his capacity as secretary during Wilson's gubernatorial years, Tumulty would likewise suggest to President Wilson that the best remedy for political opposition was taking to the stump.[71] Indeed, Wilson recognized Tumulty as "one of the ablest young Democratic politicians of the State" and someone to "have as a guide at my elbow in matters of which I know almost nothing."[72]

THE SMITH AFFAIR

The most strategic and influential of Wilson's moves followed by the press came early in his governorship, as he stared down New Jersey boss and former Democratic senator James Smith. It would become Wilson's signature experience in demonstrating popular executive leadership over his party. Wilson's "Bloody Angle" reference was a nod to this intraparty fight over the governor's influence in political matters formally outside his constitutional purview. Smith, a long-time party boss and presumed frontrunner for the Senate seat once his, miscalculated in expecting Wilson's endorsement. Instead, Wilson sought to carve out an independent executive path in Trenton. In exchange for the governor's support, Smith offered Wilson a clear route to full enactment of his legislative agenda. Wilson deflected this offer and supported a clean but unimpressive candidate in James E. Martine. "If you beat me in this fight," said a knowing Wilson to Smith, "how do I know you won't be able to beat me in everything?"[73]

Wilson was not offering mere hyperbole, given what was at stake. First and foremost, Wilson's bona fides as a true progressive leader were on the line. Martine had, in fact, been the choice of New Jerseyans in the Democratic primaries and, as such, held the popular and moral high ground as the would-be nominee. And yet his nomination was nonetheless based on party support, and Wilson was the pivotal figure in the outcome. With Smith's expectations weighing on him, Wilson wrote a brief, cryptic response to the senator, vaguely hinting at the possibility of an unexpected and stinging rebuke:

My dear Senator Smith,

Your generous telegram has given me a great deal of pleasure. I feel very deeply the confidence you have displayed in me, and the deep responsibility to the people which our success has brought with it. *I hope with all my heart that I may be able to play my part in such a way as to bring no disappointment to those who have trusted me.*

With much regard and deep appreciation,
Sincerely yours,
Woodrow Wilson[74]

This was hardly the response Smith had had in mind. Yet Wilson was beset from all sides. Progressive Democrats and "New Idea" Republicans did their best to hold his feet to the fire. One letter of support for Martine from a Republican voter exemplifies the independent streak aroused in New Jersey progressives: "We all voted the Dem[ocratic] ticket last Tuesday for the first time," wrote one Plainfield resident, warning that "we simply helped your party this time in order to punish our leaders for their sins of omission."[75] Another "ex-Republican" put it plainly: "I think [Martine] is a better man than any of the others who are the choice of the politicians and *we straight-voting and honest citizens hope that no tricksters will be allowed to get in and repudiate the will of the people as expressed in the direct primaries in which Mr. James Martine was the choice of the people.*"[76]

Winning progressive Republican support had been a goal of Wilson's at the outset of his campaign for governor. George L. Record, perhaps Wilson's leading GOP critic, had found Wilson's progressive credentials wanting. By addressing in detail some nineteen of Record's questions in print, Wilson rebuffed and, to a large extent, won over not only Record, but a good many of his fellow progressive Republicans in the state. In rallying behind Wilson's ultimate support for Martine over Smith, Record provided political cover representative of progressive affection for executive power:

Gov. Wilson showed great sagacity in forcing the [Senate] fight in the open. If he had confined himself to sending for members of the Legislature and talking to them privately, he would have made no progress, but the moment he made the fight a public one, and gave to the people his reasons, he put the machine at a big disadvantage. . . . A Governor is possessed of influence. Under our political system there must be party leaders, and the Governor, who has been retained by the people, so to speak, is duty bound to publicly say to the people from time to time, and to the Legislature as well, what he thinks would be in the public interest. Instead of such an attitude being opposed to the Constitution, it is entirely consistent with it. The Governor is acting entirely within his rights, and the universal delight with which the people have hailed his assumption of the role of leader and adviser, proves that he is performing a genuine public service.[77]

Wilson's ultimate decision to back Martine should not obscure his lengthy and, at times, difficult occupation with the issue. "I am so busy just now with this Senatorial business," he would write in response to a request for a patronage position, "that I cannot even give the matter of the appointment of my secretary the least thought at present."[78] Indeed, on the eve of his election, Wilson was reminded of the issue by William W. St. John, founder of the *Elizabeth Evening Times* and a frequent contributor to a host of newspapers in the state. "Does not party honor and party loyalty require acquiescence in the selection of Mr. Martine," St. John wrote, "equal with the acquiescence that came from Democratic affiliations *with respect to your own candidacy arising from similar political initiative and power?*"[79] St. John proved unrelenting in his advocacy for Martine, sending the governor-elect news clippings and editorials from around the state backing Martine's candidacy.[80]

For all Martine lacked in ability (he had been such an unsuccessful and lackluster candidate he would come to be known to many New Jerseyans as simply "Running Jim"), his candidacy was on the right side of progressive politics.[81] Wilson seemingly had little choice in the matter; nevertheless, he probed the crevices of state politics to see where he might be vulnerable in throwing his support to Martine. For his part, Joe Tumulty kept Wilson duly apprised of possible repercussions. "I learned from a most reliable source," he wrote Wilson, "that Mr. [Hudson County boss] Davis would not feel 'hurt' if the Hudson Delegation would refuse to take his orders on the Senatorial proposition."[82] James Kerney, Editor of the *Trenton Evening Times*, offered Wilson his own account of the situation:

Dear Mr. Wilson:
    I had a talk today with Mr. Ely, regarding the probable attitude of the Democrats in the Legislature, and we figured that the line up was, at present about as follows:

For Martine: All of Hudson, the two in Union, Walsh in Mercer, Osborne in Essex and Gebhardt in Hunterdon.

For Smith: The Assemblymen in Essex; the four votes in Middlesex; Matthews in Hunterdon; the two votes in Warren and the two in Sussex.

The Bergen, Morris, Monmouth, Ocean, Somerset, and Gloucester votes are in doubt, with the Somerset Assemblyman probably for Martine and the Gloucester vote for Smith.

If you decide to issue any statement in the matter, I would appreciate it very much if you would kindly have your secretary either phone Mr. Darrow at the University Press, or this office so that we would be certain to get it. The press associations are at times slow, and we are naturally anxious to get any matter as quickly as possible.

Yours very truly,
James Kerney

It appears Kerney's insights were not offered without regard to self-interest.[83]

Wilson issued his statement in support of Martine on December 8 with a nod to the extralegal role of the popular executive ("there are other duties besides legal duties"). Declaring the majority vote in the Democratic primary "conclusive," Wilson urged the legislature to act accordingly.[84]

The battle would have lasting impact for Wilson, who, like TR, earned his executive stripes by an act of defiance of Hudson bossism. As Wilson biographer Kendrick Clements describes:

During December and January Wilson traveled around the state as if he were campaigning, denouncing Smith and urging support for Martine. It was an unprecedented appeal to the public in a senatorial campaign, and it was effective in keeping pressure on the legislators. When the Democrats met in caucus on 23 January 1911 thirty-three were pledged to Martine, and despite last minute efforts by those Wilson denounced as Smith's "agents and partisans," the first ballot in the legislature the next day produced forty votes for Martine, just one short of the number needed for election.[85]

Wilson had made his point. Smith capitulated later that day. What is especially noteworthy from the episode is Wilson's assault on traditional party king-making. "Of whom does the Democratic Party consist?" he would ask. "Does the Democratic Party consist of a little group of gentlemen in Essex County?"[86] Wilson's early leadership credentials were no doubt built around this Democratic Party infighting—on one occasion he was reported to have kicked out of his office Boss Smith's nephew and lieutenant, James Nugent.[87] By offering such an open challenge to the party, Wilson was signaling the beginning of a new relationship. The *Times* put the implications of the fight with Smith best: "Dr. Wilson's attitude in deciding to take up the cudgels against Smith has cleared the political atmosphere marvelously and has made every one realize that the former President of Princeton University has now absolutely assumed the leadership of the Democratic Party in New Jersey."[88] The fight was not without its costs. Wilson would go on to lose the Democratic hold over the New Jersey legislature in 1912, as the Smith machine instructed its Democratic state workers to "lay down" during the election, hoping to "[destroy] Wilson's presidential chances."[89] While Wilson would go on to win the 1912 presidential election, New Jersey progressive reform would suffer a significant blow.

With progressives clamoring for executive strength, Wilson was demonstrating that the party was no longer the prime mover in either state or national politics. "Only the President represents the country as a whole," Wilson argued in *Constitutional Government*. Because of the vast powers of his office, he can "if he chooses become national boss."[90] Like Herbert Croly, Wilson believed public opinion was all that legitimately remained to restrict the president. His own record as governor in New Jersey demonstrated that American politics could be remade such that a popularly elected executive could effectively win public support while accruing enormous power in party leadership— at least at the state level—while employing extraconstitutional measures. Such leadership had proven widely popular across the country during the Progressive Era and would in time become one of the hallmarks of modern presidential leadership. It was a form of leadership that elicited Croly's admiration, if not his endorsement:

> [Wilson] has the power to write his own platform and practically repudiate the official platform of his party. He becomes the leader, almost the dictator, of his party, as no president has between Andrew Jackson and Woodrow Wilson. A wise, firm, yet conciliatory man like President Wilson can exercise his enormous power as to make his

party a more rather than a less effective instrument of government,
just as a monarchy may become, in the hands of an exceptionally able,
independent, energetic and humane administrator, a temporarily
beneficent form of government. But a Woodrow Wilson is not born
of every election.[91]

Croly represented an antiparty variant of progressivism; his fears, and
those of similarly situated progressives, were based on the premise that the
executive would ultimately succumb to the type of bossism rampant in
America's urban centers. As Richard Hofstadter suggested, the age was
largely reviled as urbanized beyond recognition. "The first city," Hofstadter
wrote, quoting Josiah Strong, "was built by the first murderer."[92] Neobossism
in the form of presidential party leadership was presumably not the answer
to the howls of the cities. Yet this strand of executive leadership, coveted by so
many progressives—one that effectively headed parties and legislatures—
was best represented by Wilson, even as governor. As Alexander and Juliette
George noted in their study of Wilson:

> The legislative session of 1911 was a triumph for Wilson. Never in the
> history of the state had there been so fruitful a session. In four months
> Wilson had succeeded in piloting his entire program through both
> houses. He had done so by eliminating the two major obstacles on
> which, in less skillful hands, the whole program might have foundered:
> boss control of the Assembly, and Republican opposition in the Senate.
> His masterful performance had increased his availability for the pres-
> idential nomination immeasurably.[93]

Wilson's leadership here is best understood in the context of the changing times. Wisconsin's Bob La Follette had demonstrated similar success,
using the same tactics as governor to great effect, and, like Wilson, helped
pave the way for far more executive-centered governance, in an era increasingly open to personalist leadership.[94] Wilson had proven he understood the
modern requisites of executive leadership—well before television, and in the
dawn before radio. Fred Greenstein's point that "the presidential activism of
FDR had been preceded by the assertive leadership of Theodore Roosevelt
and Woodrow Wilson," can be applied to their dual mastery of press rela-

tions and, for Wilson especially, the leadership of his party. The roots of such leadership are, of necessity, to be seen in the governorships of all three future presidents.[95]

Woodrow Wilson's Modern Legislative Leadership

While it is well established that Woodrow Wilson "was the first chief executive since John Adams to appear before Congress rather than sending messages in written form,"[96] what is often overlooked are the influences upon Wilson in coming to this decision. As discussed earlier, it was, in all likelihood, New York's pre-Jacksonian constitution, and Wisconsin's progressive governor, that served as the inspiration for Wilson's innovation. Besides La Follette, only one other modern executive is linked to such a daring encroachment upon legislative authority. North Carolina's Democratic governor Robert Broadnax Glenn also personally delivered his address in person in 1905.[97] Glenn and Wilson were political contemporaries—Glenn's term ended the year before Wilson was elected governor of New Jersey in 1910. An attendee of the first Governor's Conference in 1908, Glenn was a progressive typical of the era, a conservationist and a strong advocate of executive authority.[98] True to the period, Glenn opened his remarks at the conference with praise for Grover Cleveland and an attack on the laxity of Congress.[99] It stands to reason that Wilson's atavistic emulation of this Federalist-era presidential practice would emerge during a period of renewed executive authority and creativity, fostered most consciously by progressive governors. While Wilson was breaking a 113-year precedent at the national level, at the state level, the innovation was relatively fresh, a mere eight years removed from Wilson's modern presidential iconoclasm.

To appreciate the boldness of Wilson's foray into the sanctity of the legislature, one of those watershed moments that has come to distinguish the modern presidency from its predecessors, it is important to revisit Wilson's theoretical understanding of the founding.[100] As one political scientist has argued, "for Wilson, the separation of powers, and all of the other institutional remedies that the founders employed against the danger of faction, stood in the way of government's exercising its power in accord with the dictates of progress."[101] As Wilson would later explain during the presidential campaign of 1912, "You know that it was Jefferson who said that the best government is that which does as little governing as possible.... But that time has passed."[102]

While the framers feared excessive power, progressives in many ways feared powerlessness. The neat, symmetrical order of the American Constitution had to be reinterpreted as an organic one, willing to defy structural impediments for the greater good of the people. Where Madison had taken for granted that "in republican government, the legislative authority necessarily predominates," Wilson sought to "relocate administrative processes from Congress to the executive department."[103] In the end, the personally delivered message became one of the lasting symbols of executive-driven government.

WILSON'S LEGISLATIVE EXECUTIVE ENLARGED

Wilson focused his legislative agenda in New Jersey on bedrock progressive policies: the establishment of direct primaries; fighting corruption; the regulation of public utilities; and a liability act for employers.[104] To these ends, Wilson personally lobbied the Democratic Assembly. "Breaking all precedent, Wilson attended a caucus of the Democratic Assemblymen. For three hours, he lectured them about the necessity of passing the [election] bill. For the benefit of those who might remain impervious to his arguments, he warned them that if necessary he would carry the fight to the people."[105] The exchange between Wilson and the legislature was memorable, as noted by Ray Stannard Baker: "'What constitutional right has the Governor to interfere in legislation?' demanded one of the legislators bluntly. 'Since you appeal to the constitution,' responded Wilson, 'I can satisfy you.' He drew from his pocket a copy of the constitution and read the following clause: 'The governor shall communicate by message to the legislature at the opening of each session, and at such other times as he may deem necessary, the condition of the state, and recommend such measures as he may deem expedient.'"[106]

In this fight over what would become the Geran Bill for electoral reform, Wilson won outright. Twenty-seven of the thirty-eight assemblymen attending the caucus voted for the measure.[107] For his part, a truculent Wilson would boast, "A notion has gone abroad that I whipped the Legislature of New Jersey into performing certain acts, but that view of the matter is not correct. I did appeal to public opinion, and public opinion did the rest."[108]

In passing the Geran Bill for electoral reform, Wilson won himself a legislative legacy of the first order. The victory was earned with a style of personal executive leadership characteristic of the era's upstart progressive governors. Wilson had met with nearly every legislator on the Smith appointment issue,[109] and, in this instance, took to the stump to educate New Jersey voters about the provisions of the bill. "The Geran Bill is intended to clear all obstacles away and to put the whole management alike of parties and of elections in the hands of voters themselves," urged the governor.[110] Wilson specifically sought direct involvement of the people in the bill, which contained the distinctly antiparty feature of disallowing the name of any person on a primary ticket of any party, unless pledged to vote for New Jersey's top primary vote getter for the state's senate seat.[111] As the *Times* reported, "In the past New Jersey has voted with the old-fashioned party ballot containing only the names of the nominees of one party. This year [1911] every one nominated appeared on one ballot, but there were no party designation devices except the words denoting the parties name. . . . There was no way that a ballot could be prepared by a single mark."[112] If the measure put greater power in the hands of the people, it also threatened party control and, more significantly, made the governor a figure with plebiscitary power and popular authority. Nevertheless, young progressive idealists like New York's Robert Moses took note of Wilson's political innovations and theories during his governorship. "His writings show not only a clear understanding of the defects of our . . . civil service, but also a keen realization of the executive leadership necessary to remedy them," wrote New York's future power broker.[113]

Again, one critical reason Wilson and other Hudson-based executives were so vital to the era was their orchestration of national press attention. In defying their respective political machines, New York and New Jersey governors garnered greater attention than other politicians. They could be sure their legislative acts of defiance would be not only heard in greater New York, but picked up nationally. Wilson had the particular good fortune to also be a Southerner, which meant his southern brethren would be inclined to excuse his northern political lineage, while southern newspapermen covered his more favorable exploits. While Wilson certainly did not escape southern criticism, he was nonetheless politically well served by his birthplace.[114] Wilson may have joked that "compared with Princeton politicians," New Jersey's party bosses were "neophytes," but people around the country knew better, even as they presumably laughed.[115]

As Daniel Stid points out, Wilson sought an "advanced progressivism" by working to ensure the strength of the Democratic Party. He worked discreetly in both the 1914 and 1918 congressional elections in an effort to "rally support for the most promising proadministration candidates; attempting to unite factions opposed to antiadministration renegades."[116] Indeed, politics and policy were interwoven in Wilson's executive decision making. His fight as president against the railroad interests linked him to earlier reform efforts by Roosevelt and to more conservative executive exhortations from Cleveland. Whatever success Wilson had on this front was owed to his efforts to work through his party; even these victories were contingent. As Elizabeth Sanders notes:

> The political force that ultimately persuaded the agrarian Democrats to accept elements of the New Nationalist regulatory program was their party leader and president, Woodrow Wilson. In the first crucial year of the New Freedom, Wilson had put his incomparable "prime ministerial" skills behind a program that was much more the agenda of the agrarian Democratic Party than his own. . . . However, as the recession took hold in 1914 and virulent business criticism poured in, a "new Wilson"—whose principles seemed closer to the original (pre-1908) Wilson—emerged.[117]

Ultimately, Wilson's legislative and party leadership as president can in no way be detached from his tenure in Trenton. Unlike Roosevelt, however, Wilson forged a much closer and strategic relationship with his party. But this important difference should not obscure the ways in which Wilson's governorship, like TR's, meant much to the stream of modern innovations that would flow into the presidency. His use of rhetoric, directly speaking to voters—and at times openly encouraging dissent with the less progressive wing of his party—became part of a new executive manner. Not all presidents (or governors, for that matter) would employ it, but those who did quickly became pacesetters of modern executive leadership. As Theodore Lowi has noted, Wilson's call for the president to be "as big a man as a man as he can be," eventually became unnecessary, as all presidents eventually became de facto "exceptional." "The presidency grew," notes Lowi, "because it had become the center of a new governmental theory, and it became the center of a governmental theory by virtue of a whole variety of analyses and writings that were attempting to build some kind of consonance between the new, positive state and American democratic values."[118] The most telling and first practical clashes between these contending theories occurred in America's statehouses. Along with TR's, Wilson's governorship reflected this crucial dialectic in American executive political development. It was a tension common to the larger Progressive Era, and heightened by Hudson progressives, who were compelled to confront, at the crossroads of the new century, a new American state, one requiring appropriate conceptions of executive leadership. This was summed up by Wilson himself, who at once argued that the presidency was essentially a "big governorship" and reserved for himself the audacious, if not unsettling, right to execute its office "unconstitutionally" if need be.

Conclusion: Conceiving the Plebiscitary Presidency

Woodrow Wilson's governorship was the practical reflection of his political thought and a herald of future presidential practices. It was in Trenton that Wilson personally crossed the threshold of executive impropriety; hitherto, he had done so only in theory. By intruding into a Democratic legislative caucus, making popular appeals to the people outside of his constitutionally designated appointment powers, and by leading, rather than following, his party, Wilson exemplified the features of modern American executive leadership. And yet, much of this was not particularly new; La Follette had acted similarly in Wisconsin, and with more radical flair. For his part, Teddy Roosevelt continued a tradition of gubernatorial independence in New York that dated at least to Samuel J. Tilden. And other governors had been as forthrightly "executive"—indeed the word itself had changed in meaning from its tepid incarnation at the founding—as Wilson had been during the Progressive Era. But Wilson went furthest: he alone theorized a full turn from founding notions embedded in the Constitution. Theodore Roosevelt, for one, would not go so far. Also, Wilson was the first since the days of Andrew Jackson to openly advocate and fulfill a rejection of such constitutional bulwarks as the separation of powers and checks and balances. And only Wilson rhapsodized about Darwinian political change over static traditionalism. He did all of this first in his executive experience as governor.

In his Hegelian epistemology, Wilson was a true radical. In addition to having a Burkean sensibility, he was a paradigm breaker. Wilson would take Burke, modernity's archetypal conservative thinker, and embellish him with new-found intellectual stilts, such that FDR and a host of liberal policy makers could dash away from staid political forms. Custom mattered for Burke, but it was always epochal for Wilson. It lacked the continuity of political culture Burke had infused it with. Thus, with great irony, Wilson's executive-centered theory of governance embraced the Jeffersonian claim to the world of politics belonging to the living. But Jefferson had meant this as a guard against government's perpetual encroachment into the lives of its citizens, while Wilson meant it as a liberating device for popular and ever-changing executive leadership. In a sense, Wilson's was a call for government of the people, for the people, but through the executive.

In one reading into the grand narrative of history, Wilson saw a sort of "passionless"[119] austerity in Edward Gibbon's classic *Decline and Fall of the Roman Empire*. In his essay "The Historian," Wilson examined Gibbon's study of this earliest demise of a great republic. "The principles of a free constitution are irrevocably lost when the legislative power is nominated by the executive," wrote Gibbon of Rome's decline.[120] In a later salvo, Gibbon would warn, "By declaring themselves the protectors of the people, Marius and Caesar had subverted the constitution of their country."[121] What did Wilson make of Gibbon's condemnation of executive authority's abuses? Writing at the dawn of the modern republican era, Gibbon had an intriguingly contrarian project in revisiting Rome's fall.[122] Wilson's personal history in the making was a neorepublican project founded on popular executive appeal—one far removed from the republican structures so beloved by Gibbon, and, most importantly, by America's founders. In short, Wilson, appropriately enough, thought Gibbon's fears out of step with the times.

In considering the profound changes in American life, both addressed by and influencing the Progressive Era, it is worth considering just how audacious Wilson's critique of past executive practices was. Beyond an embrace of direct primaries, the recall, or referendum, Wilson was calling forth a new way of conceiving democratic governance. Despite his own more modest record in New Jersey, many saw Wilson's executive model as the only possible counter to the excesses wrought by unfettered industrial capitalism. In exemplifying the type of executive demanded at the time while governor, Wilson set not only himself, but also the presidency on a course that has known little sustained retreat in the domain of executive power. There is much to lament in pondering, as did Gibbon, where such power might lead, and has indeed led. Shortly after Wilson, even greater power was heaped upon the quintessential executive of the age—another Hudson progressive, who would come to personally identify with the complete arts of executive governance as early as his days in Albany. In so doing, much more could be ascertained at the time that was gained by progressives than had been lost in the acquisition of such demonstrable executive power. And so it was with the early political legacy of Governor Franklin Delano Roosevelt.

Chapter 4

Prince of the Hudson: FDR's Albany Executive

I want to speak not of politics but of Government. I
want to speak not of parties, but of universal principles.
—Franklin D. Roosevelt, Commonwealth Club Address,
San Francisco, 1932[1]

Every few years, say every half generation, the general
problems of civilization change in such a way that new
difficulties of adjustment are presented to government.
The forms have to catch up with the facts.
—Franklin D. Roosevelt, interview with the *New York
Times*, 1932[2]

Introduction

On September 30, 1932, in the middle of his first campaign for the presidency, Governor Franklin D. Roosevelt spoke in front of a hundred thousand people in Milwaukee, Wisconsin. Over thirty years removed from Robert M. La Follette's governorship, Roosevelt was nonetheless compelled to pay homage to what had come to be known interchangeably as the "Wisconsin Idea" and the "La Follette School" of political thought.[3] It was "Fighting Bob" La Follette who had a generation earlier personified the core tenets of progressive executive philosophy in Wisconsin. His was an avowedly executive-centered leadership—above party, plebiscitary in nature, and fiercely populist. Before Woodrow Wilson crossed the implicit line of constitutional propriety by speaking directly to Congress in person, La Follette had performed the equivalent as governor. Before FDR, while president, challenged members of his own party to follow his lead as director of the New Deal, La Follette waged a purge of his own, "reading the roll" on the campaign trail against fellow Republicans who did not conform to his progressive vision, embarrassing them into either acquiescence or defeat. Thus, Roosevelt was more earnest than pandering when he told his Milwaukee audience, "Out here in Wisconsin you do not merely protest against the teachings of the present order, you set out to correct them. You put your ideals into circulation. You set up standards to which liberals in all States have found it profitable and inspiring to repair."[4] Indeed, Roosevelt claimed La Follette's distant tutelage of him began as early as his Harvard years. It was an instruction in liberal public policy and executive-based party leadership. "The refreshing freedom from the party lock-step is a Wisconsin habit," he would say to the crowd in Milwaukee. "I hope the habit continues."[5]

FDR understood as well as anyone that he was not so much orchestrating a departure from past practices as he was cementing them. More than beginning a new order of leadership, Roosevelt was the definitive seal of America's modern executive epoch. And as much as he was the harbinger of presidential leadership to come, FDR was the last of a line of protomodern executives—progressive governors who had called into question the nature of traditional American notions of executive practice. The Hudson line, in particular, constituting the epicenter of New York and New Jersey politics and patronage, was most instructive to FDR. Western progressives from La Follette to Governor Hiram Johnson of California were no doubt important, but the generation of New York and New Jersey governors—Tilden, Grover Cleveland, Theodore Roosevelt, and Woodrow Wilson—established a governing tradition most directly pertinent to FDR. And it was his great but unlucky predecessor, Governor Alfred E. Smith of New York, who most immediately embodied the executive acumen and policies FDR would come to epitomize on the national stage.

The suggestion that FDR lacked a coherent political philosophy holds only the thinnest veneer of truth when understood with this legacy in mind. The historian Ellis Hawley, for one, argued that there was more political than economic consistency to FDR's logic as president. This "economic confusion" seen in New Deal experimentation has become one way of denying the coherence of Roosevelt's political thought.[6] A more apt interpretation suggests Roosevelt stepped into a political philosophy rather than authored one of his own. As last in a line of prophetic executives, FDR was decidedly more Joshua than Moses. In 1920, Hiram Johnson remarked somewhat cryptically, "In the end of course there will be a revolution, but it will not come in my time."[7] In his last days, Johnson proved loyal to Roosevelt and his progressive vision, writing FDR in his first year in the White House that he had "followed your gallant fight and nothing like it in courage and high endeavor has this country witnessed during my time."[8] The sentiment could only have pleased Roosevelt, who may not have originated a theory of revolution, but nevertheless centered his politics upon unapologetic executive leadership. Raymond Moley, one of the architects of the New Deal, reflected in 1939 that Roosevelt's political philosophy was "the heritage of a series of economic and social crises that began in 1873, the bywords of a progressivism that for over sixty years had preached the need for controlling the increasing concentration of economic power and the need for converting that power to social ends. These were the purposes that had activated Bryan, Altgeld, Tom Johnson, old Bob La Follette, and to a degree, TR and Wilson."[9]

By the time of his governorship, Roosevelt had become associated with progressive politics in ways that went beyond his obvious familial connections to TR. As FDR biographer Frank Freidel suggested, Roosevelt may well have "at heart always remained more a Progressive than a New Dealer."[10] In line with this progressive tradition, Roosevelt sold his antibossism to voters en route to the New York State Senate in 1911, the governorship in 1928, and the White House in 1932. Executive leadership in New York had been defined in this way since the days when Roosevelt's father backed the governorships of Samuel J. Tilden and Grover Cleveland.[11] The path to executive power in the state had often been built upon opposition to the political machine of either party on one hand, and subtle recognition of party power and influence on the other. The lure of patronage was a defining aspect of executive temptation and power. An antimachine politics that did not take this into account was not based in reality. When, in 1913, FDR was offered and declined the position of collector of the Custom House of the Port of New York, it was only because he had a better offer.[12] Like Tilden, who was offered the post decades before him, FDR would choose another path to power. Instead, he accepted a position as Assistant Secretary of the Navy in the Wilson administration. All the same, Roosevelt understood New York's party-patronage politics as well as any politician before him. As Freidel noted, "Obviously in joining the Wilson administration, Roosevelt was increasing his power in New York politics through his involvement in patronage. Through the proper dispensing of jobs he would have liked to build a strong upstate pro-Wilson and anti-Tammany organization, and he devoted a large amount of time and effort to this undertaking. He and Louis Howe, whom he had brought to the Navy Department, fought especially doggedly for postmasterships in upstate Republican congressional districts."[13]

Roosevelt ultimately failed in this early endeavor, learning that "he could not win New York primaries without Tammany support."[14] The lesson helped form Roosevelt's early understanding of party power—it cut both ways, and, in the absence of greater personal power, it could prove debilitating. The key was to hold the reins of both popular and party power and thus dissipate opposition. Good government was effectively the absence of countervailing power to executive-led progressive change. In New York, where a strong executive and party machine shared power, Roosevelt's early career was defined by a need to build personal clout while satisfying party obligations. It was a dialectic that produced an elite cadre of political leaders from the state.[15]

FDR's immediate predecessor, Al Smith, had proven himself a more than influential part of this line of progressive governors. Much of Roosevelt's legislative program was a product of Smith's tenure as governor. As the political journalist Samuel Lubell wrote, "Before the Roosevelt Revolution there was an Al Smith Revolution."[16] Smith took an already powerful office and furthered its executive reach, consolidating its one hundred departments in the state down to some twenty directly accountable to the governor. This model of administration was far from lost on Roosevelt.[17] Indeed, the entire proximate executive political history of New York had been the training ground for FDR and his vision of progressive politics and executive leadership. The increased powers of New York's governor were part of a trend toward centralization that was instrumental in Roosevelt's ultimate success in state politics. This development was summed up well years later as providing "the possibility of unity of command, of effective coordination, of internal responsibility, and of administration."[18]

For Roosevelt, the key political insight from the period was in understanding how policy opportunities could be maximized in the face of party opposition. "When I think of the difficulties of former State Chairmen with former Governors," Roosevelt remarked, "I have an idea that [James Farley] and I make a combination which has not existed since Cleveland and Lamont—and that is so long ago that neither you nor I know anything about it except from history books."[19] Roosevelt did not intend to dissolve political parties or their influence; his interest instead was in making his party a force for progressive-executive leadership. Parties should trail personal leadership, not the other way around. As Roosevelt remarked to an aide in 1932, "We shall have eight years in Washington. At the end of that time we may or may not have a Democratic party; but we will have a Progressive one."[20] While this response was partly Rooseveltian hyperbole, it nonetheless captured an equally important aspect of FDR's executive persona. The party was to follow the president if it wished to remain relevant. In an age of established executive leadership, Roosevelt was articulating the plebiscitary nature of presidential power. It was a defining sentiment for Roosevelt, one carefully honed as governor.

FDR's Albany Executive

Few New York politicians understood the rough-and-tumble nature of legislative and party relations in New York as well as Franklin Roosevelt did. FDR had been eyed for some time by party leaders to succeed Alfred E. Smith as governor. Smith himself orchestrated the move, looking to Roosevelt in 1928 as an heir apparent while girding himself for a presidential bid. Smith's idea was to govern by proxy and to use FDR's good name and "clean government" record en route to winning New York in the national election.[21] Smith would ultimately be foiled on both counts. Roosevelt would win the state for himself, becoming governor in 1928, but he could not deliver New York to Smith in the presidential election. More tellingly, he rejected Smith's efforts to govern indirectly through the appointment of old Democratic Party stalwarts. Roosevelt vowed that his governorship would be his own, even at the expense of alienating Smith and key party leaders. This early move presaged the type of independent governor FDR would be, one very much in the tradition of Al Smith, Theodore Roosevelt, and, chief among his heroes, Grover Cleveland.

Smith's tenure was perhaps most germane. It is easy to forget how critical he was to Roosevelt's governorship, and indeed for what was to come. As noted in an early postmortem on Roosevelt's political career, the Columbia historian Bernard Bellush attempted to make a point above the din of purely presidential accounts of the New Deal. "Despite the contentions of many historians," he wrote, "the seeds of the New Deal were first planted by a graduate of Tammany Hall and the Fulton fish market, the four-time Governor, Alfred E. Smith."[22] The challenge for Roosevelt was that Smith wanted to ensconce more than just his legislative reforms at the heart of FDR's governorship; he wanted his people there as well. As Arthur M. Schlesinger, Jr. recounted:

> Al Smith had been a great governor. Now denied the Presidency, he seemed disinclined to relinquish the governorship. His motives were doubly mixed. A sincere concern for Roosevelt's health and for the state's welfare mingled with a reluctance to yield power. . . . A friend told Roosevelt that Smith had said of him, "He won't live for a year." In any case, Smith informed Roosevelt that Belle Moskowitz was ready to start work on the inaugural address and the message to the legislature. Smith also suggested that Mrs. Moskowitz be appointed the Governor's secretary and that Robert Moses be kept as Secretary of State. And he reserved for himself a suite at the DeWitt Clinton Hotel in Albany to help on the big decisions.[23]

Roosevelt deflected these entreaties with characteristic deftness. Like Woodrow Wilson years before him, he rejected internal party pressures in the realm of gubernatorial appointments. Roosevelt echoed Wilson's fierce independence in his aside to Frances Perkins at the time. "I've got to be Governor of the State of New York, and I have got to be it myself," he said.[24] Moskowitz was in fact universally regarded as the best legislative insider in Albany. But she came at a price too dear for FDR. To accept her or Moses, for that matter, would violate every precept of the modern executive template laid down in Albany as early as Tilden. Roosevelt understood that national candidates, let alone state executives, could ill afford being associated with party bosses in this way, no matter how competent they might have been.

ROOSEVELT'S LEGISLATIVE LEADERSHIP

One of the gifts Al Smith bequeathed to Roosevelt was legislation placing budgetary authority in the governor's office. With a Republican-controlled legislature, Roosevelt's hands were nonetheless tied; at the very least, the details of the budget could be contested constitutionally. Indeed, the new act implemented under Smith gave the legislature power to strike out some items of the governor's budget without proposing alternatives.[25] Such revisions were the crux of executive-legislative imbroglios in the state. They were likewise part of a relatively recent trend in many states of granting budgetary authority to governors.[26] For his part, FDR upped the ante. "I raise the broad question affecting the division of governmental duties between the executive, legislative, and the judicial branches of government," Roosevelt forewarned.[27] James MacGregor Burns put the battle between FDR and the legislature in proper perspective: "The position [Roosevelt] had taken both in public and private—that he was fighting for 'Constitutional Government, carrying out the original American theory of separation of powers between executive, legislative, and judicial branches'—was a remarkable stand for a politician who in Albany and later in Washington would try to bypass some of the ancient barriers between the three branches of government."[28] Roosevelt shrewdly depicted his support for the executive-driven budget as deriving from his desire for limited government. "To the same degree that the Governor should never be given legislative functions, so the legislative members should never be given executive functions," he reasoned during the budgetary battle.[29]

Ultimately, the fight over Roosevelt's budget grew contentious enough that the issue went to the Appellate Division of the State Supreme Court. Roosevelt looked to the judicial branch to support implied executive powers. Roosevelt's Attorney General is said to have quoted Al Smith in making his case to the court. "Pay no attention to this talk about increasing the power of the Governor. Pay no attention to this talk about decreasing the power of the Legislature. Nothing in the proposed executive budget does either of these two things," quoted Attorney General Ward.[30] Pay no attention indeed. Roosevelt's executive philosophy—strident about goals, subtle in its arguments— would lose out initially: the appellate division rejected Ward and FDR's arguments. Nevertheless, Roosevelt would win in the equivalent of New York's state supreme court, the court of appeals. There, Roosevelt's executive vision was upheld. He would claim the governor's authority over New York's budget as a "victory for constitutional government."[31] As Bellush noted, FDR's executive order No. 8248, issued a decade later when he was president, likewise "transferred the United States Bureau of the Budget to the Executive Office of the nation's Chief Executive."[32] Constitutional government had proven once again, in a new age, to mean executive-centered government. For Roosevelt, the vision began in Albany.

FDR was well aware of the executive tradition he sought to advance. The political historian and Roosevelt biographer Thomas H. Greer correctly emphasized Roosevelt's executive pedigree. He was, in many respects, incapable of seeing politics through any other lens:

> Although he knew much of the judicial and legislative branches of government, Roosevelt was pre-eminently a specialist in the executive process. Counting his service as Assistant Secretary of the Navy, he spent twenty-four years in the executive branch—including sixteen as Chief Executive (of state or nation). His long hold on the presidency and the drama of history enabled him to know that office from alpha to omega. . . . As a child he once sat on Grover Cleveland's knee. His first vote for president was for his dynamic relative, "Uncle Ted." As Assistant Secretary, he served with enthusiasm under Wilson. He deeply admired these three, and they formed in his mind a highly personal, composite model of what a president should be.[33]

Quite importantly, each of these former governors led with similarly disproportionate executive backgrounds. Like his New York forebears, Roosevelt had little or no legislative experience. None of the crucial figures of the era—Cleveland, TR, and FDR—managed to spend a single day in Congress. FDR was aware of this lineage and took pride in his executive experience (as he did when bragging about his "happy association" with Cleveland's veto record as governor).[34] Roosevelt went further than Cleveland, of course, while also becoming the first president to read a veto message to Congress personally.[35]

FDR also employed personal appeals to the legislature on more than one occasion. In an early battle with the New York legislature over water power, Roosevelt addressed the chamber in person in his first term as governor.[36] Perhaps channeling Wilson in making such an appeal, Roosevelt's gubernatorial confrontation was perhaps more unnerving to New York's Republicans than to Wilson's congressional counterparts years earlier. Roosevelt's action would be the first in a protracted fight in the state over the question of power rates. Here, Roosevelt would be less successful than in his fight to win control over the budget. As the *New York Times* reported at the time, "Roosevelt, like former Governor Smith, has but one recourse—to appeal from the legislature to the people."[37] Despite many future successes, Roosevelt's popular appeals were of little avail in this instance. In June of 1929, he tried to make his case in populist terms. "In New York at the present time only the Governor and Lieutenant Governor stand between the retention by the people of their property and its alienation," he said. "We seem to have forgotten the old difference between capital going into purely private ventures and capital going into public service corporations."[38] Despite his best arguments for cheaper power rates, Roosevelt's fight resulted in a modest victory: the establishment of a state power commission.[39]

Yet Roosevelt turned what amounted to a legislative defeat into a political victory. He portrayed the creation of the commission as a signal accomplishment. Press coverage followed suit and gave Roosevelt national credentials as a progressive governor, earning him early talk as a possible candidate for the presidency in 1932. Walter Lippmann lauded the creation of the power commission as "a complete triumph."[40] It was a sign of Roosevelt's ability to curry favor with the press where support was initially lacking. Indeed, FDR's historic name, charisma, and skill with the press—and the new medium of radio— helped make him one of the more powerful political figures in the nation. Most important, Roosevelt was able to generate coverage from the platform of New York's governor on an unprecedented level. He dwarfed his immediate predecessors in this regard, including the powerful and consequential governorship of Al Smith. Only Smith would approach Roosevelt's avalanche of press coverage in the state.

In the over eighty years of *New York Times* coverage of New York governors, ending in Roosevelt's 1928 term, the newspaper's tracking of state executives increased greatly over time. *Times* coverage captured the growing significance of the governor not only in state affairs but nationally as well. In this regard, FDR followed the trajectory of former governors Tilden, Cleveland, Teddy Roosevelt, Charles Evans Hughes, and Al Smith in becoming a presidential candidate in part due to national press attention to New York's governor. The *Washington Post*'s and *Chicago Tribune*'s coverage of FDR likewise reflected his status as a national figure, as well as the value in earning a reform record as governor. The tables below provide one means of gauging what amounted to unprecedented publicity for an executive whose national appeal grew out of the dominance of New York's media coverage and political importance:

Executive leadership in antimachine politics along with progressive legislation earned Empire State candidates for the White House a level of prestige no other state could match. Roosevelt went further than any of his predecessors

Table 7. Governors of New York and *New York Times* Citations, 1851–1932

Governor	Years	Total Citations	Yearly Average	Rank
Franklin D. Roosevelt (D)	1929–1932	2445	611.2	1
Al Smith (D)	1923–1928	2628	438.0	2
Nathan L. Miller (R)	1921–1922	148	74.0	8
Al Smith (D)	1919–1920	266	133.0	4
Charles S. Whitman (R)	1915–1918	208	52.0	12
Martin H. Glynn (R)	1913–1914	98	49.0	13
John Alden Dix (D)	1911–1912	157	78.5	6
Charles Evan Hughes (R)	1907–1910	268	67.0	9
Frank W. Higgins (R)	1905–1906	11	5.5	24
Benjamin Odell (R)	1901–1904	105	26.2	16
Theodore Roosevelt (R)	1898–1900	408	204.0	3
Frank S. Black (R)	1896–1898	87	43.5	15
Levi P. Morton (R)	1894–1896	152	76.0	7
Roswell P. Flower (D)	1891–1894	133	44.3	14
David B. Hill (D)	1884–1891	642	91.7	5
Grover Cleveland (D)	1882–1884	131	65.5	11
Alonzo B. Cornell (R)	1879–1882	45	15.0	19
Lucius B. Robinson (R)	1876–1879	52	17.3	17
Samuel J. Tilden (D)	1874–1876	133	66.5	10
John Adams Dix (R)	1872–1874	33	16.5	18
John T. Hoffman (D)	1868–1872	55	13.7	21
Reuben E. Fenton (D)	1864–1868	36	9.0	22t
Horatio Seymour (D)	1861–1864	25	12.5	14
Edwin D. Morgan (R)	1858–1862	19	4.7	25
John A. King (R)	1856–1858	29	14.5	20
Myron H. Clark (Fusion-R)	1854–1856	18	9.0	22t
Horatio Seymour (D)	1852–1854	30	15.0	17
Washington Hunt (Whig Anti-Rent)	1851–1852	25	25.0	N/A

Notes: Dates are from January 1 to December 31 of years cited, 1901–1932, and from December 31 to December 31, 1851–1900. Glynn took office on October 17, 1913 upon the impeachment and removal of William Sulzer. Hughes left office on October 6, 1910 per his appointment as associate justice of the Supreme Court. The letter "t" indicates a territorial governor.

Table 8. Governors of New York and *Chicago Tribune* Citations, 1852–1932

Governor	Years	Total Citations	Yearly Average	Rank
Franklin D. Roosevelt (D)	1929–1932	7561	1890.3	1
Al Smith (D)	1923–1928	2211	368.5	2
Nathan L. Miller (R)	1921–1922	17	8.5	14
Al Smith (D)	1919–1920	20	10.0	13t
Charles S. Whitman (R)	1915–1918	30	7.5	15t
Martin H. Glynn (R)	1913–1914	15	7.5	15t
John Alden Dix (D)	1911–1912	14	7.0	17
Charles Evan Hughes (R)	1907–1910	73	18.3	8
Frank W. Higgins (R)	1905–1906	2	1.0	21t
Benjamin Odell (R)	1901–1904	4	1.0	21t
Theodore Roosevelt (R)	1898–1900	188	94.0	4
Frank S. Black (R)	1896–1898	23	11.5	12
Levi P. Morton (R)	1894–1896	65	32.5	6
Roswell P. Flower (D)	1891–1894	58	19.3	7
David B. Hill (D)	1884–1891	125	17.8	9
Grover Cleveland (D)	1882–1884	333	166.5	3
Alonzo B. Cornell (R)	1879–1882	6	2.0	19
Lucius B. Robinson (R)	1876–1879	5	1.6	20
Samuel J. Tilden (D)	1874–1876	99	49.5	5
John Adams Dix (R)	1872–1874	20	10.0	13t
John T. Hoffman (D)	1868–1872	13	3.3	18
Reuben E. Fenton (D)	1864–1868	4	1.0	21t
Horatio Seymour (D)	1861–1864	43	14.3	10
Edwin D. Morgan (R)	1858–1862	4	1.0	21t
John A. King (R)	1856–1858	2	1.0	21t
Myron H. Clark (Fusion-R)	1854–1856	0	0.0	26t
Horatio Seymour (D)	1852–1854	0	0.0	26t
Washington Hunt (Whig Anti-Rent)	1851–1852	N/A	—	—

Notes: Dates are from January 1 to December 31 of years cited, 1901–1932, and from December 31 to December 31, 1851–1900. Glynn took office on October 17, 1913 upon the impeachment and removal of William Sulzer. Hughes left office on October 6, 1910 per his appointment as associate justice of the Supreme Court. The letter "t" indicates a territorial governor.

Table 9. Governors of New York and *Washington Post* Citations, 1877–1932

Governor	Years	Total Citations	Yearly Average	Rank
Franklin D. Roosevelt (D)	1929–1932	8385	2096.3	1
Al Smith (D)	1923–1928	1359	226.5	2
Nathan L. Miller (R)	1921–1922	7	3.5	16
Al Smith (D)	1919–1920	19	9.5	13
Charles S. Whitman (R)	1915–1918	94	23.5	10
Martin H. Glynn (R)	1913–1914	50	25.0	8
John Alden Dix (D)	1911–1912	49	24.5	9
Charles Evan Hughes (R)	1907–1910	157	39.3	5
Frank W. Higgins (R)	1905–1906	13	6.5	14
Benjamin Odell (R)	1901–1904	7	1.8	17
Theodore Roosevelt (R)	1898–1900	169	84.5	3
Frank S. Black (R)	1896–1898	12	6.0	15
Levi P. Morton (R)	1894–1896	57	32.5	6
Roswell P. Flower (D)	1891–1894	20	28.5	7
David B. Hill (D)	1884–1891	106	13.3	11
Grover Cleveland (D)	1882–1884	101	50.5	4
Alonzo B. Cornell (R)	1879–1882	5	1.3	18
Lucius B. Robinson (R)	1877–1879	26	13.0	12

Notes: Dates are from January 1 to December 31 of years cited, 1901–1932, and from December 31 to December 31, 1876–1900. Glynn took office on October 17, 1913 upon the impeachment and removal of William Sulzer. Hughes left office on October 6, 1910 per his appointment as associate justice of the Supreme Court.

in enhancing his press relationships by establishing a publicity bureau at a cost of $100,000 per year, countering the largely Republican upstate press.[41] In addition to holding daily press briefings, Roosevelt astutely generated press coverage on his terms, frequently leaking information to maximize its potential benefit over time. And then there were the "fireside chats."

Like much that has come to be associated with Roosevelt's presidency, FDR's innovative use of radio for political purposes originated with his governorship.

Roosevelt thought he could circumvent a virtual state Republican monopoly of the press outside New York City with broadcasts. The Democratic Party thus contracted for an hour of radio time each month on a statewide hookup, which Roosevelt used to discuss the latest developments in Albany. As a follow-up to these monthly radio addresses, James Farley sent out questionnaires to local Democrats asking them about their reception. When faced with the 1929 legislative impasse, Roosevelt used the microphone to make a public appeal. By April 1929, Roosevelt was using his radio time in the manner of what was later called a "fireside chat," "an intimate, quiet way" of speaking.[42]

Roosevelt knew the power of speaking directly to the people. In campaigning for the governorship, he had spoken to the editors of both English-language newspapers upstate and foreign-language papers in ethnically diverse New York City.[43] By 1931, Roosevelt was cagily proposing state funding of rural newspapers to help "better educate" New York citizens. "The country paper should be the country schoolmaster for us older people," Roosevelt wrote the president of the National Editorial Association.[44] Presumably, Roosevelt would be the headmaster. It proved to be a brilliant strategy.[45]

Gaining radio listeners was a difficult task in the medium's early days. A great many people were still influenced by the written word, which often served as a filter to Roosevelt's radio addresses. Roosevelt lamented the situation in a letter touching on one of Walter Lippmann's criticisms: "I may be a little sore because a week ago I made a short radio speech on a national hookup on the broad subject of State vs. Federal Commission Rights. I talked about the broad principles and did not emphasize the Prohibition angle, but merely stated the constitutional fact of the Eighteenth Amendment. Therefore Walter hopped all over me the next morning, relegated all the rest of the speech to the discard and cursed me for not having made a speech on Prohibition alone!"[46] As Roosevelt's legislative leadership and skill with the press were cultivated during his governorship, so too was his improvisational and targeted response to America's Depression.

THE NEW DEAL PROPHESIED

FDR might have been late in recognizing the severity of the Depression, but he was the first executive in the country to tackle it head on. He already had great progressive credentials and was no stranger to supporting federal intervention in what had been distinctly seen as private life. In June of 1930, at the Governors' Conference at Salt Lake City, he was the first governor to propose unemployment insurance and old-age pensions.[47] Given the severity of the crisis but also the realities of a Republican-led legislature in New York, Roosevelt took a pragmatic approach to addressing the Depression in the state. As James MacGregor Burns noted, "Operating even then a 'little left of center,' to use his later term, he anticipated many of the New Deal programs in his continuous search for ways to meet specific problems. As the severity of the problems broadened during the Depression, so did the scope of his solutions. In his thinking he was ranging somewhat ahead of most politicians in the Northeast."[48] By August of 1931, Roosevelt had created the Temporary Emergency Relief Administration (TERA) and had pushed for unemployment insurance. New York was the first state to create such an agency and it served as a model for other states that would follow. It was the prototype for President Roosevelt's Federal Emergency Relief Administration (FERA).[49] The fact that the legislature was not fully supportive only steeled Roosevelt's resolve to defy opposition—the stuff of "politics" as he derisively called it. Unlike politics, "government," via enlightened administration, would dispense with partisan gamesmanship in the presence of such desperation. When Roosevelt declared that "to these unfortunate citizens aid must be extended by government –not as charity but as a matter of social duty," he said it as governor of a state battling him over progressive reform.[50] In short, FDR's New Deal activation of government was married early on to his sense of the need for executive political power.

In campaigning for reelection in 1930, Roosevelt lambasted the Republican legislature's opposition to his programs as "a leadership which has contented itself with a policy of blockade."[51] Later, in his second term as president, Roosevelt had opportunity to reflect on the significance of these early fights: "As Governor, it was often necessary for me to appeal for public support over the heads of the Legislature and sometimes over the almost united opposition of the newspapers of the State. In several instances, what was passed by the Legislature was literally forced from the Republican leaders by demand of public opinion which never hesitated to make its views known and which found ways of making them known."[52]

Later, in his public papers, Roosevelt characterized his gubernatorial years as "The Genesis of the New Deal." They are undoubtedly an early insight into his executive philosophy and views toward active, progressive government as understood in the first half of the twentieth century. Among the

numerous keepsakes of Rooseveltian thought is one reflection on Grover
Cleveland's lecture "The Independence of the Executive."[53] In April of 1900,
Cleveland delivered a series of lectures at Princeton on the plebiscitary role
of the president, declaring the presidency "pre-eminently the people's office."[54] Like Wilson before him, FDR revered Cleveland's executive philosophy and, in effect, replaced both Cleveland and Wilson as the quintessential
executive of the age. The Depression had provided Roosevelt political warrants unmatched by those of his predecessors. He would take advantage of
the crisis by shaping both new policy prescriptions and conceptualizations
about the limits of executive behavior.

FDR's Executive and Party Philosophies

Richard Hofstadter once wrote that despite the continuities in language that
connected the Progressive Era to the New Deal, the latter was essentially a
departure from all political philosophy that came before it.[55] This transformation was to a great extent defined by an exaltation of executive power.
Theodore Roosevelt, Woodrow Wilson, and, finally, FDR were all products
of this neoliberal thought. In his fight with the Republican legislature over
water power rates, Roosevelt inveighed against legislative intransigence.
"Executive responsibility must be armed with Executive authority," he ex-
claimed.[56] Herbert Hoover put it well when campaigning against FDR in
1932: "This campaign is more than a contest between two parties," he said.
"It is a contest between two philosophies of government."[57] The clash between
the broad ideological contours of liberalism and conservatism, as they were
being newly defined, was over executive function. As Raymond Moley evidenced in his memoir of the New Deal:

> Ernest K. Lindley, the best historian of the Roosevelt regime to date,
> has pointed out that "Mr. Roosevelt did not recruit his professorial
> advisers to provide him with a point of view; he drew them to him
> because their point of view was akin to his own. "That is perfectly true.
> It is also true that "Mr. Roosevelt had developed his political philoso-
> phy long before the depression began and long before he met any
> members of his brain trust. . . . [that] long before the presidential
> campaign of 1932 Mr. Roosevelt had emerged as the leading Demo-

cratic exponent of a modern liberalism of which the kernel was read-
iness to use the power of political government to redress the balance
of the economic world."[58]

For Roosevelt, the true "power of political government" was none other
than the executive. His interpretation of American history was decidedly
skewed in that direction, and his visionary leaders were proof of his view of
government. Roosevelt's pantheon of executives included Jefferson, Jackson, Lincoln, and, of course, "Uncle Teddy."[59] His sense of a separation of
powers was pragmatic and fluid. When the conception benefited Roosevelt,
he was keen to embrace it, as he did while governor. In admonishing New
York's Justice Ellis Staley over his handling of Roosevelt's investigation of
New York City mayor Jimmy Walker, Roosevelt was full of self-interested
restraint. "It is incumbent upon public officers, under our system, to respect
the constitutional division of authority and to remain within the limits pre-
scribed for their own action," he lectured the Justice in an indirect jibe.[60]
For his part, Justice Staley upheld the governor's power of removal.[61]

THE WALKER AFFAIR

The path to removing Walker was far from smooth. Roosevelt felt a degree
of loyalty to New York City's political machine (it was Walker who officially
nominated Roosevelt governor)[62] and he had an inherent aversion to making more out of a scandal he thought natural to the state's politics. Moreover, Walker had considerable support in the New York press, a factor both
damning and favorable to FDR. A great deal of winning the Democratic
Party nomination had to do with satisfying progressives across the nation.
And yet it was essential to curry favor with the local party organization and
machine. When, in 1931, Roosevelt rejected the entreaty to remove Walker
from office, he couched his rationale in democratic terms:

> It has ever been a fundamental principle of our government that the
> people of the state and of our various communities shall be allowed
> to exercise without restriction their right to select whomsoever they
> see fit to fill elective offices. The greatest caution must therefore be
> used in the exercise either of the impeachment power by the legisla-
> ture or the removal power by the Governor, in order not to annul the
> deliberate decision of the voters of the state or any municipality

thereof. Otherwise precedent might be established by which the will of the electorate might be set aside for partisan advantage on the part of the legislative majority or an unscrupulous Governor.[63]

It is not coincidental that Roosevelt's statement regarding Walker was preceded by broad support for retaining the mayor. "No one doubts that there are evils in the city government," opined the *New York Evening Journal*, "but [Walker's] explanation is given in detail and is sufficient for any reasoning mind, not moved by malice or party motive."[64] The *New York Sun* was blunter in its defense of Walker. "While Mr. Walker is not utterly convincing as to the absence of dust from beneath the sofa," the paper admitted, "at least his answer is more thorough than the document which provoked it."[65] Yet the Walker mess remained an albatross for Roosevelt, and as the election year of 1932 arrived, he was forced to address it once and for all.

As it was expressed by Bellush, in writing of FDR's governorship:

> Almost four years to the day he had nominated Roosevelt for Governor, Walker was fighting for his political life in the same cherry-paneled executive chamber where former Sheriff Farley had been interrogated only a few months previously. It was a charged atmosphere, for at stake was not only Walker's political future but, to an extent, the 1932 presidential race. Any indication of weakness or temerity on the part of the Governor would lose him tens of thousands of anti-Tammany votes throughout the nation. On the other hand, Walker's removal might well result in a vindictive campaign by Tammany against their national candidate – not an unfamiliar role for New York City's Democracy.[66]

Ultimately, Roosevelt knew he had to play to the crowds in Milwaukee as much as, if not more than, to the ones in Manhattan. Citing the precedent of his "illustrious predecessors, Governors Tilden, Cleveland and Hughes," FDR ruled against Walker, compelling the mayor's ultimate resignation.[67] With this move, Roosevelt affirmed the past practices of his Hudson predecessors. Tilden's chase of Tweed, TR's battles with Platt, and Wilson's fight with Smith, had now been joined by the clash between FDR and Walker. There is no doubt that removing Walker was a gamble, but it was one favored by historical circumstances. Once having partaken in this veritable rite of passage, Roosevelt was free to campaign in his own right as a "Tilden up to date." He would do so as a pragmatic politician to be sure, but also one with a greater sense of the underlying theories of politics than he is often credited.

Despite his presumed antiphilosophical stance, Roosevelt often found himself addressing the more esoteric principles of politics. "What is the State?" he asked in his opening remarks to the New York legislature on August 28, 1932. Invoking such theoretical constructs found in the state of nature as "the caveman," Roosevelt wove a story of government's responsibility to meet the basic needs of its citizenry.

> In many messages to your honorable bodies I have pointed out that [the] earlier exemplification of the State's responsibility has been sustained and enlarged from year to year as we have grown to a better understanding of governmental functions. I have mentioned specifically the general agreement of today—that upon the State falls the duty of protecting and sustaining those of its citizens who, through no fault of their own, find themselves in their old age unable to maintain life. . . . In broad terms I assert that modern society, acting through its government, owes the definite obligation to prevent the starvation and dire want of any of its fellow-men and women who try to maintain themselves but cannot.[68]

It is for good reason that this speech is said to have marked the "genesis of the New Deal."[69] In effect, it was the consolidation of decades' worth of progressive policy prescriptions and theory. What was new was that former crises and panics—of these, 1873 and 1893 loomed largest—lacked the magnitude and threat posed by the Great Depression. Moreover, it was a staple of progressivism that such crises had to be redressed by powerful executive action. Legislatures, like parties, had to be led, and if they would not follow, responsible executives would make direct appeals to the people. This was not a new playbook; what was new was the skillfulness of the practitioner, the tools available, including mass media, and the severity of the challenge. As the political scientist John Gerring notes, "Roosevelt did not advance policies any different from those of Bryan and Wilson until it became apparent that such traditional economic methods would not do the job."[70]

By January of 1932, Roosevelt was already pushing for greater latitude in policy alterations at the state level. In advocating for greater economic relief measures in New York, Roosevelt implored the legislature, "Let us not seek merely to restore. Let us restore and at the same time remodel."[71] Such remodeling was not only about expanding government's capacity to directly involve itself in the economic affairs of its citizenry; it was also tied to an expansion of executive powers and constitutional authority. Ultimately, the increase in executive influence produced by popular appeals yielded a decidedly estranged form of popular representation.[72]

Later, FDR's Commonwealth Club Address, as it has come to be known, marked the first rhetorical effort to codify these values, tying executive-led economic policy and progressive thought together. Citing German Chancellor Otto von Bismarck's command economy policies of 1880, Adolf Berle, the chief architect of the San Francisco Address, argued to Roosevelt that he had to take the reins of the economy if elected president or let private forces "tear it to pieces."[73] Berle's speech, delivered by Roosevelt on September 23, 1932, went largely unchanged by FDR, and remains the theoretical lodestar for understanding Roosevelt's public philosophy. Importantly, Roosevelt began the address with a disarming rhetorical device. "I want to speak not of politics but of Government. I want to speak not of parties, but of universal principles."[74]

For Roosevelt, politics and parties were not democratic so much as they were representative of democracy's discordant elements. They were not inherently incongruous with democracy; rather, they were potential brakes on imaginative, breakaway policies. In San Francisco, Roosevelt articulated a vision of civil life not fully divorced from the state of nature as delineated by Rousseau and other theorists. The brutishness of politics itself had to be transcended. "The creators of national Government were perforce ruthless men," he recalled.[75] To counter such raw power, early Americans expanded civil society and placed constitutional restraints on autocratic rulers. From this process emerged the American Revolution and Jeffersonian democracy— itself a measured counter to Hamiltonian impatience with popular democratic forms. This dialectic was, in Roosevelt's words, the beginning of "the day of the individual against the system."[76] While western expansion was still plausible, Roosevelt continued, so was the viability of individual prosperity and autonomy. Late nineteenth-century industrial capitalism changed all of that, and, as Roosevelt recounted, "the cry was raised against the great corporations."[77]

At last, Roosevelt invoked the progressive legacies of both TR and Wilson as exemplars of the protective role of executive authority in the interests of individual rights—indeed of "private rights"—redefined in terms of economic security and self-interest. In a world where "equality of opportunity as we know it no longer exists," Roosevelt reasoned, we must move further still to protect the interests of ordinary people.[78] This required nothing short of a new social contract between the people and their government:

> The task of statesmanship has always been the redefinition of these rights [found in the Declaration of Independence] in terms of a changing and growing social order. . . . I held, for example, in proceedings before me as Governor, the purpose of which was the removal of the Sheriff of New York, that under modern conditions it is not enough for a public official merely to evade the legal terms of official wrongdoing. He owed a positive duty as well. I said in substance that if he had acquired large sums of money, he was when accused required to explain the sources of such wealth. To that extent this wealth was colored with a public interest. . . . I feel that we are coming to a view through the drift of our legislation and our public thinking in the past quarter century that private economic power is, to enlarge an old phrase, a public trust as well.[79]

Practically, Roosevelt's stance against Sheriff Farley, like his effort to remove New York City mayor Jimmy Walker, was a calculated effort to cultivate national appeal as an anti-Tammany executive. Roosevelt did not take delight in removing Farley any more than he was personally interested in removing the adventurous Walker, but his vision of an executive in command and his desire to win the presidency were paramount. By recounting his dismissal of Farley in the Commonwealth Club Address, Roosevelt attempted to burnish his image as an independent leader, protective of the people's interests.

Arthur Schlesinger, Jr. argued that Roosevelt's speech "reflected Berle more than it did Roosevelt."[80] Nevertheless, Roosevelt understood the politics behind fashioning an image commensurate with the emergent role of the nation's chief executive. In this way, the address married theory and politics. Indeed, the politics of the 1932 campaign demanded as much attention from Roosevelt as the underlying rationales of this crucial policy speech. Winning the political support of former California governor and progressive stalwart Hiram Johnson was just as crucial to FDR as summoning an improved social contract. In fact, the Commonwealth Club Address was able to accomplish both. Shortly after FDR's inaugural, Johnson would pay Roosevelt a compliment stemming from his fondness for political experimentation.

"The admirable thing about Roosevelt," Johnson would say, "is that he has the guts to try."[81] The false choice of seeing Roosevelt as either pragmatist or grand theoretician belies the nature of executive practices of the Progressive Era. Power and theory were often wed together seamlessly. Roosevelt was fond of quoting Grover Cleveland who faced difficult, if less cataclysmic, times while president. "We are confronted with a condition, not a theory," Cleveland said in his third annual message to Congress.[82] The truth was closer to what the Commonwealth Club Address represented some thirty-five years after Cleveland uttered those words. The imperatives of crisis had been the window through which theory could skillfully come into play in American politics. That window had been opening since the presidential contest of Hayes and Tilden. In 1932, it had been blown wide open.

ROOSEVELT'S PARTY POLITICS

It has been well argued that the demands of economic centralization and liberal social policy compelled a new kind of party politics in America, one organized around presidential leadership.[83] Franklin Roosevelt under-stood this intuitively on several levels. His lesson in executive-centered party governance came first in the Wilson administration. Here, FDR was more of a student of Wilson than Theodore Roosevelt, who was more apt to contemplate the dissolution of party than personalize it. Indeed, there had been a longstanding progressive strain of executive-driven leadership dat-ing as far back as La Follette's governorship. La Follette's attempted party purge in Wisconsin exemplifies this feature of progressivism. Likewise, Hiram Johnson of California elected to lead the nascent Lincoln-Roosevelt League—an outright rebuke of the less progressive elements of his own Republican Party. The appeal of independent executive leadership at the turn of the century was frequently personified by governors who were above party—"transcendent" and fearless. By 1932, a new Roosevelt League was formed—this one in support of FDR's presidential bid. Progressives had not exactly gone away, and an executive, party-defying ethos was at the core of what spirit remained, as demonstrated in the League's backing of Roosevelt: "In his demand for social justice, his zeal to defend and conserve the people's natural resources and his intolerance of graft and corruption, Governor Roosevelt throughout his public career has been true to progres-sive principles. . . . Upon these issues the National Progressive League calls upon every independent voter to ignore party labels and join in support of

Governor Roosevelt's candidacy and the progressive principles for which he stands."[84]

The Hudson progressive tradition had long been characterized by such antiparty vigilance. Samuel Tilden's appeal was tied to the fact that he alone was powerful and independent enough to break party ties and put New York's legendary Boss Tweed in handcuffs. Roosevelt's father had been a Tilden man, and FDR's appeal as a national leader was built on the premise that he, too, was capable of standing up to the Tweed of his day, Mayor Jimmy Walker of New York. While a less than enthusiastic combatant in these matters than Tilden, in part out of recognition of how much he owed Tammany (Roosevelt's 1928 gubernatorial victory was by the thinnest of margins), Roosevelt nonetheless was quick to adopt the mantle of corruption fighter.[85] This was what Roosevelt told the throngs that met him in Chicago and Milwaukee in the fall of 1932. One *New York Times* story captured the essence of Roosevelt's rising stardom well: "Roosevelt Started Fighting Tammany," the headline read, reminding readers of FDR's independent beginning in politics.[86] While FDR's encounters with Tammany involved as many handshakes as they did fisticuffs over the years, Roosevelt remained committed to the view that the executive should lead the party; he simply had not had the power in New York to demonstrate the principle as forcefully as he would once president.

As Theodore Lowi noted, "Roosevelt had been a product of traditional Democratic party politics, was at home in such an environment, and was so lacking in hostility that he made his peace not only with the machines of New York but with those of other cities as well."[87] This is true enough, but Roosevelt also came to understand that merely playing the party game would not be sufficient for the ultimate power he sought. To accomplish national executive prestige, Roosevelt would have to become, at least in image, an executive in the progressive tradition. It is one of the reasons that Roosevelt perpetually invoked Cleveland, Tilden, and Wilson—not to mention "Uncle Teddy"—in his speeches. Not everyone bought the connection, including the former chairman of the Progressive National Committee in 1912: "[Roosevelt's] biography declaration that at Harvard he 'unequivocally stood for Bryan' and his *New York Times* interview, the year before Colonel [Theodore] Roosevelt made his second race for the Presidency, that 'I am a Democrat first, last and all the time' leaves a bad taste in the mouths of these people in the West before whom he is now posing in his attempt to show them he is strictly a non-partisan when it comes to appealing to them for their votes this year."[88]

Richard Hofstadter's accusation that FDR had no intention to end bossism or confront corrupt Democratic politicians is fair, but only to a point.[89] As far back as Tilden, protoprogressives worked to build up their own machines. This may have been done out of pragmatism but it was not done to the exclusion of reform efforts. Roosevelt's willingness to jettison Sheriff Farley or compel a resignation from Jimmy Walker was certainly not drawn from the desire for a "crusade," as Hofstadter rightly suggests. But they were tangible byproducts of personal interests conflating with a broader liberal agenda. Few were able to marry the personal and political as deftly as Roosevelt; for this he is no less "progressive." In a word, Roosevelt's chief concern was with "opposition." The politics of party machinations had to be matched by those of executive strength. It is thus not unfair to see the relationship between Roosevelt's party loyalty and "clubbiness" with his personal quest for power. Such a relationship may not speak to Roosevelt's courage as a non-partisan, but it certainly speaks to his wisdom. Again, Tilden's historic failure in 1876 may have earned him enduring admiration among Hudson progressives, but it certainly did not earn him national office. It is said that Tilden's loss inspired Woodrow Wilson. Roosevelt was more inspired by victories. As Thomas H. Greer pointed out, Roosevelt learned the hard way that opposition from within one's own party could be equally devastating to personal and progressive interests: "A decisive turning point was Roosevelt's experience in the New York Democratic primary of 1914. While serving as a Wilson appointee in Washington, he decided to test his vote appeal at home. He filed for U.S. senator against Tammany-backed James Gerard (Wilson's Ambassador to Germany). Roosevelt campaigned vigorously as the 'anti-Boss' candidate, but he was decisively beaten in the primary. Although stung by the setback, he learned his lesson well. He never again defied the Tammany organization in an election campaign."[90]

Over time, Roosevelt worked in New York to build the Democratic Party from the ground up, particularly upstate where it had done poorly historically. In the final analysis, Roosevelt not only elected not to bite the hand that fed him, but to, in essence, recreate the relationship between master and beast. As the last of the line of Hudson progressives, Roosevelt was adept enough to wait until he had accumulated enough personal power to strike out on a course not directed by his party. The forms (party-led executive action) had been surpassed by the facts, namely, power in the hands of plebiscitary leaders who understood the importance of administration, crisis leadership, and media command. Roosevelt's transformative party politics was a masterful stroke that continues to carry great implications for executive leadership today.

Conclusion

Franklin D. Roosevelt's first decisive moment as governor was an act of party defiance. In rejecting Belle Moskowitz and Robert Moses as potential appointments favored by Al Smith, Roosevelt carved for himself an independent path as governor. His last crucial act, leading an indictment against Mayor Jimmy Walker, was likewise one of defiance against Tammany Hall. Both moves showed FDR at his pragmatic and progressive best. In rejecting Moskowitz and Moses, he was making a point about power. Roosevelt made it clear that the Smith tenure had indeed come to a close. In confronting Walker, albeit late and with little relish, Roosevelt was claiming a leadership status somewhat distant from his party's most prominent figure and authority. Roosevelt's aspiration was for a new era of executive leadership, and he was willing to upend relations with Tammany Hall to attain it. Finally, Roosevelt laid out his most comprehensive prospectus on progressive values in the midst of the Depression. The Commonwealth Club Address, given in his last days as governor, was a treatise born of not only neoliberal imperatives but also Hudson progressive executive philosophy. The types of changes Roosevelt sought to usher in were not tied to some Wilson-like "spirit of the age." Roosevelt didn't think in those terms. He saw the change effected in society as the byproduct of powerful executive leadership. History was the product of the leader. Roosevelt's governorship was the last preparatory moment in this evolution, and once he had the power to declare the next epoch in America's relationship between its citizens and its government, he did so.

These bookends of the Roosevelt governorship held together other important foreshadowings of Roosevelt's executive politics. His efforts to win cheaper power rates for New Yorkers, his push to win ultimate executive authority for the state's governor over budgetary matters, and his exercise of authority in dismissing Sheriff Farley were all indicative of Roosevelt's governing philosophy. In this regard, FDR's injection of "separation of powers" discourse was as sincere as Chief Justice John Marshall's invocation of limited powers for the Court in *Marbury*. It is not coincidental that Marshall

has likewise been said to have lacked a deep penchant for founding principles or a comprehensive philosophy. Perhaps there is more in common between the Virginian federalist and the Hudson progressive than is ordinarily
thought. In a sense, Roosevelt understood executive power as a stabilizing
and countervailing power to too deeply entrenched business interests. Perhaps his patrician pedigree helped him understand better than most the ills
of oversized private interests, as Marshall's parochial background helped
him see the limits of interest rooted predominantly in the local. The crucial
difference between the two was that where Marshall lacked contemporane-
ous examples of judicial audacity, Roosevelt was predated by powerful executive iconoclasts. Roosevelt's prolific reshaping of American notions of
the presidency reflected the culmination of some fifty years of movement
toward executive supremacy in government. Roosevelt was but the last in a
line of governors who launched this trend, and the most significant figure to
emerge in the Empire State. Like those before him, FDR did so by eschewing
early nineteenth-century conceptions of executive propriety.

"People tell me that I hold to party ties less tenaciously than most of my
predecessors," Roosevelt told his audience at a Jackson Day Dinner in 1940.
"I admit the soft impeachment."[91] What Roosevelt did hold to was the acceptance of presidential leadership over his party. It was a hallmark of progressivism that he thought this the natural province of executives. And while
Roosevelt wasn't the first to contribute this vision to American executive
politics, he validated it like no other. Roosevelt transformed what Cleveland,
TR, and Wilson attempted, and he placed it in the realm of routine. As Roosevelt's efforts at reconstructing American conceptions of activist government
continue to be challenged by a host of conservative critics, it is worth remembering that no American president since—conservative or otherwise—has
called for the dismantling of the national executive along the lines reserved
for other liberal state edifices. Roosevelt made the New Deal executive, built
by Progressive Era leaders of tremendous political skill and imagination, a
permanent fixture of American politics.

When Ronald Reagan famously intoned "there you go again" in his 1980
debate with Jimmy Carter, few knew it as an old line of FDR's. Those who
draw comparisons between the two presidents frequently make note of Roosevelt's and Reagan's connections to both the New Deal and an early career in
media (Roosevelt was editor of the Harvard *Crimson*). Yet what is often overlooked in Reagan's seeming Rooseveltian style is his most substantive, enduring connection to FDR. The neofounder of American conservatism in

American politics was deeply liberal—indeed, more appropriately, *progressive*—in his understanding of executive power. And little could be more quixotically telling about Roosevelt's confirmation of the new American executive, initiated by a cadre of progressive executives. Government may have been the problem for conservatives in the last quarter of the twentieth century, but few defined the president's power as part of that problem. If anything, the president was beyond government—a unitary figure possessing popular authority and power with little specified limits. For this, Reagan, and all future presidents of whatever political stripe, must love Roosevelt. Such is the enduring, if not at times mystifying, contribution of progressive executive government—shaped most directly by the nation's governors—that culminated in the Albany-to-Washington narrative of Franklin Delano Roosevelt.

Chapter 5

"Undoing the Framers' Work": Executive Power and American Democracy

In the United States, magistrates are not elected by a
special group of citizens but by the majority of the
nation; they immediately represent the passions of the
crowd and depend entirely upon its wishes; as a result,
they inspire neither dislike nor fear: thus, I have pointed
out how little care has been taken to restrict their power
of action and how great a share of power has been left
to their discretion. This state of affairs has forged habits
which will survive it. The American magistrate would
retain his undefined power while ceasing to be
accountable and it is impossible to say where tyranny
would then end.
—Alexis de Tocqueville, *Democracy In America*, 1835[1]

Boundless intemperance in nature is a tyranny; it hath
been th'untimely emptying of the happy throne, and fall
of many kings.
—*Macbeth*[2]

Introduction

Fear of an unbound executive was at the heart of republican concerns at the
nation's founding. It was, as the biblical admonition suggests, the beginning

of all knowledge.[3] And yet that fear was overcome by progressives, as Alexis de Tocqueville—ever prescient—noted, by associating the national executive with the will of the people. In due time, the *demos* somehow became embodied in the president. To fear the national executive by this reasoning is to fear one's own self-interest. And who would willfully disarm one's own authority? Such was Tocqueville's analysis in an age with "no great parties"— one overshadowed by the reach of Andrew Jackson, whose presidency was the first to marry mass participation to primitive executive provocations.[4] And, like the great modern presidents who would emerge generations later, Jackson knew little of the legislative levers of democratic governance. An executive in war and in the blood-let Florida Territory, Jackson personified the ironic fusion of broad democratic populism and the exclusivity of executive power. And while Jackson's dominance did not suggest the immediate rise of a presidential republic, it did introduce "habits" that would be remembered long after the Age of Jackson had ended.

It is one of the subtle stories of American political development that governors were the first executives to draw broadly upon these habits. In doing so, executive-centered government emanated from below while carrying the banner of progressivism. The possibility of despotic governance envisioned and feared by many of the framers became all the more plausible in the Progressive Era's exchange of republican values for the effectiveness of personalist leadership. As Tocqueville suggested, the evolution of the presidency evidenced a troubling plebiscitary connection to the American people. Woodrow Wilson later embraced this new state of affairs when, in his essay on democracy, he attached normative value to the transition away from the founding. Whereas Tocqueville shuddered at the prospects of a radicalized popular executive, Wilson extolled its arrival, one that represented an "undoing of the framers' work."

Wilson's declaration was notable in that it came at least a decade, and, for some, a generation before the arrival of the modern presidency. For Wilson, Grover Cleveland's presidency and the combined efforts from state executives were sufficient evidence of a crossing into entirely new territory with respect to the Constitution's relevance in a new executive age.[5] The regime of governor-presidents that he was a part of, the Hayes-Cleveland-McKinley-Roosevelt-Wilson line, was revelatory of the increasing rejection of *ancien* political theories such as the separation of powers and legislative democracy. When this procession culminated in the presidency of Franklin D. Roosevelt, such power and authority had been conferred upon the nation's chief executive that all future presidents would be assumed to govern with an executive temperament. To follow Roosevelt would thus be to follow all of the combined facets of modern executive leadership—to, in short, embrace the executive-centered republic.

The two clusters of governor-presidencies in American history shed much light on American political development, but for different reasons. The first, begun by Rutherford B. Hayes and capped off by FDR, was driven by progressive policy approaches and modern executive interpretations of constitutional government. The second, initiated by President Jimmy Carter, was a reaction to the Watergate scandal and the imperial presidency. Ironically, this last regime of governor-presidents did very little to reject such imperial interpretations of the modern presidency as the "unitary executive" or the plebiscitary presidency. Tactics may have been called into question, but not the fundamental orientation of the executive-centered republic.[6] Notably, this present era has been much more about the marketing of presidential candidates as outsiders and oppositional leadership in Washington. The desire shared within this group to "change," "heal," or "cleanse" Washington reflects a domestic agenda rooted in economic or cultural disaffection of some kind.

Compared to the "kings of progressivism," as the historian Robert Wiebe described the governors of the Progressive Era, this cohort of governors has proven far less policy driven and equally less concerned with the philosophical role of the president's status in the nation's governance. That question seems to have been resolved long ago. While the Cold War helped weaken the governorship[7] as a pathway to the presidency for a time, it only inflated the position of the president as the force for national change (and, at times, recalcitrance) in both domestic and foreign affairs.[8] In the aftermath of Vietnam and in the lingering shadow of détente, American governors regained their status as junior executives with political abilities sufficient to mete out presidential leadership. The prominence of governors as presidential candidates would thus be reaffirmed in the Carter-Reagan-Clinton-Bush line.

The Lessons of the Progressive Prince

The modern presidency has been edified along four pillars of executive action, discussed throughout this book: party leadership, media command, legislative direction, and an executive-centered governing philosophy. These have been accompanied by the advance of administrative bureaucracy and government. Before these features became a hallmark of presidential leadership in the modern era, they were present in America's statehouses and executive mansions. The Progressive Era, however hard to delimit, was undoubtedly a political response to the growing influences of corporate power and social dislocation in the nation. American industrialization intensified the sense of detachment of private interests from the public good. Southern Pacific Railroad, the New York Custom House, and New York's Canal Ring emerged as some of the more profane examples of how the intermediary forces between public and private interests had become patently undemocratic or corrupt. The political party—itself an extraconstitutional invention—once looked to for protection was reduced in the popular imagination to nothing more than a vessel for the schemes of political bosses and machines. The legislatures of the states and Congress itself were increasingly seen as repositories of corruption and malfeasance.[9] As the public grew increasingly skeptical of republicanism's promise of genuine representation and fairness, social despair gave rise to attacks on both party and legislative democracy. Governors, newly empowered and given greater constitutional authority, were the initial recipients of popular power and responsibility. As Herbert Croly noted in *Progressive Democracy*, governors were fast becoming the conduits for addressing popular unrest's call for progressive policies.[10] These were executives openly challenging the ethos of the framers of the Constitution, and on occasion, claiming for themselves unexpressed powers in the name of protecting the interests of the people. American governors thus began a restorative work in executive public policy that would reshape crucial notions of what was possible for a national executive to achieve.

As governor of Ohio and later as president, Rutherford B. Hayes greatly expanded the discretionary power of the executive. His willingness to go over the heads of the state legislature and Congress by speaking directly to the people earned him the appellation "Rutherford the Rover." Having put down labor strikes as both governor and president, Hayes became associated with a brazen and relatively novel form of executive leadership. Others in the faint dawn of the modern presidency would go further. Grover Cleveland carried his executive-oriented paradigm from mayoralty to governorship to presidency, with little regard for intrusion into what was considered at the time to be the legislature's domain. Cleveland's obsession with the veto, his invocation of executive privilege, and his willingness to buck his political party made him a colossal figure of the age—beyond his well-publicized physical stature. Indeed, in New York, Cleveland's governorship, along with Samuel J. Tilden's, became the focal point of the state's growing narrative of executive leadership in the last quarter of the nineteenth century. Simply put, Cleveland was the Roosevelt of his era.

What made these early figures so striking was their propensity to eschew constitutional limits or, at a minimum, the popularly accepted notions of constitutional propriety. Governors such as Robert M. La Follette of Wisconsin and Hiram Johnson of California openly disregarded these strictures as folly. As the historian George Mowry noted, Johnson rejected "the whole system of checks and balances as a denial of popular government."[11] What mattered most in the early Progressive Era was movement toward the people, as Tocqueville had witnessed as early as the 1830s. By the turn of the century, the progressives had begun a movement to institutionalize such popular-executive proximity. The direct primary, the referendum, and the recall were all variously attempted and employed throughout the states in an effort to rein in the forces of political corruption and capitalist excess. The remedy was to unchain the executive and grant the silences of the Constitution to that individual—that "single man," as Woodrow Wilson had described Cleveland. The potential for executive domination was undervalued in the face of other more pressing threats.

Few progressives, if any, considered the implications of the demise of party as it unfolded. When Alabama's governor disparaged Wilson for standing as some errant "prophet" against the wisdom of Hamilton and Madison, Wilson only grew in the exchange. Wilson had allied himself to the will of the people; his legitimacy was therefore tied to his and other executives' ability to stand in for the public as the true representative of popular desire. Hence, Wilson and his cohort of executives indeed proved prophetic, and frequently messianic, in their constitutional views. Seeing themselves as embodying the will of the people, men like La Follette and Wilson struck a moral chord in the electorate and touched it frequently through their own rhetoric, as the plebiscitary presidency grew in its infancy. Theodore Roosevelt, for one, had grown so despondent over failed legislative leadership that he proposed biennial legislatures. Wilson belittled legislatures as parliamentary "talking shops" with little relevance to modern society, so in need of executive decisiveness.[12] Thus, deliberation, a fundamental precept of democracy, earned a disparaged place in the lexicon of the era. To speak was the prerogative of the executive. When undertaken by the legislature, it sounded as so many clanging cymbals. "Overlegislation" had become a form of overspeaking.[13]

Part of the challenge governors posed to traditional practices was in the realm of executive appointments. With increasing frequency, strong governors rejected party recommendations and bypassed legislative leadership in selecting individuals to public office they deemed accountable and graft-free. Ironically, such antiparty and antilegislative tendencies resulted in the building up of alternative local party structures and more personal political machines. From Samuel Tilden of New York in 1876 to Hiram Johnson of California in the 1900s, state executives sought to create new political forms devoted to their leadership over older institutions and party bosses. The Lincoln-Roosevelt league led by Johnson is just one such example. The beneficiaries of greater formal authority at the turn of the century, governors had become formidable in their own right as "bosses." Woodrow Wilson's nomination as president only served to cement the change from party patronage bossism to the president as ultimate party boss. Progressive Era politics did not end boss politics as much as it created a new "national Boss," as Wilson had been described by the legion of party officials who visited him in Sea Girt, New Jersey, upon his nomination.[14] The executive-party relationship had been inverted; Van Buren's conception of a closely guarded national executive died a progressive death.[15]

None, of course, theorized the "postconstitutional" presidency as carefully as Wilson. Deeply influenced by the governorship and presidencies of Theodore Roosevelt and Grover Cleveland, Wilson applied his sense of historical change to an era that was increasingly emblematic of politics as evolutionary. Hence arose Wilson's Darwinian rejection of constitutional formalism as outdated and outmoded. And with the examples of popular rhetoric and media attention cultivated by the likes of La Follette and TR, Wilson further institutionalized executive-press relations, creating a bridge between the executive and the people in a manner that large legislative bodies never could. He instituted daily press sessions as governor, following the twice-a-day model of TR, while becoming similarly disposed to using the "trial balloon" to test the feasibility of his ideas. In standing up to three party bosses in New Jersey, Wilson laid claim to broad constitutional powers in Trenton, arguing that to be his own man, the governor had to have powers and freedoms commensurate with the task. Wilson's invocations of extralegal parameters for the governor were greeted by wide popular support; they had, in fact, become a sign that someone was finally willing to do all that could be done in standing up to private interests and official corruption. He was, indeed, as the *New York Times* described him, a "Tilden, but a Tilden up to Date."[16]

But the cost of transacting for greater executive power necessarily led to withdrawals from other accounts. Once de rigeur, the separation of powers became quaint. The theory that the president is free to act unless expressly proscribed from doing so was embraced by the key executive figures during the Progressive Era. It was the atmosphere in which FDR received his political education. Among his mentors were of course "Uncle Teddy," but also Wilson, Cleveland, and La Follette. His predecessor in New York, Al Smith, provided the tangible assistance to executive authority's expansion in the Empire State, consolidating a host of agencies under the direction of the governor. The New York model proffered ever so lightly by Hamilton had grown into the preeminent executive seat in the nation, second only to the presidency itself. Importantly, progressive governors injected their broad renderings on executive powers into the presidency, grafting onto the national edifice practices and theories from their own tenures in Albany.

Franklin Roosevelt's limitations in New York were less constitutional than they were political. He was unable fully to distance himself from Tammany Hall despite early and late acts of defiance in his gubernatorial tenure. Nevertheless, FDR brokered tremendous authority to the state's governor, winning near complete authority over New York's massive budget, while addressing the State Assembly in person in an effort to lower the state's water power rates. His tenacity in making his own appointments and keeping power over his choices for removal were no small victories. New York had intermittently been in and out of the hands of bosses such as the Republican Roscoe Conkling or Democratic Tammany. Roosevelt rebuffed the party and its bosses delicately, understanding that the Hudson path to the presidency required the imprimatur of a genuinely antiestablishment candidate. Governors had been earning this distinction for some time; to continue the trend, Roosevelt would have to take the risk of opposing his own party and its leadership. This was the reason behind the unusual path TR took to the White House, as the party boss of his era pushed to get him on the 1900 ticket as McKinley's vice president. Whatever the reasons for their ascent, governors took their reform agendas and experiences with them to Washington, much to the delight of local antagonists. In Wilson's case, he had no sooner left New Jersey when his progressive reforms began to succumb to political expediency and backroom dealing.

Theoretical Implications of the Personal Presidency

The modern presidency did earn large and heretofore unforeseen concessions to the public welfare state. To a great extent, the outline of reforms such as the Square Deal and New Deal could be seen in Albany. Such reforms were not without costs. They came at the price of a heavy administrative burden[17] and a significant reduction in the meaningfulness of party. Amid the rise in presidential vetoes (launched disproportionately by governor-presidents), executive orders, and claims on prerogative power, greater distance was created between the president and the people. It is easy to forget just how far from inevitable or essential a dominant national executive was thought to be at the nation's founding. Ben Franklin had advocated for a twelve-member executive council in Pennsylvania, for example, while numerous states withheld from their governors the power of appointment.[18] The obvious association with monarchy gave credence to the dissipation of executive constitutional power. Yet, over the course of the nineteenth century, the consolidation of executive power began to be seen as natural and "organic." In a word, centralization was "progressive." This is not to suggest that the American Constitution rendered the chief executive mute; rather, the idea was that legislative dominance was such a clear given that the executive had to be fortified in the interest of balance. As Charles Thach noted, "What was feared was 'everything was being drawn into the legislative vortex,' and that the executive department would not be strong enough to fulfill its proper functions. The main thing with the majority was to strengthen the executive, whatever the argument."[19] As Publius assumed in *Federalist* 51, "in republican government, the legislative authority necessarily predominates." That famous line reads today as more anachronistic than prescient. Despite the failures and disappointments of recent presidents, with unfinished business, scandal, and even a gnawing sense of irrelevance late in their terms, presidential leadership and power remain the starting point for how the American political system unwinds or rewinds itself every fourth year.

The crucial variable used to justify the executive turn in American republicanism was, and remains, the need for "energetic" government necessitated by emergency. Dispatch and decisiveness are rationales for extending the prerogative of the president. Overly strong parliamentary systems or legislatures, it is argued, are for weak states or those that have suicide embedded in their compacts. As Harvey C. Mansfield suggests, "everyone agrees on the necessity of a strong executive."[20] Emergency power, the stuff of which the energetic strong executive is premised upon, has evolved conceptually from putting down riotous ruffians in early New York to the need to act in a perpetual state of emergency in the "War on Terror." A conflict such as the latter necessarily invokes a limitless struggle rooted in existential threat; in such a crisis, it is not that the president claims emergency powers, but that they are preexistent. They are in the ether of politics in a way that not Lincoln or FDR or any Cold War president might have strained to envision. Not only is emergency embedded with respect to foreign policy threats but it is limitless in its permeability; no single state threatens, and thus all threaten. What kind of executive power is ever sufficient to meet such a threat? While "energy in the executive" may be "a leading character in the definition of good government," as Alexander Hamilton suggested, it ought not to be seen as the equivalent of good government. Energy is morally neutral; what it is directed toward becomes a normative concern.

The progressive executives, the governors and governor-presidents who built the modern presidency, sought executive power as part of an internal struggle against political and private excesses. Clearly, progressive governors had neither the full range of tools nor political warrants associated with today's "unitary" executive. But what they did provide was a set of arguments about the centrality of executive power to American democracy, and the need for extra (or implied) constitutional authority. Today's efforts at furthering executive power are often culled from these arguments and are, in many respects, fortified by popular fears and low-level angst.[21] Thus, the modern presidency of today, some one hundred years after its inception, is sustained by a minimalist civic body. As the French political theorist Bertrand de Jouvenel remarked:

> Every authority is, by the law of its nature, essentially dualist. Being ambitious, each separate authority tends to grow; being egoistical, to consult only its immediate interest; being jealous, to pare down the role of other authorities. And this strife provides the state with its main chance. The growth of its authority strikes private individuals as being not so much a continual encroachment on their liberty as an

attempt to put down the various petty tyrannies to which they have been subjected. It looks as though the advance of the state is a means to the advance of the individual.

Such was the basis of Tocqueville's fears noted at the beginning of this chapter. This new "mild" form of despotism is best connected to broad civic indifference. It occupies the twilight between "dislike" and "fear." The incessant quality of emergency can only breed a numbed citizenry. The space between Codes Orange and Red, by way of example, proves too thin to elicit intelligible mortification. People go on with their lives, it is said.

Pointedly, Mansfield's treatise on modern executive power begins with a cryptic citation from *Macbeth*. "If it were done, when 'tis done, then 'twere well it were done quickly," is the haunting passage.[22] But one is left unsure as to whether Mansfield would have it read for its implicit warnings or on face value—a kind of shopworn advice in support of executive decisiveness. Of course, *Macbeth* is the story of a murder premised on ill-read tidings filtered through a reprobate mind. The lesson of *Macbeth* may well be that whatever is "best done quickly" should not be done at all. Dispatch has proven to be as effective a fig leaf for unbridled power as any. Emergency must therefore necessarily be defined as time-bound; to do otherwise is to blanket all political time as fearsome. As the political scientist Richard J. Ellis argues:

> In emergencies rapid action [is] necessary, but in the normal course of events speed would only empower the passions of the moment and lead to ill-considered plans. Haste was the enemy of rational dialogue and effective public policy [for the framers]. Enduring policies were to be forged through the long, laborious process of building consensus. Legislative inaction, from this perspective, is not necessarily a sign of failure. Instead, the legislature's reluctance or inability to act may be a wise and necessary response to the clash of profoundly different interests and values. The American political system is built upon a premise articulated by Cicero over two thousand years ago: "It is better that a good measure should fail than that a bad one should be allowed to pass."[23]

Civic acceptance of an imagined state of emergency in perpetuity is what fuels the power of executive leadership beyond practical restraint. Aristotle noted the tendency of democracies to devolve into such a compliant form of tyranny: "In democracies the most potent cause of revolution is the unprincipled character of popular leaders. Sometimes they bring malicious prosecutions against the owners of possessions one by one, and so cause them to join forces; for common fear makes the bitterest of foes cooperate. At other times they openly egg on the multitude against them."[24] Further detachment of the executive from constitutional accountability is fueled by the loss of party as an intermediary between the executive and the body politic. In this light, the Progressive Era brought three strands of antidemocratic material together: the deterioration of party, the rise of popular appeals, and an executive governing philosophy opposed to constitutional formalism. As Sidney M. Milkis has noted, "For Progressives, public opinion would reach fulfillment with the formation of an independent executive power, freed from provincial, special, and corrupt influence of political parties."[25] Moreover, with respect to the rise of the modern presidency in America, presidential background became disproportionately executive in nature. From Harry S. Truman to George W. Bush, presidents have been four times as likely as their counterparts from Washington to Lincoln to have spent part of their careers in public office as executives prior to the White House. The imbalance in executive, as opposed to legislative, experience, speaks to the modern presidency's relationship not only to state executive practices, but also to a core grounding in executive leadership. Part of the story of the modern presidency is the loss of the sense of constitutional balance between the legislative and executive branches, resulting in the institutional primacy of the presidency.

The earliest constitutional debates, such as those waged by Pacificus and Helvidius (Hamilton and Madison), hold a certain novelty when reconsidered today. Madison's willingness to reproach none less than President Washington for the possible usurpation of legislative authority reminds us of how far we have come in the presumption of broad presidential powers.[26] Such assumptions are difficult to square with classical democratic ideals, at best, or simple checks on personal ambition, at least. It is true that individual presidents tend to shrink in office over time; yet the presidency as an institution and its powers have not. Perhaps President Barack Obama has learned that the rhetorical strategy of staying "private," as suggested by the political scientist George C. Edwards III, leaves the president a better field to maneuver and win policy goals than does that of going public.[27] But this appears more of a swinging door than a firm commitment, to date, and it is quite hard to envision any president employing a hidden hand for very long. And while today's presidency owes much of its warrants to exercise outsized power to the president's role as commander in chief, the history of the Progressive Era offers a complementary, if not alternative, view. As Stephen Skowronek notes, "for most of American history, the cutting edge of the assault on the constitutional principle of checks and balances—and the most potent engine elevating the presidency in the American system—was not the exercise of war powers but political democratization."[28]

The Executive Turn Toward the Imperial Presidency

We are now over thirty-five years removed from the publication of Arthur M. Schlesinger, Jr.'s *The Imperial Presidency*. Schlesinger's work focused on the growth of presidential power primarily as a byproduct of greater authority in foreign affairs and war. Schlesinger thought the Second World War particularly instrumental in bolstering presidential prerogative. Interestingly, Schlesinger did not directly address the Progressive Era's influence on the dissolution of the power of parties in America, nor the rise of mass media during the period. On the contrary, Schlesinger took these two phenomena and placed them in the context of the 1960s and 1970s in explaining the impetus for the modern presidency's outsized quality:

> As the parties wasted away, the Presidency stood out in solitary majesty as the central focus of political emotion, the ever more potent symbol of the national community. When parties were strong and media weak, Presidents were objects of respect but not veneration. There were no great personality cults of Rutherford B. Hayes and Benjamin Harrison. . . . For their part historians and political scientists discovered in the image of the two Roosevelts and Wilson strong presidents using power for enlightened ends, the model of the Presidency to teach their students and hold up before the aspiring politicians.[29]

While Schlesinger saw the imperial presidency truly born in the 1940s and 1950s, he paid only passing attention to the Progressive Era as a force for unleashing the plebiscitary presidency that would later emerge. While Hayes was no great charismatic figure, he did represent a bolder move toward the restoration of presidential power. The executive careers of TR and later Wilson did in fact set the stage for the more transparent and unapologetic executive excesses generations later. It is not happanstance that four of the five figures referenced by Schlesinger were once governors, Harrison having lost an unsuccessful bid at the office. Numerous governor-presidents were responsible for injecting imperial tendencies into the presidency; later, overwhelming factors provided oxygen to the conflagration of little-restrained executive power. As Andrew Rudalevige wisely instructs, "there is no 'imperial presidency' in the structure of American government. Any such creature is conditional, fragile, and revocable. The presidency, in other words, is contingently imperial."[30]

This is perhaps why the more critical element in Schlesinger's narrative is the role he assigns the body politic as civic enablers of presidential prerogative and extraconstitutional action. Here, Schlesinger captures the challenge of granting so much in the way of emergency power to the president, under the faulty notion that citizens can somehow remain unaffected and yet disconnected from the vagaries of personalist leadership. "What kept a strong President constitutional, in addition to checks and balances incorporated in his own breast," instructed Schlesinger, "was the vigilance of the nation." "Neither impeachment nor repentance would make much difference if the people themselves had come to the unconscious acceptance of the imperial Presidency."[31]

The relationship between representative democracy and executive power is at the heart of classical discourse on politics. It reflects one of democratic inquiry's great and persistent challenges. As Sheldon Wolin expressed it, "Locke's famous proviso that authority can be 'taken back' if the governors violate the terms of the contract suggests mistrust, suspicion that political power will evade direct control. With the introduction of administration and the centralization of power, it will be virtually impossible for the citizen to recognize these powers as his own. He has resigned them and become resigned to their loss."[32] For Wolin and other democratic theorists, this is the great challenge of democratic society today. And yet, as suggestive of recent presidential history as such analysis may be, the age of administration and centralization was primarily an endeavor launched during the Progressive Era. At the state level, governors witnessed the growth of the administrative state before it took hold on the national level.[33] And it was governors in their own right, or later as presidents, who made the distant administrative state and plebiscitary presidency all the more plausible. This was part of the exchange for progressive public policies and security against the excesses of corporate capitalism and municipal corruption.

While the postwar presidency furnished presidents with the broadest possible range of executive authority and extraconstitutional mandates, the Progressive Era opened the doorway. Thus, one of the abiding ironies of American democracy was reinforced: democratic ideals were juxtaposed with the realities of contingent democratic processes and politics. In his concluding discussion in *Democracy in America*, Alexis de Tocqueville ventured an opinion on what he saw as a looming administrative despotism: "At the present time, many people very easily fall in with this type of compromise between a despotic administration and the sovereignty of the people and they think they have sufficiently safeguarded individual freedom when they surrendered it to a national authority. That is not good enough for me. The character of the master is much less important to me than the fact of obedience."[34] As with much of what was to transpire in the latter part of the nineteenth and early twentieth centuries, Alexis de Tocqueville saw the shape of things to come.

Conclusion: "Our American Governors"

Patrick Henry was chief among the skeptics of America's constitutional president. The pledges of modest executive rule and checks and balances left him deeply dissatisfied. "Where are your checks in this Government?" he lamented. "It is on a supposition that our American Governors shall be honest, that all the good qualities of this Government are founded: But its defective, and imperfect construction, puts it in their power to perpetrate the worst of mischiefs, should they be bad men."[35] In the end, Henry and the antifederalists would lose this argument, among other significant battles over both the content and meaning of the Constitution. But this early struggle over the nature of American executive power—the terms "governor" and "president" were interchangeable in early American usage—was far from the last. Henry had himself been a colonial governor, one inclined to show deference to the Virginia legislature.[36] A century later, similar lines of argument would fall into disfavor. It was at "The House of Governors," one of the earliest meetings of the nation's governors, that Woodrow Wilson argued down one of his colleagues about the extension of the governor's executive power. "There is nothing inconsistent between the strengthening of the powers of the Executive and the direct power of the people," Wilson implored. Some present were unimpressed. "I would rather stand with Madison and Hamilton, than to stand with some modern prophets," Alabama's governor retorted.[37] By the early 1900s, Hamilton and Madison would be seen as moderates on the executive question, a fact Henry would no doubt have found curious.

The ties between the people and the executive had been so strongly forged as inseparable by progressives that foundational principles such as separation of powers had to be reconsidered, if not jettisoned altogether. Herbert Croly, for one, sought examples of executive power in the nation's governors, and in praising Oregon's efforts to embolden the power of its governor, launched a line of argument at odds with founding notions of representative government, declaring legislative representation "minor."[38] James P. Young expressed the exchange of progressivism's public policies for the somewhat lessened quality of democratic life in America well. "We are all probably better off in the regulated world the Progressives created than in what went before," he noted. "Yet it cannot be claimed that democracy is more secure than it was seventy years ago. By many standards it is weaker."[39]

For all of the presidency's limitations, we are all too often reminded of just how consequential the president's power is—more for ill than for good with respect to the preservation of democratic values. Woodrow Wilson's and Herbert Croly's quite tortured views of the public suggest an executive power built upon the most creative imagining of majorities, composed of the frailest minorities of those who participate in presidential elections. When 60 percent of the eligible voting population turns out in presidential elections and is hailed as a restoration of participant democracy, serious questions are begged regarding the nature of present-day republicanism. A theoretical "public" of one is plausible if the term is stretched to ultimate plasticity, but this hardly constitutes democratic government. This is why the parallel phenomena of the ascendancy of executive power and the decline of party power and civic participation hold such foreboding prospects for American democracy. "The weakening of the two-party system as a check on power," reminds Wolin, "was one manifestation of a general weakening of institutions intended to limit or balance power."[40]

In an August 1932 memo, Adolf Berle wrote to convince FDR that his campaign for president needed an anchoring intellectual address. What became known as the Commonwealth Club Address stands as the most coherent theoretical text outlining Roosevelt's perspective on the New Deal's public mission. It is therefore interesting to note the executive template suggested by Berle. "In a word," he wrote, "it is necessary to do for this system what Bismarck did for the German system in 1880, as result of conditions not unlike these."[41] The richness found by way of analogy is evident in analyses of what Bismarck's policies suggested for democratic values in Germany. As James T. Kloppenberg noted:

> The centralization of power in Germany under Bismarck's strategy of *Sammlungspolitik* (coalition politics) was thus accompanied by the simultaneous and fateful corruption of the democratic process and the polarization of the voting public. Ironically, German liberals were initially attracted to Bismarck because he seemed to offer an effective barrier against the perceived threat to *Bildung*—the ideal of cultivation cherished by the German middle class. . . . [D]espite its ostensibly democratic institutions, government in imperial Germany became a tool of elite domination.[42]

Personalist power's growth enabled progressive change, but it also enfeebled participatory democracy and political parties in the process. Finding a way back seems hardly tenable in a climate devoid of popular institutional vigor. As Schlesinger reflected, "As the parties wasted away, the Presidency stood out in solitary majesty as the central focus of political emotion, the ever more potent symbol of national community."[43]

The modern presidency emerged over considerable time and took shape in ways that are less obvious than its effects on the nature of political power in America's presidential republic. As executive power's demands grew in the latter part of the nineteenth century, state executives were most often the earliest claimants. Governors launched bold experiments in the expansion of executive authority, and, during the high tide of progressivism, they were the chief institutional representatives of practices ever removed from the nation's earliest notions of executive propriety. When some became presidents in their own right, as did the crucial figures of the period, including Cleveland, TR, Wilson, and FDR, they brought with them the executive habits and predilections learned while state executives. They injected into the presidency an easy acceptance of executive-centered governance and prerogative power. In large part, the imbalance in prepresidential background reflected in the disproportionate time spent in executive administration suggests that the modern presidency is best understood when tied to the entirety of executive behavior in a federal republic such as ours. In looking at the presidency in this light, we can see not only the character of modern presidential power at its dawn, but also possible approaches toward its restraint. The modern presidency was largely the creation of popular support for executive action in the face of powerful and antidemocratic market and political forces. It could not have blossomed fully, however, without the concomitant decline, if not decimation, of parties as an intermediary force in American politics.

It is therefore difficult, if not impossible, to envision the reining in of the imperial presidency absent a substantive elevation in the participatory character of American life and the further revitalization of political parties. The American citizen's relationship to executive power must be reconsidered. In so doing, we must first apprehend the circumstances of its deterioration. Perhaps, even as Americans remain in what might still be just the first act of a new presidency, marked by the exclusively legislative character of its chief executive, there may yet be hope for a different paradigm of leadership, one that could suggest the birth of a postmodern presidency. The question of whether or not popularly based support for a powerful president in times of great crises can be met by presidential restraint may only be answered years from now—and with a strong historic appreciation of its challenges and imposing record of failure.

Notes

Introduction

1. Alexander Hamilton, James Madison, and John Jay, *The Federalist Papers* (commentary by Garry Wills) (New York: Bantam Dell, 1982), 425.

2. Remarks by Ambassador James Bryce of England, *Proceedings of the Second Meeting of the Governors of the States of the Union* (Lakewood, N.J.: Lakewood Press, 1910), 87.

3. The first conference was held to address the specifics of TR's conservation plan. See Edmund Morris, *Theodore Rex* (New York: Random House, 2001), 514–18.

4. "Governors Clash on the Referendum," *New York Times*, September 13, 1911.

5. Perhaps no work offers a more damaging refutation to this notion than Richard J. Ellis, *Democratic Delusions: The Initiative Process in America* (Lawrence: University of Kansas, 2002).

6. See John Gerring, *Party Ideologies in America, 1828–1996* (Cambridge: Cambridge University Press, 1998), for a summary of the Progressive Era's assault on parties and the rise of presidential campaigning.

7. "Governors Clash on Referendum," *New York Times*, September 13, 1911.

8. Ibid.

9. Ibid.

10. John J. Dinan, *The American State Constitutional Tradition* (Lawrence: University of Kansas Press, 2006), 98.

11. See Bryce, *The American Commonwealth* (New York: Macmillan Company, 1904).

12. *Proceedings of the Second Meeting of the Governors*, 88.

13. "Dr. Wilson Speaks to Many Governors," *New York Times*, November 30, 1910.

14. John F. Reynolds, *The Demise of the American Convention System, 1880–1911* (New York: Cambridge University Press, 2006), 229.

15. Scott C. James is right to caution against exaggerating the reach of the "president-centered polity." Its reality is not without its own attendant limitations and counterweights. See James, *Presidents, Parties, and the State: A Party System Perspective on Democratic Regulatory Change, 1884–1936* (New York: Cambridge University Press, 2000), 270–71.

16. On presidential leadership in legislative matters, see, for example, Andrew Rudalevige's *Managing the President's Program: Presidential Leadership and Legislative Policy Formulation* (Princeton: Princeton University Press), 2002. For an account of the lessening of the role of the two-party system and the related rise of executive leadership, see Sidney M. Milkis, *The President and the Parties: The Transformation of the American Party System Since the New Deal* (New York: Oxford University Press, 1993).

17. See Richard E. Neustadt's discussion of presidential reputation and the press. Richard E. Neustadt, *Presidential Power and the Modern Presidents: The Politics of Leadership from Roosevelt to Reagan* (New York: Free Press, 1990), 53.

18. For such a comprehensive list of modern presidential characteristics, see Clinton Rossiter, *The American Presidency* (Baltimore: Johns Hopkins University Press, 1987), 95–127.

19. The arbor-filled analogy was provided by Virginia's Edmund Randolph. James Madison, *Notes of Debates in the Federal Convention of 1787 Reported by James Madison* (Athens: Ohio University Press, 1966), 93–94.

20. Hamilton, 424–25.

21. Charles Thach noted that New York was the one exception to the revolutionary trend in state constitutions towards the subordination of executive power. See Charles C. Thach, Jr., *The Creation of the Presidency, 1775–1789: A Study in Constitutional History* (New York: Da Capo Press, 1969), 27–28.

22. Hamilton had practical reasons for referencing New York's governor, to be sure; he was also hoping to convince his reluctant fellow New Yorkers to ratify the new Constitution.

23. One of David Mayhew's more intriguing conclusions in his classic work on Congress is that the American reform tradition (and progressivism in particular) has eroded the relative authority of legislatures while bolstering executive power. See *Congress: The Electoral Connection* (New Haven: Yale University Press, 1974), 165–72.

24. Joseph E. Kallenbach, *The American Chief Executive: The Presidency and the Governorship* (New York: Harper and Row Publishers, 1966), 174.

25. See, for example, Sidney Milkis (with Marc Landy), *Presidential Greatness* (Lawrence: University of Kansas Press, 2000) and Stephen Skowronek, *Presidential Leadership in Political Time: Reprise and Reappraisal* (Lawrence: University of Kansas Press, 2008).

26. Mayer's recent work, for example, focuses on executive orders. See Kenneth R. Mayer, *With the Stroke of a Pen: Executive Orders and Presidential Power* (Princeton: Princeton University Press, 2002).

27. See Tables 1 and 2.

28. This cohort spent 171 years in prior public office, but actually one year more than the Washington to Grant cohort, with respect to prior elective executive office.

29. Ware argues that the Democratic Party was best positioned to take advantage of these changes. See Alan Ware, *The Democratic Party Heads North, 1877–1962* (New York: Cambridge University Press, 2006), 109–11.

30. Durkheim's *The Division of Labor in Society* offers but one example of how modern social discontent has been closely tied to new forms of political authority.

31. The period in question (1876–1932) was characterized by a cluster of governors elected to the White House and the marked rise in constitutional authority at the state level to governors, and the concomitant rise in presidential leadership at the national level.

32. Hayes was instrumental, for example, in mentoring William McKinley. His early progressivism was part of McKinley's formative executive education. See Kevin Phillips, *William McKinley* (New York: Times Books, 2003), 39–42.

33. Where Alan Ware argues for an emergent and different twentieth-century "separation of national from state-level politics," I make the case that this is not quite so with regard to the executive-centered policy orientation of state and national governments in the later stages of the Gilded Age. See Ware, 178.

34. Cited in Dinan, from the *Proceedings and Debates of the Constitutional Convention of the State of Ohio [1912]*, 117.

35. A more formal discussion of the use of the veto by governor-presidents will be taken up in Chapter 2.

36. Scott C. James's insight about presidents "going public" was part of an evolving trend initiated by state executives. See James, 236–37.

37. Neustadt, 6.

38. Jeffrey Tulis, *The Rhetorical Presidency* (Princeton: Princeton University Press, 1987), 14.

39. Mel Laracey, for example, argues that those who side with the "rhetorical presidency" hypothesis do not consider "how presidents might have sought to appeal to the people through the newspapers of the times or other means." See Laracey, *Presidents and the People: The Partisan Story of Going Public* (College Station: Texas A & M University Press, 2002), 8.

40. Ibid., 87.

41. Governor-presidents average 18 speeches per year, while presidents lacking gubernatorial experience average 10. If the statistical anomalies of Benjamin Harrison and Grover Cleveland are removed, the averages still favor governor-presidents, 8.5 to 5.5 speeches per year.

42. Reynolds, 231.

Chapter 1

1. Lou Cannon, *Governor Reagan: His Rise to Power* (New York: Public Affairs, 2003), 158.

2. Arthur M. Schlesinger, Jr., *The Crisis of the Old Order, 1919–1933* (Boston: Houghton Mifflin Company, 1957), 45.

3. Richard L. McCormick, *From Realignment to Reform: Political Change in New York State, 1893–1910* (Ithaca: Cornell University Press, 1981), 83.

4. See "Statement to the Attorney-General in the Matter of the Charges Against James J. Walker, Mayor of the City of New York," signed by Governor Roosevelt, December 29, 1932, Vertical File: Walker, James J. (1881–1946), Franklin D. Roosevelt Library, Hyde Park, N.Y.

5. Ibid.

6. "Wilson—A Tilden, But a Tilden Up to Date," *New York Times*, September 25, 1910.

7. Arthur Link argues that Wilson derived his American political philosophy from Tilden and Grover Cleveland. See Arthur S. Link, "Woodrow Wilson: The American as Southerner," *Journal of Southern History* 36, no. 1 (February 1970): 11.

8. See Jon C. Teaford, *The Rise of the States: Evolution of American State Government* (Baltimore: Johns Hopkins University Press, 2002), 16–20.

9. My use of "Republic" is intended to connote a more general governing philosophy, marked in the "Second" by the rise of strong executives, national power, and political centralization. The term probably owes its most recent persuasive influence to Theodore Lowi and his *The End of Liberalism: The Second Republic of the United States* (New York: W. W. Norton and Company, 1979). Lowi viewed the New Deal as the beginning of a Second Republic, but for different reasons. Others, such as Wilson Carey McWilliams, took the view of the New Deal as a *Third* Republic, following those launched by the Constitutional Convention and the Civil War.

10. The approach was reinforced by nominations. Richard M. Pious notes, "from 1800 to 1820 all the [presidential] nominees of the congressional caucus were Virginians." The legacy would extend beyond birthplace, coming to represent a more conservative understanding of presidential authority. See Richard M. Pious, "The Presidency and the Nominating Process: Politics and Power," in Michael Nelson, ed., *The Presidency and the Political System* (Washington, D.C.: CQ Press, 2006), 197.

11. Larry Sabato, *Goodbye to Goodtime Charlie: The American Governorship Transformed* (Washington, D.C.: CQ Press, 1983), 4.

12. Teaford, 19.

13. James Madison, *Notes of Debates in the Federal Convention of 1787 Reported by James Madison* (Athens: Ohio University Press, 1985), 291.

14. Jack Rakove, *Original Meanings: Politics and Ideas in the Making of the Constitution* (New York: Vintage Books, 1996), 287.

15. Peri Arnold's history of the presidencies of Roosevelt, Taft, and Wilson captures this altered terrain quite well, along with the relationship between presidential practice and executive background. See his *Remaking the Presidency: Roosevelt, Taft, and Wilson, 1901–1916* (Lawrence: University Press of Kansas, 2009).

16. Robert H. Wiebe, *The Search for Order: 1877–1920* (New York: Hill and Wang, 1967), 179–80.

17. Richard Hofstadter, *The Age of Reform: From Bryan to FDR* (New York: Vintage Books, 1955), 266.

18. Ibid., 265.

19. Cannon, 158.

20. Woodrow Wilson, *Congressional Government* (Houghton, Mifflin, and Company, 1901), 253.

21. See W. Barksdale Maynard's account of this affair in his *Woodrow Wilson: Princeton to the Presidency* (New Haven: Yale University Press, 2008), 265–66.

22. Woodrow Wilson, letter to Mary Allen Hubert Peck, January 7, 1912, *The Papers of Woodrow Wilson*, vol. 24, ed. Arthur S. Link (Princeton: Princeton University Press, 1977), 5–6.

23. See Horace Samuel Merrill, *Bourbon Leader: Grover Cleveland and the Democratic Party* (Boston: Little, Brown, and Company, 1957), 130–33.

24. Mario R. DiNunzio, ed., cited in Wilson, "The Making of the Nation," originally in *Atlantic Monthly*, July 1897. *Woodrow Wilson: Essential Writings and Speeches of the Scholar-President* (New York: New York University Press, 2006), 180.

25. Herbert F. Margulies, *The Decline of the Progressive Movement in Wisconsin, 1890–1920* (Madison: State Historical Society of Wisconsin, 1969), v.

26. Address before the Commercial Club of Portland, Oregon, May 18, 1911, cited in Sabato, 6, 11.

27. William Jennings Bryan attended as a 16-year-old. Morris, 108.

28. Alexander Clarence Flick, *Samuel Jones Tilden: A Study in Political Sagacity* (Westport: Greenwood Press, 1973), 293.

29. Morris, 179.

30. Hans L. Trefousse, *Rutherford B. Hayes* (New York: Times Books), 99, 122.

31. Morris, 146. The emphasis is mine.

32. Ibid., 122.

33. Flick, 281–82.

34. William C. Hudson, *Random Reflections of an Old Political Reporter* (New York: Cupples and Leon Company, 1911), 46.

35. Morris, 105.

36. Henry Adams, *Democracy* (New York: Feather Trail Press, 2009), 9.

37. Joseph E. Kallenbach, *The American Chief Executive: The Presidency and the Governorship* (New York: Harper and Row, 1966), 174. The geography was so deterministic that Richard M. Pious described it as the Republicans' "old New York/Ohio combination." See Nelson, 206.

38. Flick, 307.

39. Ibid., 317.

40. Trefousse, 73.

41. Edwin G. Burrows and Mike Wallace, *Gotham: A History of New York City to 1898* (New York: Oxford University Press, 1999), 572.

42. Ari Hoogenboom, *Rutherford B. Hayes: Warrior and President* (Lawrence: University of Kansas Press, 1995), 324.

43. Edmund Morris, *The Rise of Theodore Roosevelt* (New York: Modern Library, 1979), 68–69, 124–25.

44. H. J. Eckenrode, *Rutherford B. Hayes: Statesman of Reunion* (Port Washington: Kennikat Press, 1963), 269.

45. H. Wayne Morgan, *From Hayes to McKinley: National Party Politics, 1877–1896* (Syracuse: Syracuse University Press, 1969), 55–56.

46. Morris, Roy, 91.

47. David McCullough, *The Great Bridge: The Epic Story of the Building of the Brooklyn Bridge* (New York: Simon and Schuster, 1972), 257.

48. Flick, 258.

49. Edmund Morris, 772.

50. Roy Morris, Jr., 104. See "Centennial Sam," chapter 3, for coverage of Tilden's emergence as a preeminent reformer.

51. The immensely wealthy Tilden purchased the governor's mansion for the state of New York (Flick, 254); meanwhile, Hayes moved into Columbus Judge Noah H. Swayne's house (Trefousse, 51).

52. Kallenbach, 18–19.

53. Joel Tyler Headley, *The Great Riots of New York, 1712–1873* (New York: Cosimo Classics, 2009), 33.

54. Ibid., 35.

55. Charles C. Thach, *The Creation of the Presidency, 1775–1789* (New York: Da Capo Press, 1922), 41.

56. "There is a close analogy between him [the President] and a Governor of New York," wrote Alexander Hamilton in making the case for a single strong executive, in *Federalist* 69. If New Yorkers, to whom *The Federalist* was directed, could stomach their own governor, they presumably ought to have been able to accept Hamilton's executive.

57. Harry Barnard, *Rutherford B. Hayes and His America* (Newtown, Conn.: American Political Biography Press, 1994), 244–45.

58. Ibid., 310.

59. Roy Morris, Jr., 145.

60. Flick, 263.

61. Hoogenboom, 327.

62. Barnard, 445–46.

63. Trefousse, 95.

64. Hoogenboom, 318.

65. Ibid., 346.

66. Jeffrey K. Tulis, *The Rhetorical Presidency* (Princeton: Princeton University Press, 1987), 64. This takes into account the unprecedented administration of Andrew Johnson and his 60 speeches, the grossest "violation" of the tacit premodern prohibition against the president's direct appeals to the people. Hayes's speeches more than double Johnson's, 126 to 60.

67. Hoogenboom, 303.

68. Barnard, 246.

69. Trefousse, 141.

70. Merrill, 44.

71. Henry Graff, *Grover Cleveland* (New York: Henry Holt, 2002), 55.

72. Merrill, 29.

73. For a full discussion of Clinton and Cleveland compared and the politics of preemption, see Stephen Skowronek, *The Politics Presidents Make: Leadership from John Adams to Bill Clinton* (Cambridge: Belknap Press, 1997), 447–64.

74. See, for example, Attorney General Homer Cummings's letter to FDR on Cleveland's use of the pardon, December 19, 1936, which had been requested by Roosevelt "sometime ago." President's Personal File, 1346, Cleveland, Grover, FDR Presidential Library, Hyde Park.

75. Alyn Brodsky, *Grover Cleveland: A Study in Character* (New York: St. Martin's Press, 2000), 135.

76. David A. Crockett, *The Opposition Presidency: Leadership and the Constraints of History* (College Station: Texas A&M University Press, 2002), 99–100.

77. Brodsky, 137.

78. Crockett, 100.

79. H. Paul. Jeffers, *An Honest President: The Life and Presidencies of Grover Cleveland* (New York: William Morrow, 2000), 146. The emphasis is mine.

80. Richard E. Welch, Jr., *The Presidencies of Grover Cleveland* (Lawrence: University Press of Kansas, 1988), 57.

81. Crockett, 98.

82. Welch, 9–10.

83. Brodsky, 58.

84. Edmund Morris, 176–77.

85. Jeffers, 6.

86. See *The American Presidency Project* (http://www.presidency.ucsb.edu/index .php), Gerhard Peters and John Woolley, 1999–2005, University of California, Santa Barbara. The Office of the Clerk of the U.S. House of Representatives likewise keeps an updated count of presidential vetoes (http://clerk.house.gov/art_history/house_history /vetoes.html).

87. Letter to Mrs. Thomas J. Preston, April 4, 1941, President's Personal File, 1346: Cleveland, Grover, FDR Presidential Library, Hyde Park, N.Y.

88. Crockett, 215. Crockett is interested in "oppositional presidents," a term loosely inspired by Robert Dahl's and Stephen Skowronek's "preemptive" presidents. Here, I argue for prepresidential background as an equally useful explanatory variable for assessing, in part, the underlying disposition toward employing the veto, above and beyond political context or "time."

89. Jeffers, 48.

90. Theda Skocpol, *Protecting Soldiers and Mothers: The Political Origins of Social Policy in the United States* (Cambridge: Harvard University Press, 1992), 124–27.

91. See John J. Dinan on the executive veto in the states. *The American State Constitutional Tradition* (Lawrence: University of Kansas Press, 2006), 99–113.

92. Morgan, 196.

93. Graff, 33–34.

94. Stephen Skowronek, *Building a New American State: The Expansion of National Administrative Capacities, 1877–1920* (Cambridge: Cambridge University Press, 1990), 66.

95. Wiebe, viii.

96. Ibid., 93.

97. Clinton Rossiter, *The American Presidency* (Baltimore: Johns Hopkins University Press, 1987), 105.

98. Ibid., 94.

99. Merrill, 195.

100. This is Lewis L. Gould's aversion to ranking Cleveland among the "moderns." See *The Modern American Presidency* (Lawrence: University of Kansas Press, 2003), 1.

101. See Mark Wahlgren Summers, *Rum, Romanism, and Rebellion: The Making of the President, 1884* (Chapel Hill: University of North Carolina Press, 2000).

102. See, for example, Steve Benen, "High Infidelity: What If Three Adulterers Run for Public Office and No One Cares?" *Washington Monthly*, July/August 2006.

103. "History insured that the linkage between Cleveland and FDR would be defined to Cleveland's disadvantage," wrote Cleveland biographer Geoffrey Blodgett, cited in William E. Leuchtenburg, *In the Shadow of FDR: From Harry Truman to Ronald Reagan* (Ithaca: Cornell University Press, 1983), 240, 346.

104. Brandeis was particularly enamored with New York's and Wisconsin's progressive ideas, which found their way readily into New Deal policies. It is difficult to imagine the legislative success emanating from these and other progressive states without executive leadership from those progressive governors who dotted the landscape in the years leading up to the New Deal. David Osborne first reprised this premise during the heart of the second wave of governor-presidents in 1988. See David Osborne, *Laboratories of Democracy* (Boston: Harvard Business School, 1990).

105. Tulis, 55–59.

106. Kallenbach, 335–36.

107. Ibid., 336.

108. Nancy C. Unger, *Fighting Bob La Follette: The Righteous Reformer* (Chapel Hill: University of North Carolina Press, 2000), 122.

109. David P. Thelen, *Robert M. La Follette and the Insurgent Spirit* (Boston: Little Brown, and Company, 1976), 50.

110. Ibid., 51.

111. Allen Fraser Lovejoy, *La Follette and the Establishment of the Direct Primary in Wisconsin, 1890–1904* (New Haven: Yale University Press, 1941), 66–67.

112. Ibid., 67.

113. Ibid., 66.

114. Unger, 123.

115. Robert S. Maxwell, *La Follette and the Rise of the Progressives in Wisconsin* (Madison: State Historical Society of Wisconsin, 1956), 12.

116. Unger, 33.

117. See Alfred D. Chandler, Jr., *The Visible Hand: The Managerial Revolution in American Business* (Cambridge: Harvard University Press, 1977), on railroad cooperation and competition, 122–44.

118. Skowronek, 258.

119. Unger, 143.

120. Edmund Morris, *Theodore Rex* (New York: Random House, 2001), 434.

121. Skowronek, 125.

122. Maxwell, 7–8.

123. Carl R. Burgchardt, *Robert La Follette, Sr.: The Voice of Conscience* (New York: Greenwood Press, 1992), 64.

124. Maxwell, 6.

125. La Follette did employ other means, including the distortion of political events. See Herbert F. Margulies's account of La Follette's (false) accusation of bribery against the Wisconsin legislature. Margulies, 53–54.

126. Fred Greenbaum, *Robert Marion La Follette* (Boston: Twayne Publishers, 1975), 42–43.

127. Maxwell, 29.

128. Unger, 109.

129. Lovejoy, 72.

130. Forrest McDonald, *The American Presidency: An Intellectual History* (Lawrence: University of Kansas Press, 1994), 359–60. Emphasis original.

131. Thelen, 35.

132. John F. Reynolds, *The Demise of the American Convention System, 1880–1911* (New York: Cambridge University Press, 2006), 180–90.

133. Greenbaum, 53.

134. Unger, 123.

135. Burgchardt, 62.

136. Unger, 121–22.

137. Ibid., 307.

138. Louis Hartz, *The Liberal Tradition in America: An Interpretation of American Political Thought Since the Revolution* (San Diego: Harcourt Brace and Company, 1991), 209.

139. Maxwell, 5.

140. Geoffrey Blodgett, *The Gentle Reformers: Massachusetts Democrats in the Cleveland Era* (Cambridge: Harvard University Press, 1966), xii.

141. Herbert Margulies rightly cautions against turning Wisconsin into too much of a catalyst for later national progressive change. But he also critically notes, "no adequate picture of the national progressive movement can be drawn without reference to Wisconsin." And while no straight path from progressivism to the New Deal can be

drawn to satisfy all, the emergence of New Deal politics must be discerned, at least in part, by the enormous influence of La Follette on not only his own era but the one to come. See Margulies, 288–89.

142. Carey McWilliams, *California: The Great Exception* (Berkeley: University of California Press, 1999).

143. Spencer C. Olin, *California's Prodigal Sons: Hiram* Johnson and the Progressives, 1911–1917 (Berkeley: University of California Press, 1968), 27.

144. Ibid., 27–28.

145. George E. Mowry, *The California Progressives* (Berkeley: University of California Press, 1951), 9.

146. Alan Trachtenberg, *The Incorporation of America: Culture and Society in the Gilded Age* (New York: Hill and Wang, 1986), 76–77.

147. Olin, 3.

148. R. Hal Williams, *The Democratic Party and California Politics, 1880–1896* (Stanford: Stanford University Press, 1973), 207.

149. Richard Coke Lower, *A Bloc of One: The Political Career of Hiram W.* Johnson (Stanford: Stanford University Press, 1993), 17.

150. A very young and armed Hiram once confronted Sacramento boss Frank Rhoades with both his father and brother in a saloon. The elder Grove would one day campaign against Hiram. See Michael A. Weatherson and Hal Bochin, *Hiram Johnson: A Bio-Bibliography* (New York: Greenwood Press, 1988), 4–7.

151. Mowry, 7.

152. Weatherson, 9.

153. Lower, 27.

154. Weatherson, 9.

155. Ibid., 149.

156. See Olin's critique of Croly's executive philosophy, 43.

157. Cannon, 162.

158. Ibid., 370.

159. Mowry, 135.

160. Ibid., 138.

161. Weatherson, 12.

162. Lower, 37.

163. Dinan, 296.

164. For a detailed account of how this election reflected the Progressive Era's confluence of executive visions for America, see Sidney M. Milkis, *Theodore Roosevelt, The Progressive Party, and the Transformation of American Democracy* (Lawrence: University of Kansas Press, 2009).

165. Sidney M. Milkis, *The President and the Parties: The Transformation of the American Party System Since the New Deal* (New York: Oxford University Press, 1993), 38.

166. "Governor Woodrow Wilson's Speech at Passaic, New Jersey," November 1, 1910, Woodrow Wilson Papers Project, Box 79, Princeton University Library, Department of Rare Books and Special Collections, Seeley G. Mudd Manuscript Library.

Chapter 2

1. Herbert Croly, *Progressive Democracy* (New York: Macmillan Company, 1914), 296.

2. Thomas Platt, *Letter to Theodore Roosevelt*, May 6, 1899, Theodore Roosevelt Papers, Presidential Papers Microfilm, Reel 2, Washington, D.C., 1967.

3. As the *New York Press* reported at the time of Roosevelt's fight, Grover Cleveland was once in a nearly identical predicament. See "Governor Puzzled Over Payn's Case," *New York Press*, December 14, 1899, Theodore Roosevelt Papers, Presidential Papers Microfilm, Reel 457, Washington, D.C., 1967.

4. "Breakfast," *New York World*, January 21, 1900, Theodore Roosevelt Papers, Presidential Papers Microfilm, Reel 457, Washington, D.C., 1967.

5. Nathan Miller, *Theodore Roosevelt: A Life* (New York: William Morrrow, 1992), 336–37.

6. Croly, 12.

7. Roosevelt's New Nationalism was derived from Croly's *The Promise of American Life*. See Sidney M. Milkis, *Theodore Roosevelt, The Progressive Party, and the Transformation of American Democracy* (Lawrence: University of Kansas Press, 2009), 38.

8. Ibid., 297.

9. Ibid., 296.

10. Ibid., 297–98.

11. Ibid., 301.

12. Ibid., 314.

13. Herbert Croly, *The Promise of American Life* (New York: BiblioBazaar, 2006), 172.

14. Ibid., 328.

15. Ibid., 322.

16. Richard L. McCormick, *From Realignment to Reform: Political Change in New York State, 1893–1910* (Ithaca: Cornell University Press, 1981), 82.

17. See Thomas E. Cronin, *The State of the Presidency* (Little, Brown: Boston, 1980). Gary L. Gregg II also uses the term in his *The Presidential Republic: Executive Representation and Deliberative Democracy* (New York: Rowan and Littlefield, 1997).

18. James P. Young, *Reconsidering American Liberalism: The Troubled Odyssey of the Liberal Idea* (Boulder: Westview Press, 1996), 151.

19. Robert H. Wiebe, *The Search for Order, 1877–1920* (New York: Hill and Wang, 1967), 133.

20. Cited in Alan Trachtenberg, *The Incorporation of America: Culture and Society in the Gilded Age* (New York: Hill and Wang, 1982), 70.

21. See Sidney M. Milkis and "The Roots of New Deal Reform," in *The Presidents and the Parties* (Oxford: New York), 1993.

22. From Woodrow Wilson, *The State* (1889), quoted in Martin J. Sklar, *The Corporate Reconstruction of American Capitalism, 1890–1916* (New York: Cambridge University, 1988), 405.

23. Maxine N. Lurie, and Marc Mappen, eds., *Encyclopedia of New Jersey* (New Brunswick: Rutgers University Press, 2004), 327.

24. Tom Lewis, *The Hudson: A History* (New Haven: Yale University Press, 2005), 236.

25. See Charles Thach on the historic strength of the New York governorship since the colonial era. Charles Thach, *The Creation of the Presidency, 1775–1789* (New York: Da Capo Press, 1922).

26. "The Reform Work at Albany," *New York Times*, February 1, 1899.

27. Stephen Skowronek, *Building a New American State: The Expansion of National Administrative Capacities, 1877–1920* (New York: Cambridge University Press, 1982), 59–61.

28. Sidney M. Milkis and Michael Nelson, *The American Presidency: Origins and Development, 1776–2002* (Washington, D.C.: CQ Press, 2003), 210.

29. John Gerring, *Party Ideologies in America, 1828–1996* (Cambridge: Cambridge University Press, 1998), 190.

30. "Roosevelt a Cog in the Political Machine," *New York Herald*, April 10, 1899, Theodore Roosevelt Papers, Presidential Papers Microfilm, Reel 456, Washington, D.C., 1967.

31. Letter to Adolph Brandeis, in Melvin I. Urofsky and David W. Levy, eds., *Letters of Louis D. Brandeis, Volume I (1870–1907)* (Albany: State University of New York Press, 1971), 387.

32. Lewis, 248.

33. Croly, *The Promise of American Life*, 330.

34. See Edmund Morris on Roosevelt and the weaving of a national reputation, especially chapters 13 and 24. Edmund Morris, *The Rise of Theodore Roosevelt* (New York: Modern Library: New York, 1979).

35. Jeffrey Tulis, *The Rhetorical Presidency* (Princeton: Princeton University Press, 1987), 19–20.

36. G. Wallace Chessman, *Governor Theodore Roosevelt: The Albany Apprenticeship, 1898–1900* (Cambridge: Harvard University Press, 1965), 153.

37. Theodore Roosevelt, *An Autobiography* (United Kingdom: Dodo Press, 2006), 235.

38. Sidney M. Milkis sees this as a new incarnation of Hamilton, as "the development of industrial capitalism had led to the formation of a national economy and concentration of 'private economic power,' requiring strong countervailing action to

ameliorate unacceptable political and economic inequality." See Milkis, "The Presidency, Democratic Reform, and Constitutional Change," *Political Science* 20, no. 3 (Summer 1987): 630.

39. For Tilden's, Cleveland's, and TR's influence on FDR's progressive governorship, see Frank Freidel, *Franklin D. Roosevelt: A Rendezvous with Destiny* (Boston: Little, Brown and Company, 1990), 18–19.

40. G. Wallace Chessman, *Governor Theodore Roosevelt: The Albany Apprenticeship, 1898–1900* (Cambridge: Harvard University Press, 1965), 4.

41. John Milton Cooper, *The Warrior and the Priest: Woodrow Wilson and Theodore Roosevelt* (Cambridge: Harvard University Press, 1983), 39.

42. Morris, 728–29.

43. Nathan Miller, *Theodore Roosevelt: A Life* (New York: William Morrow, 1992), 327.

44. "A Day with Gov. Roosevelt," *New York Times*, April 23, 1899.

45. Mario R. Dinunzio, *Theodore Roosevelt* (Washington, D.C.: CQ Press, 2003), 214.

46. Miller, 326.

47. Roosevelt, 233.

48. Stephen Ponder, *Managing the Press: Origins of the Media Presidency, 1897–1933* (New York: St. Martin's Press, 1999), 21.

49. Morris, 731.

50. Cooper, 162.

51. From Roosevelt's speech, "The Menace of the Demagogue," Chicago, October 15, 1896. See Mario R. DiNunzio, ed., *Theodore Roosevelt: An American Mind* (New York: St. Martin's Press, 1994), 116.

52. Theodore Roosevelt, *Public Papers of Theodore Roosevelt, Governor, 1899-[1900]* (Danvers, Mass.: General Books, 2009), 64.

53. Chessman, 15

54. "Roosevelt Wins on Every Point," May 20, 1899, *New York Herald*, Theodore Roosevelt Papers, Presidential Papers Microfilm, Reel 456, Washington, D.C., 1967.

55. Kathleen Dalton, Theodore *Roosevelt: A Strenuous Life* (Vintage Books: New York, 2002), 185.

56. Miller, 322.

57. Tulis, 112.

58. Theodore Roosevelt, letter to John Daniel Crimmins, May 1, 1899, *The Letters of Theodore Roosevelt*, ed. Elting E. Morrison (Cambridge: Harvard University Press, 1951), 1000.

59. Theodore Roosevelt, *State Papers as Governor and President, 1899–1909* (New York: Charles Scribner's Sons, 1926), 21.

60. See John J. Dinan, *The American State Constitutional Tradition* (Lawrence: University of Kansas Press, 2006), 160–71.

61. Croly, *The Promise of American Life*, 324.

62. Roosevelt, *Autobiography*, 235.

63. Theodore Roosevelt, letter to Senator Hobart Krum, May 24, 1899, Theodore Roosevelt Papers, Presidential Papers Microfilm, Reel 317, Washington, D.C., 1967.

64. "Expected Defeat of the Ford Franchise Bill," *New York Times*, April 15, 1899.

65. Roosevelt, *Autobiography*, 251.

66. See Roosevelt biographer William Draper Lewis, The *Life of Theodore Roosevelt* (Philadelphia: The John C. Winston Company, 1919), 161.

67. Theodore Roosevelt, "Letter to Henry Cabot Lodge," May 27, 1899, in *Letters and Speeches*, ed. Louis Auchincloss (New York: Library of America, 2004), 176.

68. Miller, 322.

69. "Review of the Session About to Close," *New York Times*, April 28, 1899.

70. McCormick, 161.

71. Carl Schurz, letter to *Evening Post*, October 22, 1898, Theodore Roosevelt Papers, Presidential Papers Microfilm, Reel 2, Washington, D.C., 1967.

72. See Sven Beckert, "Democracy in the Age of Capital: Contesting Suffrage Rights in Gilded Age New York," in *The Democratic Experiment*, ed. Meg Jacobs, William J. Novak, and Julian E. Zelizer (Princeton: Princeton University Press, 2003).

73. Ponder, 21.

74. "Governor Roosevelt is Inaugurated," *New York Times*, January 3, 1899.

75. Ibid.

76. "Citizens Dine Roosevelt," *New York Times*, March 25, 1899.

77. Thomas Platt, *Letter to Theodore Roosevelt*, May 6, 1899, Theodore Roosevelt Papers, Presidential Papers Microfilm, Reel 2, Washington, D.C., 1967.

78. John A. Corry, *A Rough Ride to Albany: Teddy Runs for Governor* (New York: Fordham University Press, 2000), 27.

79. Platt, *letter to Theodore Roosevelt*, May 6, 1899, Theodore Roosevelt Papers, Presidential Papers Microfilm, Reel 2, Washington, D.C., 1967.

80. "Franchises to be Taxed," *New York Times*, April 29, 1899.

81. "Victory for Roosevelt," *New York Sun*, May 26, 1899, Theodore Roosevelt Papers, Presidential Papers Microfilm, Reel 456, Washington, D.C., 1967.

82. "Gov. Roosevelt's Views," *New York Times*, January 5, 1899.

83. McCormick, 82.

84. Theodore J. Lowi, *The Personal President: Power Invested, Promise Unfulfilled* (Ithaca: Cornel University Press, 1985), 38, 41.

85. Roosevelt, *Autobiography*, 264.

86. Ibid., 301–2.

87. Miller, 326.

88. Theodore Roosevelt, letter to John A. Sleicher, April 6, 1899., Theodore Roosevelt Papers, Presidential Papers Microfilm, Reel 317, Washington, D.C., 1967.

89. Chessman, 166.

90. Croly, *Progressive Democracy*, 347.

91. As Sid Milkis notes, "Theodore Roosevelt and Woodrow Wilson had begun the construction of a new political order; the task of the New Deal was to consolidate the gains of FDR's progressive predecessors." See Sidney M. Milkis, *The President and the Parties: The Transformation of the American Party System Since the New Deal* (New York: Oxford University Press, 1993), 43.

92. Wiebe, 197.

93. Milkis, 26.

94. Kallenbach, 381–82.

95. Skowronek, 82.

96. See Daniel P. Carpenter, *The Forging of Bureaucratic Autonomy: Reputations, Networks, and Policy Innovation in Executive Agencies, 1862–1928* (Princeton: Princeton University Press, 2001), for discussion on "The Clerical State."

97. Skowronek, 67.

98. Ibid., 172.

99. Chessman, 304–5.

100. Cooper, 41.

101. Milkis, *Political Science*, 635.

102. Lewis L. Gould, *The Presidency of Theodore Roosevelt* (Lawrence: University of Kansas Press, 1991), 300–301.

103. Alan Rosenthal, *Governors and Legislators: Contending Powers* (Washington, D.C.: CQ Press, 1990), 25.

104. "A Role Model [Woodrow Wilson] for Governor Corzine," editorial, *Trenton Times*, November 10, 2005.

105. Joseph E. Kallenbach, *The American Chief Executive: The Presidency and the Governorship* (New York: Harper and Row Publishers, 1966), 567.

106. Kraig, 117.

107. Young, 155, 159–60.

108. Lowi, x.

Chapter 3

1. Address delivered January 5, 1911. Joseph E. Kallenbach, *The American Chief Executive: The Presidency and the Governorship* (New York: Harper and Row, 1966), 174.

2. Woodrow Wilson, "The Law and the Facts: Presidential Address, Seventh Annual Meeting of the American Political Science Association," *American Political Science Review* 5, no. 1 (February 1911): 10.

3. "Governors and Senators," *The New York Evening Post*, November 29, 1910.

4. "Red Blooded Governors," *Jersey Journal*, November 23, 1910.

5. Ibid.

6. "Dr. Wilson Criticizes the Appetite for Legislation," *Trenton Evening Times*, November 25, 1910.

7. Woodrow Wilson, "Mr. Cleveland as President," *Atlantic Monthly* 79, no. 478 (March 1897).

8. Ibid., 289.

9. Ibid., 296.

10. Ibid., 289.

11. Ibid., 294.

12. Ibid., 293.

13. See David Hirst, *Woodrow Wilson: Reform Governor: A Documentary Narrative* (Princeton: D. Van Nostrand Company, Inc., 1965), 32.

14. See Thorsen, 50.

15. Wilson, *Atlantic Monthly*, 300.

16. "The House of Governors," *New York Times*, January 19, 1910.

17. Ibid.

18. "Dr. Wilson Speaks to Many Governors," *New York Times*, November 30, 1910.

19. "Proceedings of the Third Meeting of the Governors of the States of the Union held at Frankfort and Louisville, KY," November 29–December 1, 1910, Woodrow Wilson Papers Project, Box 81, Princeton University Library, Department of Rare Books and Special Collections, Seeley G. Mudd Manuscript Library.

20. John Milton Cooper, Jr.'s most recent biography of Wilson places his New Jersey legislative record in the broader context of a national progressive movement among governors. See Cooper, *Woodrow Wilson: A Biography* (New York: Alfred A. Knopf, 2009), 135

21. The veto power was particularly salient in this regard. See Frank W. Prescott, "The Executive Veto in American States," *Western Political Quarterly* 3, no. 1 (March 1950).

22. "Governor Wilson Takes Office in New Jersey," *New York Times*, January 18, 1911.

23. See Ray Stannard Baker on U'Ren's meeting with Wilson and his influence on his thinking in *Woodrow Wilson: Life and Letters, Governor, 1910–1913* (New York: Charles Scribner's Sons, 1931), 130–31.

24. Richard J. Ellis, *Democratic Delusions: The Initiative Process in America* (Lawrence: University of Kansas, 2002), 183.

25. Arthur S. Link, *Wilson: The Road to the White House* (Princeton: Princeton University Press, 1947), 269.

26. Barbara G. and Stephen A. Salmore, *New Jersey Politics and Government: Suburban Politics Comes of Age* (Lincoln: University of Nebraska Press, 1998), 127.

27. Ibid., 128.

28. Charles Thach notes that New Jersey was the only state for a time with no restrictions regarding reeligibility for office. Charles C. Thach, *The Creation of the*

Presidency, 1775–1789 (New York: Da Capo Press, 1922), 28. This changed in 1844, but the governor was now popularly elected.

29. This perhaps explains why New Jersey was "the birthplace of the national initiative and referendum movement in America, even though direct legislation was never enacted there." See Ellis, 27.

30. Wilson actually appropriated the phrase from a conversation with a "prominent" but unnamed public figure in New Jersey. Hirst, 146.

31. Diary citation found in Niels Aage Thorsen, *The Political Thought of Woodrow Wilson, 1875–1910* (Princeton: Princeton University Press, 1988), 11.

32. "Wilson—A Tilden, But a Tilden Up to Date," *New York Times*, September 25, 1910.

33. Arthur Link argues that Wilson in fact derived his American political philosophy from Tilden and Grover Cleveland. See Arthur S. Link, "Woodrow Wilson: The American as Southerner," *Journal of Southern History* 36, no. 1 (February 1970): 11.

34. George W. Smith, Letter to Woodrow Wilson, November 9, 1910, Woodrow Wilson Papers Project, Box 79, Princeton University Library, Department of Rare Books and Special Collections, Seeley G. Mudd Manuscript Library.

35. If Wilson was billed as a "Tilden up to date," he was also billed as a "safer" version of La Follette. See Robert A. Kraig, *Woodrow Wilson and the Lost World of the Oratorical Statesman* (College Station: Texas A&M University Press, 2004), 122.

36. Link, 271–72.

37. Woodrow Wilson, *Constitutional Government in the United States* (New York: Columbia University Press, 1908), 63.

38. Mario Di Nunzio, ed., *Woodrow Wilson: Essential Writings and Speeches of the Scholar-President* (New York: New York University Press, 2006), 298.

39. Ronald J. Pestritto, *Woodrow Wilson and the Roots of Modern Liberalism* (Lanham, Md.: Rowman and Littlefield, 2005), 8.

40. The phrase is from Hegel's *Philosophy of History.*

41. Pestritto, 14.

42. See Gary L. Gregg II, *The Presidential Republic: Executive Representation and Deliberative Democracy* (Lanham, Md.: Rowman and Littlefield, 1997), 101.

43. Di Nunzio, 90.

44. Ibid.

45. Jeffrey Tulis, *The Rhetorical Presidency* (Princeton: Princeton University Press, 1987), 122.

46. See Pestritto, 167–72.

47. Sidney M. Milkis and Michael Nelson, The *American Presidency: Origins and Development, 1776–2002* (Washington, D.C.: CQ Press, 2003), 232–33.

48. "Dr. Wilson Says He Is Owned by No One," *New York Times*, October 4, 1910.

49. See Ray Stannard Baker, 134. Baker called New Jersey's constitution "one of the most antiquated in the Union, following the French revolutionary model."

Importantly, the document nonetheless held significant implied powers, and Wilson exploited them.

50. "Dr. Wilson Says He Is Owned by No One."

51. Baker, 155.

52. Wilson, *Constitutional Government*, 4.

53. Ibid., 4.

54. Governor Woodrow Wilson's Speech (stenographic report supplied by F. P. Stockbridge), Auditorium of the Hillside School, Montclair, N.J., November 2, 1910, Woodrow Wilson Papers Project, Box79, Princeton University Library, Department of Rare Books and Special Collections, Seeley G. Mudd Manuscript Library.

55. Wilson, *Constitutional Government*, 55–56.

56. Ibid., 64.

57. Lewis L. Gould, *The Modern American Presidency* (Lawrence: University of Kansas, 2003), 54.

58. "The Exponent of the New Stateism," *New York Times*, November 14, 1910.

59. Stephen Skowronek, "The Conservative Insurgency and Presidential Power: A Developmental Perspective on the Unitary Executive," *Harvard Law Review* (June 2009): 2070–2103.

60. "Bow to Wilson as Party Leader," *New York Times*, July 5, 1912.

61. Sidney M. Milkis, *The President and the Parties: The Transformation of the American Party System Since the New Deal* (New York: Oxford University Press, 1993), 5.

62. "Bow to Wilson as Party Leader," *New York Times*, July 5, 1912.

63. James D. Startt, *Woodrow Wilson and the Press: Prelude to the Presidency* (New York: Palgrave Macmillan, 2004), 67.

64. Ibid., 68.

65. As Robert A. Kraig notes, "New Jersey's proximity to the most influential newspapers and magazines had kept a constant national spotlight on [Wilson's] state battles." Kraig, 120.

66. Roosevelt averaged 204 annual citations in the *Times*, while Wilson averaged over 322.

67. Startt, 75–76.

68. Ibid., 101.

69. Gould, 45.

70. Baker, 458.

71. Kraig, 137.

72. Hirst, 140.

73. Clements, 61.

74. Woodrow Wilson, Letter to James Smith, Jr., November 9, 1910, Woodrow Wilson Papers Project, Box 79, Princeton University Library, Department of Rare Books and Special Collections, Seeley G. Mudd Manuscript Library. Emphasis added.

75. Letter to Woodrow Wilson [unspecified sender], November 10, 1910, Woodrow Wilson Papers Project, Box 79, Princeton University Library, Department of Rare Books and Special Collections, Seeley G. Mudd Manuscript Library.

76. E. Runyan, Letter to Woodrow Wilson, November 17, 1910, Woodrow Wilson Papers Project, Box 79, Princeton University Library, Department of Rare Books and Special Collections, Seeley G. Mudd Manuscript Library. Emphasis added.

77. "Governor Wilson as a Dictator and Destroyer of the Constitution," *Jersey Journal*, December 5, 1910.

78. Woodrow Wilson, Letter to Oswald Garrison Villard, December 5, 1910, Woodrow Wilson Papers Project, Box 81, Princeton University Library, Department of Rare Books and Special Collections, Seeley G. Mudd Manuscript Library.

79. William St. John, Letter to Woodrow Wilson, November 7, 1910, Woodrow Wilson Papers Project, Box 79, Princeton University Library, Department of Rare Books and Special Collections, Seeley G. Mudd Manuscript Library. Emphasis added.

80. William St. John, Letter to Woodrow Wilson, November 12, 1910, Woodrow Wilson Papers Project, Box 79, Princeton University Library, Department of Rare Books and Special Collections, Seeley G. Mudd Manuscript Library.

81. "James E. Martine, Who Hopes to Be Senator," *Newark Sunday Call*, November 20, 1910.

82. Joseph P. Tumulty, Letter to Woodrow Wilson, November 30, 1910, Woodrow Wilson Papers Project, Box 81, Princeton University Library, Department of Rare Books and Special Collections, Seeley G. Mudd Manuscript Library.

83. James Kerney, Letter to Woodrow Wilson, December 6, 1910, Woodrow Wilson Papers Project, Box 81, Princeton University Library, Department of Rare Books and Special Collections, Seeley G. Mudd Manuscript Library.

84. "Statement by Mr. Woodrow Wilson regarding the senatorship," December 8, 1910, Woodrow Wilson Papers Project, Box 81, Princeton University Library, Department of Rare Books and Special Collections, Seeley G. Mudd Manuscript Library.

85. Ibid., 61–62.

86. "Wilson Acclaimed in Attack on Smith," *New York Times*, January 6, 1911.

87. For his part, Nugent referred to Wilson as "an ingrate and a liar." "Governor Wilson Opens Attack on Nugent," *New York Times*, September 16, 1912.

88. "Wilson Tells Smith He Will Fight Him," *New York Times*, November 29, 1910.

89. "Predicting Defeat for Gov. Wilson," *New York Times*, October 30, 1911.

90. Wilson, 215.

91. Herbert Croly, *Progressive Democracy* (New York: Macmillan Company, 1914), 344.

92. Richard Hofstadter, *The Age of Reform: From Bryan to FDR* (New York: Vintage Books, 1955), 176.

93. Clements, 69.

94. Carl R. Burgchardt, *Robert La Follette, Sr.: The Voice of Conscience* (New York: Greenwood Press, 1992), 62.

95. Fred I. Greenstein, *The Presidential Difference: Leadership Style from FDR to Clinton* (New York: Free Press, 2000), 28.

96. Mary E. Stuckey, "The Domain of Public Conscience: Woodrow Wilson and the Establishment of a Transcendent Political Order," *Rhetoric and Public Affairs* 6, no. 1 (2003): 1–24.

97. See Kraig, 131 and notes, 209.

98. Robert Sobel and John Raimo, *Biographical Directory of the Governors of the United States, 1789–1978*, vol. 3 (Westport, Conn.: Meckler Books, 1978).

99. Newton C. Blanchard et al., eds., *Proceedings of a Conference of Governors: In the White House, Washington, D.C., May 13–15, 1908* (Washington, D.C.: Government Printing Office, 1909), 119–23.

100. On Wilson's break with tradition, see Tulis, 133, 134.

101. Pestritto, 6.

102. Ibid., 255.

103. Thorsen, 60.

104. See Alexander and Juliette George, *Woodrow Wilson and Colonel House: A Personality Study* (New York: Dover Publications, 1964), 66.

105. Ibid., 67.

106. Baker, 141.

107. Ibid., 193.

108. Pestritto, 170.

109. Hirst, 131.

110. "Woodrow Wilson's Victory," *New York Times*, January 26, 1911.

111. Ibid.

112. "New Jersey Carried by Republicans," *New York Times*, November 8, 1911.

113. Moses cites Wilson here in his 1913 Columbia University dissertation, "The Civil Service of Great Britain." See Robert Caro, *The Power Broker: Robert Moses and the Fall of New York* (New York: Vintage Books, 1974), 55.

114. John Milton Cooper, Jr., is right to point out that Wilson's English mother and Ohioan father hardly made him the near caricature of a southern politician he has on occasion become. See Cooper, *Woodrow Wilson: A Biography* (New York: Alfred A. Knopf, 2009).

115. John Milton Cooper, Jr., *The Warrior and the Priest: Woodrow Wilson and Theodore Roosevelt* (Cambridge: Harvard University Press, 1983), 170.

116. Daniel Stid, *The President as Statesman: Woodrow Wilson and the Constitution* (Lawrence: University Press of Kansas, 1998), 144.

117. See Elizabeth Sanders, *Roots of Reform: Farmers, Workers, and the American State, 1877–1917* (Chicago: University of Chicago Press, 1999), 394 (for quote) and 387–97 (Wilson's party leadership).

118. Theodore J. Lowi, *The Personal President: Power Invested, Promise Unfulfilled* (Ithaca: Cornell University Press, 1985), 57.

119. See Wilson, "The Historian," referenced here in Di Nunzio, 153.

120. Edward Gibbon, *The Decline and Fall of the Roman Empire*, ed. Hans-Friedrich Mueller (New York: Modern Library, 2003), 39.

121. Ibid., 44.

122. Along with the *Declaration* and Adam Smith's *The Wealth of Nations*, Gibbon's work was published in 1776.

Chapter 4

1. Cited in J. B. S. Hardman, *Rendezvous with Destiny: Addresses and Opinions of Franklin Delano Roosevelt* (New York: Dryden Press, 1944), 27.

2. "Roosevelt's View of the Big Job," *New York Times*, September 11, 1932.

3. The latter was the preference of the *Times*'s coverage of FDR's fall Midwestern campaign tour. "Roosevelt Hailed by Chicago Throng," *New York Times*, October 1, 1932.

4. "Governor Roosevelt's Address in Milwaukee," *New York Times*, October 1, 1932.

5. "Roosevelt Hailed by Chicago Throng."

6. Ellis W. Hawley, *The New Deal and the Problem of Monopoly: A Study in Economic Ambivalence* (Princeton: Princeton University Press, 1966), 15. Hawley also suggests that the Brandesian turn in New Deal economic policy revealed a more fragmentary philosophy of governance.

7. Arthur M. Schlesinger, Jr., *The Crisis of the Old Order, 1919–1933* (Boston: Houghton Mifflin Company, 1957), 45.

8. Hiram Johnson, Letter to Roosevelt, November 16, 1933, President's Personal File, 1134, Franklin D. Roosevelt Library, Hyde Park, N.Y.

9. Raymond Moley, *After Seven Years* (Lincoln: University of Nebraska Press, 1939), 14.

10. Frank Freidel, *Franklin D. Roosevelt: A Rendezvous with Destiny* (Boston: Little, Brown, and Company, 1990), 16.

11. Ibid., 18.

12. Jean Edwards Smith, *FDR* (New York: Random House, 2007), 97–98.

13. Freidel, 25.

14. Ibid., 25.

15. Smith, 229–30.

16. Cited in Richard Hofstadter, *The Age of Reform: From Bryan to FDR* (New York: Vintage Books, 1955), 300–301.

17. Thomas H. Greer, *What Roosevelt Thought: The Social and Political Ideas of Franklin Roosevelt* (East Lansing: Michigan State University Press, 1958), 90–91.

18. The quotation is found in Leonard D. White, *Introduction to the Study of Public Administration* (New York: Macmillan Company, 1939). The citation is from Bernard Bellush, *Franklin D. Roosevelt as Governor of New York* (New York: Columbia University Press, 1955), 38.

19. James MacGregor Burns, *Roosevelt: The Lion and the Fox* (New York: Harcourt, Brace, and World, 1956), 122.

20. The aside was delivered to Rex Tugwell. Schlesinger, Jr., 504.

21. Conrad Black, *Franklin Delano Roosevelt: Champion of Freedom* (New York: Public Affairs, 2003), 180.

22. Bernard Bellush, *Franklin D. Roosevelt as Governor of New York* (New York: Columbia University Press, 1955), 282.

23. Schlesinger, 386.

24. Ibid.

25. In actuality, the power extended to the governor was finalized under an amendment to the state constitution. See Bellush, 38–40.

26. See John Dinan, *The American State Constitutional Tradition* (Lawrence: University of Kansas Press, 2006), 117.

27. Burns, 111.

28. Ibid., 112.

29. Bellush, 42.

30. Ibid., 47–48.

31. Ibid., 55.

32. Ibid., 57.

33. Greer, 88.

34. Ibid., 95.

35. William E. Leuchtenburg, *The FDR Years: On Roosevelt and His Legacy* (New York: Columbia University Press, 1995), 18.

36. Bellush, 210.

37. "Gov. Roosevelt Puts in a Long Workday," *New York Times*, March 24, 1929.

38. "Roosevelt Calls Power Main Issue," *New York Times*, June 21, 1929.

39. Freidel, 58.

40. Black, 192.

41. Ibid., 190.

42. Betty Houchin Winfield, *FDR and the News Media* (Urbana: University of Illinois Press, 1990), 17.

43. "Roosevelt Hails Democratic Unity," *New York Times*, October 16, 1931.

44. "Roosevelt Wants State-Aided Press," *New York Times*, June 5, 1931

45. Roosevelt, in fact, starred in the first talking movie about a politician, the 1930 film *The Roosevelt Record*.

46. Letter to Columbia University Professor James C. Bonbright, March 11, 1930, in Eleanor Roosevelt, ed., *FDR: His Personal Letters* (New York: Duell, Sloan and Pearce, 1950), 98.

47. Black, 204.

48. Burns, 117.

49. Smith, 251.

50. Bellush, 140.

51. Franklin D. Roosevelt, *Public Papers of Governor, 1930* (Albany: J. B. Lyon Company, 1930), 774.

52. Franklin D. Roosevelt, The *Public Papers and Addresses,* vol. 1: *The Genesis of the New Deal, 1928–1932* (New York: Random House, 1938), 8.

53. Ibid., 619.

54. "Grover Cleveland Lectures," *New York Times*, April 10, 1900.

55. Hofstadter, 303.

56. Burns, 114.

57. Freidel, 77.

58. Moley, 13.

59. See "Foundation Principles of Jefferson and Their Relation to the Social and Political Structure of the Republic, at Jefferson Day Dinner, St. Paul, Minnesota, April 18, 1932," in Roosevelt, *Public Papers of Governor of New York, 1932* (Albany: J. B. Lyon Company, 1939), 577–83.

60. See Thomas Greer's account of the confrontation between FDR and Staley in Greer, 76–77.

61. Bellush, 278.

62. Ibid., 10.

63. Governor Roosevelt's Decision, April 28, 1931, Container 125, Franklin D. Roosevelt Library, Hyde Park, N.Y.

64. "Citizens Should Read Walker's Answer," *New York Evening Journal*, April 21, 1931.

65. "Mayor Walker's Answer," *New York Sun*, April 21, 1931.

66. Bellush, 277.

67. "Statement to the Attorney-General in the Matter of the Charges Against James J. Walker, Mayor of the City of New York," signed by Governor Roosevelt, December 29, 1932, Vertical File: Walker, James J. (1881–1946), Franklin D. Roosevelt Library, Hyde Park, N.Y.

68. "Text of Gov. Roosevelt's Message on Unemployment Relief," *New York Times*, August 29, 1931.

69. Smith, 251.

70. John Gerring, *Party Ideologies in America, 1828–1996* (Cambridge: Cambridge University Press, 1998), 228.

71. "Text of Governor Roosevelt's Message Urging State Action on Economic Measures," *New York Times*, January 7, 1932.

72. Sidney M. Milkis, "Franklin D. Roosevelt and the Transcendence of Partisan Politics," *Political Science Quarterly* 100, no. 3 (Autumn 1985): 502.

73. Bismarck began to put Germany on a welfare state path in the early 1880s. Jordan A. Schwarz, *Liberal: Adolf A. Berle and the Vision of an American Era* (New York: Free Press, 1987), 78.

74. Hardman, 27.

75. Roosevelt, *PP: 1928–1932*, 744.

76. Ibid., 746.

77. Ibid., 749.

78. Ibid., 750.

79. Ibid., 753.

80. Schlesinger, 426.

81. Leuchtenburg, 7.

82. See http://millercenter.virginia.edu/scripps/digitalarchive/speeches/spe_1887
_1206_cleveland.

83. Milkis, 484.

84. "Progressives Start a Roosevelt League," *New York Times*, September 26, 1932.

85. Out of more than 4 million votes cast, Roosevelt's margin of victory was 25,608. Smith, 228.

86. "Roosevelt Started Fighting Tammany," *New York Times*, November 9, 1932.

87. Theodore J. Lowi, *The Personal President: Power Invested, Promise Unfulfilled* (Ithaca: Cornell University Press, 1985), 59–60.

88. The indictment was launched by one J. M. Dixon. See "Doubts Roosevelt Ever Voted for T.R.," *New York Times*, September 26, 1932. Dixon went so far as to accuse FDR of shamelessly appropriating TR's famous "dee-lighted." See Dixon again in "Asserts Roosevelt Is Imitating 'T.R.,'" *New York Times*, September 22, 1932.

89. Hofstadter, *The Age of Reform*, 310.

90. Greer, 115.

91. Franklin D. Roosevelt, *Our Democracy in Action: The Philosophy of President Franklin D. Roosevelt* (Washington, D.C.: National Home Library Foundation, 1940), 161–62.

Chapter 5

1. Alexis de Tocqueville, *Democracy in America and Two Essays on America* (London: Penguin Books, 2003), 469.

2. William Shakespeare, *William Shakespeare: The Complete Works* (New York: Dorset Press, 1988), 877.

3. The presumption of legislative power was so entrenched in the minds of the framers that countervailing executive power was a reaction to legislative supremacy, not an isolated initiative. With this in mind, the legislative branch was to be the only one armed with what Garry Wills has referred to as "shoot-out" power, the ability to overcome the initiatives of either of the other two branches of government. See Garry Wills, *Explaining America: The Federalist* (New York: Penguin Books, 2001), 128.

4. As Stephen Skowronek notes, "By the time of Andrew Jackson, the presidency had become in [Henry Jones] Ford's famous phrase, 'the work of the people breaking

through the constitutional form.'" Stephen Skowronek, *Presidential Leadership in Political Time: Reprise and Reappraisal* (Lawrence: University of Kansas Press, 2008), 156.

5. Wilson was particularly fond of Cleveland's executive acumen, noting his tendency to defy his own party and the legislature as both mayor and governor. See Woodrow Wilson, "Mr. Cleveland as President," *Atlantic Monthly* 79, no. 478 (March 1897).

6. None have, for instance, called for the "building down" of the presidency, as has Theodore Lowi, for example. The "middle way" advocated by President Bill Clinton was about policy direction and political compromise, not the rechanneling of presidential authority to Congress.

7. See Lou Harris, "Why the Odds Are Against a Governor Becoming President," *Public Opinion Quarterly* 23, no. 3 (1959): 361–70.

8. For an analysis of the presidency as more in line with order-preserving projects, see Russell Riley, *The Presidency and the Politics of Racial Inequality: Nation-Keeping from 1831–1965* (New York: Columbia University Press, 1999).

9. Such attitudes toward Congress persist. See John R. Hibbing and Elizabeth Thiess-Morse, *Congress as Public Enemy: Public Attitudes Toward American Political Institutions* (Cambridge: Cambridge University Press, 1999).

10. Herbert Croly, *Progressive Democracy* (New York: Macmillan Company, 1914), 296.

11. George E. Mowry, *The California Progressives* (Berkeley: University of California Press, 1951), 149.

12. Woodrow Wilson, *Constitutional Government in the United States* (New York: Columbia University Press, 1908), 11.

13. The term was a favorite of Roosevelt's (he introduced it in his first annual message as governor) and was used on occasion by progressive executives. Theodore Roosevelt, *State Papers as Governor and President, 1899–1909* (New York: Charles Scribner's Sons, 1926), 21.

14. "Bow to Wilson as Party Leader," *New York Times*, July 5, 1912.

15. Sidney M. Milkis describes Van Buren's efforts to "republicanize" the executive, for example. See Sidney M. Milkis, *The President and the Parties: The Transformation of the American Party System Since the New Deal* (Oxford: Oxford University Press, 1993), 102–3. See also Marc Landy and Sidney Milkis, *Presidential Greatness* (Lawrence: University of Kansas Press, 2000), 88–94.

16. "Wilson—A Tilden But a Tilden Up to Date," *New York Times*, September 25, 1910.

17. Theodore Lowi has described the administrative nature of modern government in America as a product of popular capitulation to personalist leadership and the "plebiscitary presidency." See Theodore J. Lowi, *The Personal President: Power Invested, Promise Unfulfilled* (Ithaca: Cornell University Press, 1985).

18. See Sean Wilentz, for example, on early republican governance in America. *The Rise of American Democracy: Jefferson to Lincoln* (New York: W. W. Norton and Company, 2006), 15, 29.

19. Charles Thach, *The Creation of the Presidency, 1775–1789: A Study in Constitutional History* (New York: Da Capo Press, 1969), 172–73.

20. Harvey C. Mansfield, *Taming the Prince: The Ambivalence of Modern Executive Power* (Baltimore: Johns Hopkins University Press, 1993), 17.

21. See Haynes Johnson, *The Age of Anxiety: McCarthyism to Terrorism* (Orlando: Harcourt, Inc, 2005).

22. Mansfield. The line is the epigraph to the book.

23. Richard J. Ellis, *Democratic Delusions: The Initiative Process in America* (Lawrence: University of Kansas Press, 2002), 200.

24. T. A. Sinclair, *Aristotle: The Politics* (London: Penguin Books, 1981), 310–11.

25. See Sidney M. Milkis, "Executive Power and Political Parties: The Dilemmas of Scale in American Democracy," in Joel D. Aberbach and Mark A. Peterson, eds., *The Executive Branch, Institutions of American Democracy Series* (Oxford: Oxford University Press, 2005), 386.

26. This debate was over Washington's Proclamation of Neutrality in 1793.

27. George C. Edwards III, *On Deaf Ears: The Limits of the Bully Pulpit* (New Haven: Yale University Press, 2003), 246–54.

28. Skowronek, 156.

29. Arthur M. Schlesinger, Jr., *The Imperial Presidency* (New York: Popular Library, 1973), 206–7.

30. Andrew Rudalevige, *The New Imperial Presidency: Renewing Presidential Power after Watergate* (Ann Arbor: University of Michigan Press, 2005), 15.

31. Ibid., 396–97.

32. Sheldon Wolin, *Politics and Vision: Continuity and Innovation in Western Political Thought* (Princeton: Princeton University Press, 2004), 429.

33. Thad L. Beyle, and Lynn Muchmore, eds., Being *Governor: The View From the Office* (Durham: Duke University Press, 1983), 112.

34. Tocqueville, 807.

35. Herbert J. Storing, *The Anti-Federalist: An Abridgement by Murray Dry, of the Complete Anti-Federalist* (Chicago: University of Chicago Press, 1985), 310.

36. Joseph E. Kallenbach, *The American Chief Executive: The Presidency and the Governorship* (New York: Harper and Row, Publishers, 1966), 27–28.

37. The exchange can be found in "Governors Clash on Referendum," *New York Times*, September 13, 1911.

38. Herbert Croly, *Progressive Democracy* (New York: Macmillan Company, 1914), 301.

39. James P. Young, *Reconsidering American Liberalism: The Troubled Odyssey of the Liberal Idea* (Boulder: Westview Press, 1996), 159–60.

40. Wolin, 593–94.

41. Jordan A. Schwarz, *Liberal: Adolf A. Berle and the Vision of an American Era* (New York: Free Press, 1987), 78.

42. James T. Kloppenberg, *Uncertain Victory: Social Democracy and Progressivism in European and American Thought, 1870–1920* (Oxford: Oxford University Press, 1986), 167–68.

43. Schlesinger, 210.

Bibliography

Adams, Henry. *Democracy*. New York: Feather Trail Press, 2009.

Baker, Ray Stannard. *Woodrow Wilson: Life and Letters, Governor, 1910–1913*. New York: Charles Scribner's Sons, 1931.

Barnard, Harry. *Rutherford B. Hayes and His America*. Newtown, Conn.: American Political Biography Press, 1994.

Beckert, Sven. "Democracy in the Age of Capital: Contesting Suffrage Rights in Gilded Age New York." In Meg Jacobs, William Novak, and Julian Zelizer, eds., *The Democratic Experiment*. Princeton: Princeton University Press, 2003.

Bellush, Bernard. *Franklin D. Roosevelt as Governor of New York*. New York: Columbia University Press, 1955.

Beyle, Thad and Lynn Muchmore. *Being Governor: The View from the Office*. Durham, N.C.: Duke University Press, 1983.

Bishop, Joseph Bucklin. *Theodore Roosevelt and His Time: Shown in His Own Letters*. Vol. 1. New York: Charles Scribner's Sons, 1920.

Black, Conrad. *Franklin Delano Roosevelt: Champion of Freedom*. New York: Public Affairs, 2003.

Blanchard, Newton C., John Franklin Fort, et al., eds. *Proceedings of a Conference of Governors: In the White House, Washington, D.C., May 13–15, 1908*. Washington, D.C.: Government Printing Office, 1909.

Blodgett, Geoffrey. *The Gentle Reformers: Massachusetts Democrats in the Cleveland Era*. Cambridge, Mass.: Harvard University Press, 1966.

Brodsky, Alyn. *Grover Cleveland: A Study in Character*. New York: St. Martin's Press, 2000.

Burgchardt, Carl R. *Robert La Follette, Sr.: The Voice of Conscience*. New York: Greenwood Press, 1992.

Bryce, James. *Proceedings of the Second Meeting of the Governors of the States of the Union*. Lakewood, N.J.: The Lakewood Press, 1910.

Burns, James MacGregor. *Roosevelt: The Lion and the Fox*. New York: Harcourt, Brace, and World, Inc., 1956.

Burrows, Edwin G. and Mike Wallace. *Gotham: A History of New York City to 1898*. New York: Oxford University Press, 1999.

Cannon, Lou. *Governor Reagan: His Rise to Power*. New York: Public Affairs, 2003.

Caro, Robert. *The Power Broker: Robert Moses and the Fall of New York*. New York: Vintage Books, 1974.

Carpenter, Daniel P. *The Forging of Bureaucratic Autonomy: Reputations, Networks, and Policy Innovation in Executive Agencies, 1862–1928*. Princeton: Princeton University Press, 2001.

Chessman, G. Wallace. *Governor Theodore Roosevelt: The Albany Apprenticeship, 1898–1900*. Cambridge, Mass.: Harvard University Press, 1965.

Cooper, John Milton, Jr.. *The Warrior and the Priest: Woodrow Wilson and Theodore Roosevelt*. Cambridge, Mass.: Harvard University Press, 1983.

———. *Woodrow Wilson: A Biography*. New York: Alfred A. Knopf, 2009.

Corry, John A. *A Rough Ride to Albany: Teddy Runs for Governor*. New York: Fordham University Press, 2000.

Crockett, David A. *The Opposition Presidency: Leadership and the Constraints of History*. College Station: Texas A&M University Press, 2002.

Croly, Herbert. *Progressive Democracy*. New York: The Macmillan Company, 1914.

———. *The Promise of American Life*. New York: BiblioBazaar, 2006.

Cronin, Thomas E. *The State of the Presidency*. Boston: Little, Brown and Company, 1980.

Dinan, John J. *The American State Constitutional Tradition*. Lawrence: University of Kansas Press, 2006.

Di Nunzio, Mario. *Theodore Roosevelt*. Washington, D.C.: CQ Press, 2003.

———, ed. *Theodore Roosevelt: An American Mind*. New York: St. Martin's Press, 1994.

———, ed. *Woodrow Wilson: Essential Writings and Speeches of the Scholar-President*. New York: New York University Press, 2006.

Eckenrode, H. J. *Rutherford B. Hayes: Statesman of Reunion*. Port Washington: Kennikat Press, 1963.

Edwards, George. *On Deaf Ears: The Limits of the Bully Pulpit*. New Haven, Conn.: Yale University Press, 2006.

Ehrenhalt, Alan. "Woodrow Wilson and the Modern American Governorship," Paper delivered at "Woodrow Wilson in the Nation's Service," a colloqium at the Woodrow Wilson School of Public and International Affairs, Princeton University, April 28, 2006.

Ellis, Richard J. *Democratic Delusions: The Initiative Process in America*. Lawrence: University of Kansas, 2002.

Flick, Alexander Clarence Flick. *Samuel Jones Tilden: A Study in Political Sagacity*. Westport: Greenwood Press, 1973.

Freidel, Frank. *Franklin D. Roosevelt: A Rendezvous with Destiny*. Boston: Little, Brown and Company, 1990.

George, Alexander and Juliette. *Woodrow Wilson and Colonel House: A Personality Study*. New York: Dover Publications, 1964.

Gerring, John. *Party Ideologies in America, 1828–1996*. Cambridge: Cambridge University Press, 1998.

Gibbon, Edward. *The Decline and Fall of the Roman Empire*. Ed. Hans-Friedrich Mueller. New York: Modern Library, 2003.

Gould, Lewis L. *The Modern American Presidency*. Lawrence: University of Kansas Press, 2003.

——. *The Presidency of Theodore Roosevelt*. Lawrence: University of Kansas Press, 1991.

Graff, Henry. *Grover Cleveland*. New York: Henry Holt and Company, 2002.

Greenstein, Fred I. *The Presidential Difference: Leadership Style from FDR to Clinton*. New York: Free Press, 2000.

Greer, Thomas H. *What Roosevelt Thought: The Social and Political Ideas of Franklin Roosevelt* East Lansing: Michigan State University Press, 1958.

Gregg, Gary L., II. *The Presidential Republic: Executive Representation and Deliberative Democracy*. Lanham, Md.: Rowman and Littlefield, 1997.

Hamilton, Alexander, James Madison, and John Jay. *The Federalist Papers*. Commentary by Garry Wills. New York: Bantam Dell, 1982.

Hardman, J. B. S. *Rendezvous with Destiny: Addresses and Opinions of Franklin Delano Roosevelt*. New York: Dryden Press, 1944.

Hawley, Ellis W. *The New Deal and the Problem of Monopoly: A Study in Economic Ambivalence*. Princeton: Princeton University Press, 1966.

Headley, Joel Tyler. *The Great Riots of New York, 1712–1873*. New York: Thunder Mouth Press, 2004.

Hibbing, John R. and Elizabeth Thiess-Morse. *Congress as Public Enemy: Public Attitudes Toward American Political Institutions*. Cambridge: Cambridge University Press, 1999.

Hirst, David W. *Woodrow Wilson: Reform Governor: A Documentary Narrative*. Princeton: D. Van Nostrand Company, 1965.

Hofstadter, Richard. *The Age of Reform: From Bryan to FDR*. New York: Vintage Books, 1955.

Hoogenboom, Ari. *Rutherford B. Hayes: Warrior and President*. Lawrence: University of Kansas Press, 1995.

James, Scott C. *Presidents, Parties, and the State: A Party System Perspective on Democratic Regulatory Change, 1884–1936*. New York: Cambridge University Press, 2000.

Jeffers, H. Paul. *An Honest President: The Life and Presidencies of Grover Cleveland*. New York: William Morrow, 2000.

Johnson, Haynes. *The Age of Anxiety: McCarthyism to Terrorism*. Orlando: Harcourt, Inc, 2005.

Kallenbach, Joseph E. *The American Chief Executive: The Presidency and the Governorship* New York: Harper and Row, 1966.

Kendricks, Clement A. *Woodrow Wilson: World Statesman*. Chicago: Ivan R. Dee, 1999.

Kloppenberg, James T. *Uncertain Victory: Social Democracy and Progressivism in European and American Thought, 1870–1920*. Oxford: Oxford University Press, 1986.

Kraig, Robert A. *Woodrow Wilson and the Lost World of the Oratorical Statesman*. College Station: Texas A&M University Press, 2004.

Leuchtenburg, William E. *In the Shadow of FDR: From Harry Truman to Ronald Reagan*. Ithaca: Cornell University Press, 1983.

Lewis, Tom. *The Hudson: A History*. New Haven: Yale University Press, 2005.

Lewis, William Draper. *The Life of Theodore Roosevelt*. Philadelphia: John C. Winston Company, 1919.

Link, Arthur S. "Woodrow Wilson: The American as Southerner." *Journal of Southern History* 36, no. 1 (February 1970): 3–17.

———. *Wilson: The Road to the White House*. Princeton: Princeton University Press, 1947.

Lowi, Theodore J. *The End of Liberalism: The Second Republic of the United States*. New York: W. W. Norton and Company, 1979.

———. *The Personal President: Power Invested, Promise Unfulfilled*. Ithaca: Cornell University Press, 1985.

Lurie, Maxine N. and Marc Mappen, eds. *Encyclopedia of New Jersey*. New Brunswick: Rutgers University Press, 2004.

Madison, James. *Notes of Debates in the Federal Convention of 1787 Reported by James Madison*. Athens: Ohio University Press, 1966.

Mansfield, Harvey C. *Taming the Prince: The Ambivalence of Modern Executive Power*. Baltimore: Johns Hopkins University Press, 1993.

Mayer, Kenneth R. *With the Stroke of a Pen: Executive Orders and Presidential Power*. Princeton: Princeton University Press, 2002.

Mayhew, David. *Congress: The Electoral Connection*. New Haven, Conn.: Yale University Press, 1974.

McCullough, David. *The Great Bridge: The Epic Story of the Building of the Brooklyn Bridge*. New York: Simon and Schuster, 1972.

McWilliams, Carey. *California: The Great Exception*. Berkeley: University of California Press, 1999.

Merrill, Horace Samuel. *Bourbon Leader: Grover Cleveland and the Democratic Party*. Boston: Little, Brown and Company.

Milkis, Sidney M. and Michael Nelson. *The American Presidency: Origins and Development, 1776–2002*. Washington, D.C.: CQ Press, 2003.

———. "Executive Power and Political Parties: The Dilemmas of Scale in American Democracy." In Joel D. Aberbach and Mark A. Peterson, eds., *The Executive Branch*. Institutions of American Democracy Series. Oxford: Oxford University Press, 2005.

———. "Franklin D. Roosevelt and the Transcendence of Partisan Politics." *Political Science Quarterly* 100, no. 3 (Autumn 1985): 479–504.

———. "The Presidency, Democratic Reform, and Constitutional Change." *Political Science* 20, no. 3 (Summer 1987): 628–36.

——. *The President and the Parties: The Transformation of the American Party System Since the New Deal.* New York: Oxford University Press, 1993.

——. *Presidential Greatness.* Lawrence: University of Kansas Press, 2000.

Miller, Nathan. *Theodore Roosevelt: A Life.* New York: William Morrow, 1992.

Moley, Raymond. *After Seven Years.* Lincoln: University of Nebraska Press, 1939.

Morris, Edmund. *Theodore Rex.* New York: Random House, 2001.

Morris, Roy, Jr. *Fraud of the Century: Rutherford B. Hayes, Samuel Tilden, and the Stolen Election of 1876.* New York: Simon and Schuster, 2003.

Mowry, George E. *The California Progressives.* Berkeley: University of California Press, 1951.

Osborne, David. *Laboratories of Democracy.* Boston: Harvard Business School, 1990.

Pestritto, Ronald J. *Woodrow Wilson and the Roots of Modern Liberalism* Lanham, Md.: Rowman and Littlefield, 2005.

Pious, Richard M. "The Presidency and the Nominating Process: Politics and Power." In Michael Nelson, ed., *The Presidency and the Political System.* Washington, D.C.: CQ Press, 2006.

Ponder, Stephen. *Managing the Press: Origins of the Media Presidency, 1897–1933.* New York: St. Martin's Press, 1999.

Prescott, Frank W. "The Executive Veto in American States." *Western Political Quarterly* 3, no. 1 (March 1950): 98–112.

Rakove, Jack. *Original Meanings: Politics and Ideas in the Making of the Constitution.* New York: Vintage Books, 1996.

Reynolds, John F. *The Demise of the American Convention System, 1880–1911.* New York: Cambridge University Press, 2006.

Riley, Russell. *The Presidency and the Politics of Racial Inequality: Nation-Keeping from 1831–1965.* New York: Columbia University Press, 1999.

Roosevelt, Eleanor, ed. *FDR: His Personal Letters.* New York: Duell, Sloan and Pearce, 1950.

Roosevelt, Franklin D. *Our Democracy in Action: The Philosophy of President Franklin D. Roosevelt.* Washington, D.C.: National Home Library Foundation, 1940.

——. *The Public Papers and Addresses.* Vol. 1: *The Genesis of the New Deal, 1928–1932.* New York: Random House, 1938.

——. *Public Papers of Governor of New York, 1932.* Albany: J. B. Lyon Company, 1939.

——. *Public Papers of Governor, 1930.* Albany: J. B. Lyon Company, 1930.

Roosevelt, Theodore. *An Autobiography.* New York: Macmillan, 1913.

——. *Letters and Speeches.* Ed. Louis Auchincloss. New York: Library of America, 2004.

——. *State Papers as Governor and President, 1899–1909.* New York: Charles Scribner's Sons, 1926.

Rosenthal, Alan. *Governors and Legislators: Contending Powers.* Washington, D.C.: CQ Press, 1990.

Rossiter, Clinton. *The American Presidency*. Baltimore: Johns Hopkins University Press, 1987.

Rudalevige, Andrew. *Managing the President's Program: Presidential Leadership and Legislative Policy Formulation*. Princeton: Princeton University Press, 2002.

———. *The New Imperial Presidency: Renewing Presidential Power after Watergate*. Ann Arbor: University of Michigan Press, 2005.

Sabato, Larry. *Goodbye to Goodtime Charlie: The American Governorship Transformed*. Washington, D.C.: CQ Press, 1983.

Salmore, Barbara G. and Stephen A. Salmore. *New Jersey Politics and Government: Suburban Politics Comes of Age*. Lincoln: University of Nebraska Press, 1998.

Sanders, Elizabeth. *Roots of Reform: Farmers, Workers, and the American State, 1877–1917*. Chicago: University of Chicago Press, 1999.

Schlesinger, Arthur M., Jr. *The Crisis of the Old Order, 1919–1933*. Boston: Houghton Mifflin Company, 1957.

———. *The Imperial Presidency*. New York: Popular Library, 1973.

Schwarz, Jordan A. *Liberal: Adolf A. Berle and the Vision of an American Era*. New York: Free Press, 1987.

Skocpol, Theda. *Protecting Soldiers and Mothers: The Political Origins of Social Policy in the United States*. Cambridge, Mass.: Harvard University Press, 1992.

Sklar, Martin J. *The Corporate Reconstruction of American Capitalism, 1890–1916*. New York: Cambridge University Press, 1988.

Skowronek, Stephen. *Building a New American State: The Expansion of National Administrative Capacities, 1877–1920*. Cambridge: Cambridge University Press, 1990.

———. *The Politics Presidents Make: Leadership from John Adams to Bill Clinton*. Cambridge: Belknap Press, 1997.

———. *Presidential Leadership in Political Time: Reprise and Reappraisal*. Lawrence: University of Kansas Press, 2008.

Smith, Jean Edwards. *FDR*. New York: Random House, 2007.

Sobel, Robert and John Raimo. *Biographical Directory of the Governors of the United States*. Vol. 3: *1789–1978*. Westport, Conn.: Meckler Books, 1978.

Startt, James D. *Woodrow Wilson and the Press: Prelude to the Presidency*. New York: Palgrave Macmillan, 2004.

Stid. Daniel D. *The President as Statesman: Woodrow Wilson and the Constitution*. Lawrence: University of Kansas Press, 1998.

Storing, Herbert J. *The Anti-Federalist: An Abridgement by Murray Dry, of the Complete Anti-Federalist*. Chicago: University of Chicago Press, 1985.

Stuckey, Mary E. "The Domain of Public Conscience: Woodrow Wilson and the Establishment of a Transcendent Political Order." *Rhetoric and Public Affair* 6, no. 1 (2003).

Summers, Mark Wahlgren. *Rum, Romanism, and Rebellion: The Making of the President, 1884*. Chapel Hill: University of North Carolina Press, 2000.

Tulis, Jeffrey. *The Rhetorical Presidency*. Princeton: Princeton University Press, 1987.

Thach, Charles C. *The Creation of the Presidency, 1775–1789*. New York: Da Capo Press, 1922.

Trefousse, Hans L. *Rutherford B. Hayes*. New York: Times Books, 2002.

Thorsen, Niels Aage. *The Political Thought of Woodrow Wilson, 1875–1910*. Princeton: Princeton University Press, 1988.

Tocqueville, Alexis de. *Democracy in America and Two Essays on America*. London: Penguin Books, 2003.

Trachtenberg, Alan. *The Incorporation of America: Culture and Society in the Gilded Age*. New York: Hill and Wang, 1982.

Urofsky, Melvin I. and David W. Levy, eds. *Letters of Louis D. Brandeis*. Vol. 1: *1870–1907*. Albany: State University of New York Press, 1971.

Ware, Alan. *The Democratic Party Heads North, 1877–1962*. New York: Cambridge University Press, 2006.

Welch, Richard E., Jr. *The Presidencies of Grover Cleveland*. Lawrence: University Press of Kansas, 1988.

White, Leonard D. *Introduction to the Study of Public Administration*. New York: Macmillan Company, 1939.

Wiebe, Robert H. *The Search for Order: 1877-1920*. New York: Hill and Wang, 1967.

Wilentz, Sean. *The Rise of American Democracy: Jefferson to Lincoln*. New York: W. W. Norton and Company, 2006.

Wilson, Woodrow. *Constitutional Government in the United States* New York: Columbia University Press, 1908.

———. "The Law and the Facts: Presidential Address, Seventh Annual Meeting of the American Political Science Association." *American Political Science Review* 5, no. 1 (February 1911): 1–11.

———. "Mr. Cleveland as President," *Atlantic Monthly* 79, no. 478 (March 1897).

Winfield, Betty Houchin. *FDR and the News Media*. Urbana: University of Illinois Press, 1990.

Wolin, Sheldon. *Politics and Vision: Continuity and Innovation in Western Political Thought*. Princeton: Princeton University Press, 2004.

Woodward, C. Vann. *Reunion and Reaction: The Compromise of 1877 and the End of Reconstruction*. Boston: Little, Brown and Company, 1951.

Young, James P. *Reconsidering American Liberalism: The Troubled Odyssey of the Liberal Idea*. Boulder: Westview Press, 1996.

Index

A *t* preceding a number indicates a table. *FDR* stands for Franklin Delano Roosevelt; *TR*, for Theodore Roosevelt.